DISCARDED

People Only Die
of Love in Movies

People Only Die of Love in Movies

Film Writing by Jim Ridley

Edited by Steve Haruch

VANDERBILT UNIVERSITY PRESS

NASHVILLE

© 2018 by Vanderbilt University Press
Nashville, Tennessee 37235
All rights reserved
First printing 2018

This book is printed on acid-free paper.
Manufactured in the United States of America

Library of Congress Cataloging-in-Publication Data on file

LC control number 2017037747
LC classification number PN1995 .R535 2018
Dewey classification number 791.43/75—dc23
LC record available at lccn.loc.gov/2017037747

ISBN 978-0-8265-2206-1 (cloth)

For Alicia, Kat and Jamie

Contents

Introduction *by Steve Haruch*   **1**

1   The Nouvelle Vague   **13**
   Lola
   Band of Outsiders
   Two English Girls
   Private Fears in Public Places
   Notre Musique

2   How the Western Won   **27**
   Once Upon a Time in the West
   Four films by Sergio Corbucci
   McCabe & Mrs. Miller
   The Wild Bunch
   The Ballad of Little Jo
   Meek's Cutoff

3   Heroes and Anti-Heroes   **41**
   Batman Begins
   Le Samouraï
   Dragon: The Bruce Lee Story
   Bonnie and Clyde
   Thelma & Louise
   Star Wars: Episode III — Revenge of the Sith

4   Shorts   **57**
   Rio Bravo
   Meet Me in St. Louis
   Point Blank
   Taxi Driver
   The Devil's Rejects
   Four films featuring Ray Harryhausen

Point Break
The Warriors
Rock 'n' Roll High School
The Big Lebowski
300
Swept from the Sea
The Order of Myths
I Like It Like That
Sugar Hill
Tony Takitani
The Scent of Green Papaya
Ikiru

5   Twin Cinema / Double Visions   73
Full Frontal / Signs
Singin' in the Rain / Chicago
Darwin's Nightmare / Grizzly Man
Boys Don't Cry / Fight Club
Femme Fatale
Point of No Return
A History of Violence
Summer of Sam
Passion
Touch of Evil
Actress
Mulholland Drive

6   Phoners & Shoe Leather   103
Look Back in Anger: Robert Altman's
     Nashville, 20 Years Later
Fade to Black: Can the Watkins Belcourt Be Saved?

Intermission   123
Bruce Springsteen and the E Street Band
at Bridgestone Arena, 4/17/14

Photo Gallery   129

7   Innocence and Experience   137
Toy Story 2
Son of Rambow
Little Man Tate

Akeelah and the Bee
Pump Up the Volume
Boyz N the Hood
Moonrise Kingdom
Mister Lonely

8   That Obscure Object   **157**
Turn Me On, Dammit!
Afterglow
The Notorious Bettie Page
The Piano
Gloria
Eyes Wide Shut
Carol

9   A Boot the Size of Nebraska   **175**
Playtime
Rumble in the Bronx
Serial Mom
Jackass: The Movie
Pulp Fiction
Wayne's World
Orlando
The Fifth Element
Hot Fuzz

10   Panning for Gold   **197**
Bad Boys II
Little Miss Sunshine
Texasville
The Messenger: The Story of Joan of Arc
Schindler's List
8MM

11   Problem Pictures   **213**
Triumph of the Will
American History X
Army of Shadows
The Untold Story of Emmett Louis Till
Xiu Xiu: The Sent-Down Girl
Underground
To Live

12 Forever Changes   **229**

    After Life
    The Last Picture Show
    Mother and Son
    Daughters of the Dust
    The Long Goodbye: Robert Altman, 1925–2006
    Taste of Cherry
    The Umbrellas of Cherbourg

Acknowledgments   **247**

Index   **249**

Introduction

The first time I met Jim Ridley, I couldn't quite see him.

It was 2004, and I had come to the *Nashville Scene* to pitch a story, after which I got a tour of the office. I had been regularly knocked flat by the quicksilver wit of Jim's deeply informed film reviews since before making the drive from Seattle, so I was eager to finally meet him.

Jim was barely visible — the top of his head, haloed by a big scribble of curls, broke above an ad hoc skyline of precariously balanced books, CDs, DVDs, flyers, newspapers, comics, vinyl records and all manner of packaging. Then Jim, a staff writer at the time, wheeled around in his chair, fixed his blue eyes on me and exclaimed through a wildly friendly grin, "Oh, hey!"

It was the tone of voice you might use when you turn an unfamiliar corner in a strange city and stumble into a friend you have not seen in a decade. Jim introduced himself to everyone this way, but I'm not sure I'd ever been greeted so warmly by a stranger, and don't expect to be again. Whether parsing the nuances of perplexing obscurities or reveling in the joys of thunderous megaplex fodder, Jim's reviews share that atmosphere of warmth. This collection aims to have a similar effect: to pull readers into an embrace, so to speak — as Jim was so fond of doing — and to showcase his uncommon knack for writing as rangy and vivid as it is clear and precise.

As Jim rose from his chair and navigated the vertical detritus, he looked kind of like an actor without his Godzilla suit on, stalking a miniature film-set version of Tokyo. For as long as I knew him, Jim's office would be like this: a cross between a record store cutout bin, a dead letter office and the belly of a Jawa sandcrawler (the occasional purge notwithstanding), a testament to his varied enthusiasms and attachments, which he was always happy to share. If he saw your eye land on something, he immediately plucked it from the pile and offered it to you as he rattled off commentary often better than the liner notes.

Some months later, Jim showed up at my door with an advance DVD copy of Gregg Araki's *Mysterious Skin*, starring a young Joseph Gordon-Levitt. Jim's arrival at my door was not typical behavior for an editor, but it was of a piece with his generosity. He made his writers feel like it was an honor to edit them, not the other way around. So it feels like an unthinkable reversal to be introducing his work, just as it feels unthinkable, still, that he is not here to do it himself. But let's not start there.

By the time Jim Ridley was 13 years old, he was already reviewing books for the *Tennessean*, Nashville's daily newspaper. A family friend owned a movie theatre near his house, so he and his brother Read were regulars there from a young age. In his first and only year at Vanderbilt University — "glorious and study-free," as he would later describe it — Jim wrote film and album reviews for the campus newspaper and magazine. Then it was on to Middle Tennessee State University — or back, depending on your point of view; the campus sits in Jim's hometown of Murfreesboro. There he earned a bachelor's in mass communications and a major in English, and wrote for *Fireplace Whiskey Journal*, which he would later characterize as a "Xeroxed local zine . . . fueled by beer, Obie's Pizza and Diet Dr. Pepper in the waning days of Ronald Reagan's second term."[1] He also worked at a video store, the whole time devouring all manner of books, albums and movies as quickly as he could find them. Then the *Nashville Scene* came along.

In 1989, the *Scene* was an upstart publication, an attempt at alternative journalism (more on that in a moment) in a city that, as then-publisher Albie Del Favero said at the time, struck analysts as "basically a downscale market where the favorite leisure activities were Bible/devotional reading and entering sweepstakes."[2] Jim, like others on the *Scene* staff, wanted something different for Nashville, and was champing at the bit to convey his passions in print — starting with an alternately bold and self-effacing inquiry to the paper's arts editor.

"If I had to choose my favorite movies I would tear out my hair," Jim wrote in that letter, "but off the top of my head I'd say I never get sick of *Repo Man*, *Shoot the Piano Player*, *Citizen Kane*, *Married to the Mob*, *After Hours* and *Jules and Jim*." His favorite directors: François Truffaut, David Cronenberg, Akira Kurosawa, Martin Scorsese, Alfred Hitchcock, David Lynch and Brian De Palma. His favorite critics: Pauline Kael, John Simon, Dwight Macdonald and James Agee. This, from a baby-faced 23 year old in an age before YouTube,

---

1   "It Was Twenty Years Ago Today . . . or Something Like That," *Nashville Scene*, Jan. 25, 2008, *www.nashvillescene.com*.
2   Albie Del Favero, "Rebirth of a Paper," *Nashville Scene*, June 29, 1989, *www.nashvillescene.com*.

IMDb or Netflix. Jim closed his missive with a parting shot at the paragon of milquetoast mainstream movie reviewers of the time: "Remember: Gene Shalit is a disease, and we are the cure."

Needless to say, the *Scene* was happy to welcome him aboard.

● ● ● ● ●

For the uninitiated, an "alt-weekly" is a particular subspecies of newspaper, printed in tabloid format and distributed weekly for free thanks to a surfeit of advertising. The best-known alt-weekly, and the spiritual ancestor of the format, is New York's *Village Voice*, founded by Norman Mailer, Dan Wolf and Edwin Fancher in 1955. As Louis Menand observes in the *New Yorker*, the *Voice* "was doing what the Internet does now long before there was an Internet"[3]— a prototype of blogging and Craigslist 50 years before their time. The *Voice* took the notion of the "shopper" — a bundle of advertisements with a few strands of editorial — and transformed it into something urgent. Furthermore, Menand says, "the *Voice* also helped to create the romance of the journalistic vocation by making journalism seem a calling, a means of self-expression, a creative medium."

Alt-weeklies differ greatly by market, but they tend to share an interest in hyperlocal reporting, arts coverage, under-the-radar music and what might be called muckraking journalism, otherwise known as reporting with a point of view. Though often dismissed as a "liberal rag" for its progressive social politics, the *Scene* suffers its share of criticism from the left as well. At the end of the week, it is still a for-profit venture, which some readers see as fostering too-cozy relationships with advertisers and other capitalists. Fans of the paper admire its advocacy of outsiders, misfits and underdogs, and its commitment to independent arts coverage in a city whose media overwhelmingly veer toward red carpets and rhinestones. Over the years, there's been a (mostly) collegial rivalry between the *Scene* and the *Tennessean*. Staffers recall a 1990s *Scene* slogan, "[w]hen news breaks, we fix it," as a subtle jab at 1100 Broadway. In other words, the alt-weekly's job is to go deeper on stories that might get only a passing mention in the daily, to contextualize the facts in order to explain why they matter. But the alt-weekly is also an endangered species. Between the time this book was accepted for publication and the time it was printed, the *Village Voice* discontinued its print edition; the *L.A. Weekly* was sold and

---

3   Louis Menand, "It Took a Village: How the *Voice* Changed Journalism," *New Yorker*, Jan. 5, 2009, *www.newyorker.com*.

its staff almost entirely eliminated; and the *Nashville Scene* itself cut a quarter of its staff and was put up for sale.

Twenty years after joining the staff as its resident film critic, Jim became the *Nashville Scene*'s top editor. By 2009, it had been bought and sold four times, and changed office locations five. (At one point in the early 2000s, the *Village Voice* and the *Scene* were sister papers in a nationwide chain.) Jim took the helm almost reluctantly at first, but never shied from its many duties both on and off the page. The Association of Alternative Newsweeklies (now the Association of Alternative Newsmedia), a confederation of roughly 125 alt-weeklies, convenes each summer to discuss the state of the industry and to confer awards for writing and design. Under Jim's editorship, the *Scene* won 40 such awards, averaging better than five per year. Jim took home first place in arts criticism twice himself, despite also juggling managerial duties.

Over his nearly three-decade tenure, Jim fielded countless letters like the one he wrote to the *Scene*. He kept his office door open unless he was on a sensitive call or under an urgent deadline. (And even then, he'd usually wave you in with a smile.) He interviewed interns and took them out for lunch on their last day. He gave hugs full heartedly and with abandon. As anyone who works in an alt-weekly newsroom as part of a dedicated skeleton crew, Jim wore many hats: editor, boss, cheerleader, proofreader, arbitrator, customer service agent, barista, friend. He also wrote, not just about movies, but also about bands, clubs, records, novels, plays, poetry, politics, coffee shops, playgrounds, fried chicken and burlesque shows, among other topics. Long before Nashville ever appeared on the national hip-city radar, Jim saw and highlighted the city's strengths while also holding the city and the people in it to the highest standards.

● ● ● ● ●

In 1999, a decade after he began writing for the Scene, Jim Ridley wrote a sentence in the paper's January 21 cover story that hung like a cloud over his newfound profession: "One week from today, Nashville's only art-movie theater will close its doors for good." The situation was beyond bleak. Unsustainable losses, an effect of miserable attendance, had driven the Belcourt to the brink.

> I might as well share the moment that broke my heart: The Belcourt was
> showing an amazing double bill of Jean-Luc Godard's *Contempt* and
> François Truffaut's *Day for Night* — two movies available on TV and video
> only in the most washed-out, dispiriting condition. I was seeing a movie

on the other screen, but I snuck for a moment into *Day for Night*, which I'd seen earlier. Onscreen was the scene in which Truffaut, playing a movie director, dreams that he is a child again, swiping stills of *Citizen Kane* from the lobby of a neighborhood movie theater. Truffaut the director deepened my love of movies; Truffaut the critic made me want to write. I wondered how many other people in the auditorium were sharing this impossibly perfect moment. The room held 400. I counted eight. I bought two more tickets, just to make it 10.

As it turned out, it was not the end for the Belcourt. A community of film lovers, Jim among them, banded together to save the theater, and with it, a vital pillar of the city's arts scene. Many consider his cover story ("Fade to Black," included here in Chapter 6) to be the spark that helped the Belcourt survive its darkest hour: "Local audiences don't receive better because they haven't been demanding or supporting it," he wrote. He led the way by doing both.

Jim's writing reminds aspiring journalists that the printed word can and should be used as a bully pulpit to demand better. During a period when the Belcourt was under corporate ownership, Jim sometimes wove his critiques of the theater's conditions into his reviews. In a 1997 assessment of *Breaking the Waves*, Jim decried "a great filmmaker's work kneecapped by indifferent projection and lousy facilities." He even included the phone number for *Breaking the Waves'* distributor so readers could complain. We don't often hear about critics in big cities contending with such conditions just to see movies worth writing about. To do the work he loved, in other words, Jim could not focus solely on film reviewing but also on coverage of the venues that mattered to him.

In the end, the Belcourt did more than just survive. In July 2016, just months after Jim left us, it reopened after undergoing a massive six-month, $5 million renovation that modernized the building, restored the facade and, importantly, added a third screen. Also among the many improvements: a seat bearing Jim's name, eternally reserved in the third row, where he always sat. (There are also seats for his wife, Alicia Adkerson, and his kids, Kat and Jamie.) They also named the lobby after him — a place he had spent countless hours discussing what he'd just seen, with everyone from film students to friends.

But Jim's work on behalf of the Belcourt is just a tiny piece of his film-writing oeuvre, which included some 600 reviews and reported features. Ninety-four are collected in this volume. They are not grouped chronologically, but according to cinematic movement, genre and review format, as well as around associative themes that include innocence, social engagement, memory and heroism. They are arranged to give a sense of Jim's loves and his sensibilities as a critic, and to heighten connections both between films and between reviews. Aside from very minor editing, such as removing references to specific screening times or other extraneous information, they appear here as they were originally published. Some reviews have been out of print and unavailable online for decades. This slate represents the best of Jim's film writing, even if it doesn't represent a diversity of cinematic talent as broad as I might have hoped.

In 2016, just seven of the 250 top-grossing films were directed by women — the same number as in 1998. According to a study by the University of Southern California's Annenberg Media, Diversity & Social Change Initiative, fewer than 10 percent of the top-grossing fiction films released between 2007 and 2016 were directed by people of color.[4] In the 25 years since Wayne Wang's *The Joy Luck Club*, for example, no major studio has backed a live-action film featuring an Asian-American director and majority Asian-American cast. Jim was aware of these imbalances, and often addressed them head-on. In a 1994 review, he notes: "Darnell Martin is the first African-American woman ever to direct a major-studio release; once you see *I Like It Like That*, you'll be thrilled she got a chance to share her voice — even as you wonder about the other voices that have never been heard."

Add to this dilemma the relative smallness of Nashville as a film market in the 1980s and '90s, and it's not hard to see why the pool of reviews from which this book was drawn skewed heavily white and male. Even so, it's remarkable just how inclusive Jim's writing still manages to be. He strove to amplify marginalized voices when he could, as evidenced by his stories about small and upstart enterprises such as the International Black Film Festival of Nashville, which in its second year Jim observed as showing "signs of becoming a major boon to the city and its perpetually struggling film industry."[5] The festival recently completed its eleventh run. As Jim's career advanced and Nashville's stature grew, the duties of running the paper limited the number of films he had time to review, but he used this as a way to encourage other writers, myself included, to cover movies that mattered and spoke to them.

---

4   Stacy L. Smith, Marc Choueiti, Katherine Pieper, Traci Gillig, Carmen Lee, and Dylan DeLuca, "Inequality in 700 Popular Films: Examining Portrayals of Gender, Race, & LGBT Status from 2007 to 2014," USC Annenberg Media, Diversity & Social Change Initiative, *annenberg.usc.edu*.

5   Jim Ridley, "Betting on Black: Second IBFF Brings Bigger Stars, Films to Nashville," *Nashville Scene*, Oct. 4, 2007, *www.nashvillescene.com*.

● ● ● ● ●

On March 28, 2016, Jim collapsed in his office at the *Scene*. His heart had failed, and he was rushed to the hospital in a coma. A few days later, as doctors eased him off sedatives, his eyes fluttered when Alicia played Elvis Costello songs for him on her computer. So we flooded his Facebook page with songs we knew he loved, or hoped he would love enough to hear again. But Jim never regained consciousness. He died on April 8.

For days after his death, you could search the national trending topics on Twitter and find the name Jim Ridley there alongside the likes of *Star Wars* (the first *Rogue One* trailer had arrived) and Bruce Springsteen (one of Jim's heroes, who had just canceled a North Carolina date to protest the state's anti-transgender bathroom law). Nashville mayor Megan Barry called him "one of those rare individuals who effortlessly coupled genius and insight with infectious enthusiasm and unbridled generosity of spirit."[6] In Washington, D.C., Nashville Congressman Jim Cooper entered a statement into the record of the 114th Congress that read, in part, "Jim Ridley made our city better, and it will not be the same without him."[7]

As Noel Murray, a former *Scene* colleague, wrote in a tribute to Jim on Roger Ebert's website:

> Critics around the country are mourning Jim because many of them were on the receiving end of phone calls or emails from him during some of the lowest times in their careers. If they'd just lost a gig, he'd ask if they wanted to contribute something to the *Scene*, and would make it seem like they'd be doing *him* a favor. Even after he had the responsibility of running the entire paper, Jim still edited the film section, and managed a stable of contributors that at times has included some of the best-known critics in the country: Bilge Ebiri, Mike D'Angelo, David Fear and Joshua Rothkopf. He paid attention to what his friends and colleagues loved, and tried to match them to reviews where they could shine.[8]

---

6   *Nashville Scene* staff and contributors, "Jim Ridley, 1965–2016: Saying Goodbye to Our Friend and Leader, *Scene* editor Jim Ridley," *Nashville Scene*, April 14, 2016, *www.nashvillescene*.

7   Rep. Jim Cooper, "Honoring Jim Ridley (Extensions of Remarks – April 13, 2016)," *Congressional Record*, Vol. 162, No. 56 — Daily Edition, April 13, 2016, 114th Congress, 2nd Session, *www.congress.gov*.

8   Noel Murray, "A Farewell to Nashville Film Critic Jim Ridley: A Civic Institution and Everybody's Friend," *Balder & Dash*, April 9, 2016, *www.rogerebert.com/balder-and-dash/a-farewell-to-nashville-film-critic-jim-ridley-a-civic-institution-and-everybodys-friend*.

Even as he worked to buoy the careers of others, Jim turned down numerous opportunities over the years to write for bigger audiences. He chose to remain committed to Nashville and to the *Scene*.

In his final blog post, Jim, in just a few words, vividly evokes the jittery feel of the comic-drama *The Mend*: "[John] Magary, making his feature debut, uses a jarring cutting style that keeps you edgy and off-balance, as if someone were tossing lit firecrackers with fuses of varied lengths." That's an image that stays with you. Here's another: "Like Burt Reynolds, his face got thicker and heavier, with a drugged lion's eyes," Jim writes, describing Eddie Murphy post–*Beverly Hills Cop*, "while he flashed his dimming smile like someone plugging in a beer sign." Watching Wong Kar-wai's *Fallen Angels* is "like looking at the world from the inside of a jukebox," a perfect summation of the movie's whirling pop delirium.

That is to say, Jim was able to pull seemingly disparate elements into the same review and make them sing — sometimes in unison, sometimes in harmony, sometimes in counterpoint. The farther apart in time and sphere of knowledge the references, the more delight the recombinant sentences yield. (A word of caution to budding critics: It doesn't matter how colorful or out-of-the-blue a comparison is if it doesn't illuminate something about the subject.) In a review of *Stranger Than Fiction*, Jim observes Will Ferrell's "Bullwinkle frame" and "those boyish, faintly blobby features that suggest an ice-cream sculpture of James Caan in hot August sun." Jim likens a sequence in *Superman Returns*, in which Superman uses his X-ray vision to follow Lois' elevator up the *Daily Planet* skyscraper, to the silent movies of Louis Feuillade — finding an unexpected grace note in a summer tentpole crowd-pleaser. Jim's analysis of *The Matrix Reloaded* uses imagery you might associate with the film anyway, but in a vividly new way: He likens the way it alternates jarringly between furious action scenes and not-at-all-furious talking scenes to "passing from one Philosophy 101 lecture to another through a campus full of somersaulting ninjas." And so on. It speaks to Jim's prolific phrase-turning that these examples are all taken from reviews that, for reasons of space or thematic cohesion, didn't even make it into this volume. The writings that did make it stand as something more than simply movie reviews.

• • • • •

A review — or, for that matter, a numerical score culled from dozens or even hundreds of reviews — can inform the decision to pay or not to pay to see a movie. Jim expressed his own sense of the distinction between reviewer and critic in his tribute to the *New Yorker*'s Pauline Kael, on the occasion of her death in 2001.

> Kael made her readers want to be critics, not reviewers. It's a small but important distinction. A reviewer, first and foremost, is a consumer advocate. From a good reviewer, you will typically get a brief synopsis, a comment on the stars and maybe the director, and a firm thumbs-up or thumbs-down. That last is most important. A reviewer's job is to sift through the half-dozen movies that open every week and tell you which ones to skip or see. A good example is Roger Ebert: a writer with generally well-defined mainstream likes and dislikes, a keen understanding of film history, and a clear love of the medium.
>
> A critic, on the other hand, is someone you read to sharpen your own opinions, either in agreement or opposition. A first-rate piece of film criticism — like Jonathan Rosenbaum's rousing defense of *The Circle* this summer in the *Chicago Reader*, or Kent Jones' mock-celebratory flip-of-the-bird to director Michael Bay in the last *Film Comment* — is less interesting for the writer's ultimate yea-or-nay than for the argument that backs it up. A critic holds your interest whether you give a damn about the movie or not. Perhaps this is the crucial distinction: A reviewer is someone you look to for advice, while a critic is someone you read for affirmation.[9]

Not just for affirmation of one's own opinions, but also for guidance — for a sense of ethics about what matters in cinema, and what the stakes are for both viewer and director. A review, like the jacket-flap copy on a novel, proves mainly useful before the fact. A good piece of criticism, like the film it describes, is worth reliving. It makes and deepens connections between films and the histories that surround them.

"One of the amazing things about Pauline Kael," Jim continues, "is how often, and with what consistency, she was able to practice a critic's craft on a reviewer's deadline." For his part, Jim often caught a Monday-night press screening and turned in his review the following afternoon, with the *Scene* office in the throes of assembling the paper in order to send it off to the printer

---

9   Jim Ridley, "When the Lights Go Down: Pauline Kael carried on a 30-year conversation with movie lovers," *Nashville Scene*, Sept. 13, 2001, www.nashvillescene.com/arts-culture/article/13006207/when-the-lights-go-down.

in time. Later in his career, he was responsible for writing his reviews while simultaneously overseeing the assembly line — and while he was editor-in-chief, he insisted on reading the entire issue, front to back, before approving it to go to the press. This made for some long nights, and I knew the issue was an especially good one if I heard more outbursts than usual of his singularly high-pitched laugh, ringing out of his office and over the mostly abandoned cubicles.

When a film he already knew well came through Nashville for reasons of an anniversary screening, a refurbished print, a festival, or inclusion in one of the Belcourt's many inspired series, Jim could conjure vivid reviews, sometimes even if it had been years since he last saw the work in question. And as blogging afforded the ability to expand beyond the limitations of the weekly print edition, Jim would often bang out quick heads-up posts for movies coming to Nashville. Then he would wade gleefully into the cinephile back-and-forth that often ensued below — where even the most acerbic, button-pushing commenters were known to lower their usual rhetorical weapons and engage in serious film discussions, to the amazement of anyone familiar with their usual hijinks. Jim carried on these conversations under his *nom de blogeur*, Mr. Pink, a reference to the jittery jewel thief in *Reservoir Dogs*. Every so often, a commenter would assail Mr. Pink for his bad taste or lack of movie knowledge, much to the delight of regulars who knew the mind behind the sunglasses-clad Steve Buscemi avatar. These trolls would inevitably get their comeuppance, but never in an overly nasty way.

He could be withering, too, and this book dedicates a chapter to such reviews, but Jim's preferred mode of discourse was praise. He liked to nestle critiques inside accolades. To illustrate a point about storytelling, he jabs at the hasty editing shorthand in *Legends of the Fall*:

> Brad Pitt says goodbye to his lover on the Wyoming prairie, and in the very next shot he's commandeering a pirate ship somewhere on the high seas. A 19th-century novelist would have spent 100 pages explaining the information crucial to that narrative development. Now we're expected to assume the screenwriter's role along with the viewer's; in the process, the very things that hold our attention in a story — character development, anecdotes and incidental asides — are abandoned.

This is not to bury *Legends of the Fall* but to praise Zhang Yimou's *To Live* — by showing what it is not. Zhang's film, by contrast, "restores the thematic richness and detail so lacking in most contemporary films — and so crucial to our enjoyment." Notice the word "enjoyment." No doubt, Jim loved plenty of films that were difficult — or at the very least, not what most would call "accessible." (His most broken-in T-shirt bore the logo of the dystopic Japanese cult thriller *Battle Royale*, in which teenagers are forced to kill or be killed in a sadistic game show run by the government.) But Jim didn't think difficulty necessarily correlated with value, and he loved so-called low art as much as the lofty, challenging stuff. Jim the reviewer could tell you if a film was worth seeing; Jim the critic could tell you why it was worth remembering.

"He was a critic as populist," filmmaker Harmony Korine wrote after his death. "He allowed for love to creep in, he said if you give yourself over to cinema it will return the magic tenfold."[10] The writer and theology professor, David Dark, an occasional *Nashville Scene* contributor, once remarked that the lesson Jim taught him was that "you can find your voice by loving things."[11]

● ● ● ● ●

This book ends with movies about memory, loss and death — in other words, movies about life. These reviews examine the ways people carry on. They also explore how the people we love continue on after they die, in the objects that in some form or other bear their signature: a film of a single memory; a dresser with their height measured in ascending hash marks over the years; a volume of film criticism. In the case of Robert Altman, eulogized by Jim in 2006, it's a hugely influential body of work that treated a movie as a way of making something, rather than simply a thing to be made. Put all of Altman's movies together, Jim writes, "the grand and the misshapen, all overlapping and crisscrossing, and out of that entropic maelstrom comes something the movies rarely evoke: a sense of life's richness." The same could be said of Jim's writing. Instead of undercutting his review of *Taste of Cherry*, a personal remembrance of a friend who took his own life makes Jim's review resonate even more deeply.

There's a scene in Jacques Demy's particolored 1964 movie musical *The Umbrellas of Cherbourg* in which a grief-stricken Geneviève (Catherine Deneuve) agonizes over the loss of her love. Guy (Nino Castelnuovo) has been conscripted into the French army and shipped off to Algeria. He's only a

---

10 "Jim Ridley, 1965–2016."

11 David Dark, "Can I Get a Witness?: Nashville's Righteously Radical Campbellite Core," Nashville Summer Foodways Symposium, July 8, 2016, *www.southernfoodways.org*.

few months into a two-year deployment, but already his letters have begun to sound less ardent and arrive less frequently. "I would have died for him," Geneviève wails. "So why aren't I dead?"

Her mother's response betrays exasperation with her teenage daughter: "People only die of love in movies," she trills. It's a curt reply, but there's something else in there, like a crushed flower at the center of a balled-up fist. Jim locates it in "A Finite Forever," one of the most beautiful film essays I've ever read. "Her pronouncement," Jim observes, "has an unmistakable note of regret." The movies, alas, are the only place where love can be so powerful.

The movies are also the only place where belief can be suspended so far as to allow for light sabers, and for characters bursting into song when words alone are no longer enough. Considering *Meet Me in St. Louis*, as a way into talking about movie musicals more broadly, Jim writes, "This is not the real world; this is a world with the veil of realism parted, allowing the passions beneath to peek through." Sometimes art gifts us a vision that is more true than it is accurate.

This idea of "the veil of realism" also calls to mind Samhain, or El Día de Los Muertos — the season when the veil between this world and the next is said to be at its thinnest, and the living can commune with the dead, if only for a short time. I think of Jim ducking into an almost-empty hall at the Belcourt as *Day for Night* plays larger than life on the screen. He looks up, his face illuminated by the projector's reflected light. He's watching Truffaut, transported back into childhood as Jim allowed himself to be so many times. Maybe in this moment, and in moments like it, the world of film and the world we live in are not so much separated by the silver veil that shows us these moving pictures, as they are joined by it.

The Nouvelle Vague 1

This chapter on films of the Nouvelle Vague serves as a kind of way station from which some of the book's larger themes embark. Also known as the French New Wave, the Nouvelle Vague was a "tendency" whose playfully experimental trajectory peaked between 1959 and 1962. The fascinations and attitudes kicked up by the young French critics-turned-moviemakers and their compatriots resonate both through Jim's body of work and the films he writes about. For instance, Jim identifies Jean-Luc Godard's *Bande à part* as "the precursor of what film critic Rob Nelson calls the 'DJ movie,' a young man's cinematic mixtape of the cool things in life." Jim didn't make movies, aside from the ones he would dream up in film-geek reveries with friends and colleagues. But this mixmaster spirit animates his writing, as evidenced by the way he thrills in flipping through far-flung cultural references.

There's a reason this book begins with Jacques Demy. As an underrated artist outshone by his own celebrated milieu, he's a loveable underdog of a director. In that sense, it's expected for a writer of Jim's broad knowledge to sing the praises of a relatively obscure figure. But there isn't a hint of more-knowledgeable-than-thou arrogance here. Of the densely allusive *Lola*, Jim writes, "Demy's first feature creates a world in which the movies and life intermingle like elation and disappointment. An awareness of one deepens the other." This intermingling of film and life suffuses Jim's writing, especially in his deft inclusion of personal anecdotes — though only when they deepen our understanding.

Demy remains largely unsung because of his unflagging devotion to beauty and grace in a time when cinema moved toward coarser themes; some critics have derided Demy's films as old fashioned and sentimental. So it's fitting that Jim saw so much to admire in them — an appreciation that only intensified over time and repeated viewings.

• • • • • • • • • •

Lola
Dir. Jacques Demy
1961, NR, 90 min.

Demy Monde

In an interview last fall with critic Sam Adams, Gaulywood poster boy
Jean-Pierre Jeunet bristled at the mention of the Nouvelle Vague. It's the way
the Strokes must feel when somebody brings up the Velvet Underground. "Oh,
I hate the New Wave, except for the first Truffaut movies," Jeunet complained.
"It's all sad stories, couples fighting in the kitchen." Uh-huh. Leaving aside
the fact that he's, well, off his rocker with regard to the New Wave's frequently
playful films, it's understandable why the director of *Amélie* wouldn't rush to
hip audiences to Jacques Demy. After all, Julian Casablancas doesn't go around
handing out copies of *White Light, White Heat*.

Ironically, Demy's very lightness — his bittersweet effervescence, his
embrace of the swooniest tropes of Hollywood musicals and romantic
trifles — made him a dim star in the Nouvelle Vague firmament. He was
outshone by the more insistent charm of Truffaut and Rohmer, the sinister
elegance of Chabrol, the ground-breaking experimentation of Godard and
Resnais. By the time of his early death at age 59 in 1990, he was routinely
dismissed as the movement's twee miniaturist: that guy who made Gene Kelly
movies and fairy tales while the world was at the ramparts. Try convincing
ideologues that upholding grace and beauty in times of ugliness is itself a
revolutionary act.

It wasn't until the mid-1990s, when a restored version of his 1964 musical
The Umbrellas of Cherbourg returned to dazzle anew, that contemporary
viewers started to see Demy as something more than a dabbler in moribund
genres. Demy's first film, 1961's *Lola*, comes to Nashville in a breathtaking
restoration supervised by his widow, Agnès Varda. Encountering it in this
form is like running into a childhood love after 40 years, only to find her youth
undimmed by a second.

The analogy isn't as gushy as it sounds. To see such a person would make
our hearts leap, sure. But the sight would also carry a piercing pang of our own
mortality. The other person's perfection would only intensify the awareness of
our imperfection. Demy's films have the same inextricable formula of elation
and melancholy, of mundaneness and magic. Yes, *The Umbrellas of Cherbourg*
is a cinematic lollipop in which lovers float down the street, and every line of
dialogue is sung to a Michel Legrand score sweet as cherry Coke. At the same

time, those very musical conventions are used to evoke the delusions of young lovers and the fragility of romantic ideals against the battering of war, economic necessity and fate. The power of the film's heartrending finale comes not from a sugarcoating of life's disappointments but from an acceptance of them.

Lola is neither a musical nor in color, and yet it's scarcely less lilting than the rain-misted *Umbrellas*. If his later films (including 1967's criminally underrated *The Young Girls of Rochefort*) scale the Hollywood musical down to the modest particulars of daily life, Demy's first feature imbues kitchen-sink subject matter with the intensity and heightened emotion of a knock-'em-dead production number.

Shot in sumptuous B&W 'Scope by Raoul Coutard — the Nouvelle Vague's secret weapon — *Lola* establishes the motifs and boundaries of the Demy *monde*. The setting is Nantes, the seaside town of Demy's youth, to which he would return in subsequent films. Sailors swagger the streets, as if searching for an MGM back lot. Here, single-mom dancer Cécile, played with sad-clown radiance by Anouk Aimée, plies her trade in a waterfront dance hall under the name Lola — a nod to Dietrich as well as to *Lola Montès* director Max Ophüls, to whom the film is dedicated. Men flit in and out of her life and her bed while she awaits the return of her child's father and her true love, who vanished years ago to seek his fortune.

The gold-hearted dance-hall gal is a movie staple as old as sprockets. But Aimée plays Lola with a sexual pragmatism, a casual, nonjudgmental awareness of her desires, that blows the dust off the type. She's what an old-movie archetype would be if she wandered off the screen and settled into our world. The Nouvelle Vague directors, in movies like *Shoot the Piano Player* and *Breathless*, lifted situations and genre conventions from matinees but used them in deliberately artificial ways that exposed the difference between life and movie-fed fantasies. Here, the glossy photography of grubby apartments and shabby saloons evokes the transformative power of Lola's optimism.

The effect may be disconcerting, but it is not ironic. Dense with film allusions, Demy's first feature creates a world in which the movies and life intermingle like elation and disappointment. An awareness of one deepens the other. The whims of chance may whisk characters into each other's paths with the geometric precision of screwball comedy, as when another girl named Cécile (Annie Duperoux) and a sailor (Alan Scott) share a flirtation that mirrors Lola's own sexual awakening years earlier. The twist here is that the sailor has just left Lola's bed a short time before, but the results are less funny than poignant. This scene, shot in languid slow motion against an amusement park backdrop, shimmers with a summery, innocent eroticism. And even when

Lola gets her happily-ever-after ending, riding off into the sunset in a white convertible, she can't help but look back — at a chance not taken trudging off in the opposite direction.

Demy would revisit the world of *Lola* throughout his career. The sailors bound for Cherbourg become a platoon bound for Algiers in *The Umbrellas of Cherbourg*, and a character from his first film meets a bizarre fate offscreen in *The Young Girls of Rochefort*. Each film ends with a quote-unquote happy ending, but always in a way that leaves a pang of regret and missed opportunity. The pang is what lingers. In Demy's second film, *Bay of Angels*, a gambling drama drunk on the power of chance and the exhilaration of risk, a couple drift from luxury to poverty on the Riviera. Yet the thrill of the gamble makes even the losses worthwhile. "What counts is to want something," the movie's bank-clerk hero tells his compulsive partner, "no matter what the cost is." It is a sentiment full of illusion-free optimism, of impractical hope and foolhardy risk, of a passion undeterred by disdain and despair. Which makes it a fitting career statement for Jacques Demy, a filmmaker who saw no value in placing small bets when the heart was at stake. (*Nashville Scene*, July 11, 2002)

• • • • • • • • • •

Band of Outsiders
Dir. Jean-Luc Godard
1964, NR, 95 min.

A Band Apart

"The cinema is truth 24 frames a second," goes the famous dictum expressed by the deserter hero of Jean-Luc Godard's 1960 political tract *Le petit soldat*. Yet in Godard's *Band of Outsiders*, made four years later, there's a famous instance of a "minute of silence" that takes up only 35 actual seconds of screen time. So what gives? If truth involves the accurate representation of space and time, where are those missing 600 frames?

The truth is that in the alchemy of cinema — in the persistence of vision that draws an imitation of life from 24 separate snapshots flipping past a projector beam in sequence — 35 seconds add up to a minute. Movies aren't a photographic record of unassailable veracity; their truth lies in their engagement of the world as it is perceived and experienced. Thus when a bored kid in a Parisian café sighs, "A real minute of silence takes forever" — and the entire soundtrack of background chatter and ambient noise goes dead, leaving nothing but a sullen void — the equation of seconds to minutes to forever couldn't seem truer.

Or maybe it's just that 35 of Godard's seconds are worth 60 of most film-makers'. *Band of Outsiders*, his 1964 gangster fantasia is a breathless jumble of film allusions, literary shout-outs and exuberant pop-culture riffing. Dense with the director's personal checkpoints, from Fritz Lang films and American cartoons to his own mother's maiden name, this is the precursor of what film critic Rob Nelson calls the "DJ movie," a young man's cinematic mixtape of the cool things in life. Small wonder Quentin Tarantino named his production company A Band Apart, in homage to the film's French title. It could stand for the band of misfits and dreamers who make up the obsessive militant front of film culture, for whom this restored print is practically a grail.

Watching *Band of Outsiders* today, though, you're struck by the melancholy that underlines and offsets every burst of fancy, every mad dash of beauty. Godard shot it when he was 33, in the midst of a creative damburst scarcely equaled in movie history. At the time, he was married to his leading lady, Anna Karina, as bewitching a subject of scrutiny as a camera could seek. And yet in 1964, after its revolutionary initial films, the Nouvelle Vague of which he was a part was already approaching ebb tide. In just a few years France would explode in war protest and student revolt. The raw dynamism of American pop culture, once championed by French cineastes, would be seen as another form of hegemony as the U.S. stepped up its presence in Vietnam. Even Godard's marriage would not last another two years.

Fittingly, there is a constant tension in *Band of Outsiders* between the immediacy of the moment and the threat of what is to come. It's established in the break between the jazzy title sequence and the location shooting that follows on gray Parisian streets. Godard took the basic plot of an American pulp novel, Dolores Hitchens' *Fools' Gold*, about two crooks who hook up with a girl so they can rob her aunt's house. The novel's crooks were professionals, but Godard's popgun outlaws, Arthur Rimbaud (Claude Brasseur) and Franz (Sami Frey), seem more like play-actors — they delight in pretend shoot-outs, like kids playing cowboy.

The pop-stoked heroes wander through a postmodern Paris where the civilizing traditions of high art and literature are fading. In an English class, the two buddies meet Odile (Karina) — who, under the gaze of Godard and Nouvelle Vague mainstay Raoul Coutard, manages to look like a different, equally fascinating woman in every shot. The class lesson is *Romeo and Juliet*, and while the teacher swoons over the love poetry, Arthur propositions Odile with crude Shakespearean puns. (Classics in Godard don't translate well into modern love — check out the treatment that the *Odyssey* gets in

Contempt.) The teacher wants the class to learn literary English; the class wants only phrases that matter — e.g., "a big $1 million film."

Later, in a gag, the three companions sprint through the Louvre, ignoring the masterworks and beating "the record set by Jimmy Johnson of San Francisco." Rimbaud *classique*, invoked in Godard's murmured narration, sang of crystal skies and impassive rivers. Brasseur's Rimbaud *moderne* dreams of Ferraris.

Even when nothing is happening, the director sustains the illusion of forward momentum: in the pans that follow the characters' leapfrogging positions within the frame, in the use of moving vehicles as settings. And yet Godard the narrator distances us from the characters even as he's ostensibly bringing them closer — as in the movie's centerpiece, the wondrous sequence in which the three principals do a swivel-hipped "Madison" line dance. (It looks improvised on the spot; it actually took weeks of rehearsal.) As the finger-popping leads jive around a makeshift dance floor, the jukebox suddenly cuts out, leaving only Godard's voice and the tramp-tramp-*clap!* of the dancers' feet. The effect is of being awakened from a reverie — of the poignant instant that perception ushers the present into the past. "Franz thinks of everything and nothing," Godard narrates. "He wonders if the world is becoming a dream or a dream is becoming the world."

The dream is ruptured when the dormant crime plot reemerges. Arthur hits Odile with real violence, and it seems to shake even him. As Pauline Kael noted, the movie's earlier playfulness doesn't prepare us for this jolt; the characters seem to lack any psychological context beyond their immediate surroundings. During a train ride, Arthur and Odile watch a scowling passenger, and Arthur says his expression could mean anything, depending on the story he concocts around it. It's the Kuleshov editing principle extended to life, and it may also be Godard's comment on the blatant narrative manipulation that's a staple of the gangster thrillers he's imitating. Like the extras in our lives who pass us on the street, Godard's characters have facets and motivations we will never understand from the short time we're watching them. Our movie-fed fantasies are fragile things. When these abstractions collide with a concrete world, sometimes they shatter.

That scarcely makes them less pleasurable. If anything, Godard's lyrical fondness for the fleeting youth and beauty of his band of outsiders is even more touching because it seems so delicate, so threatened — so *pop*. The Madison sequence wouldn't be nearly as affecting without the bittersweet intimations of transience that precede it — like his beloved Karina catching a glimpse of a newspaper headline that reads, "Keep Your Youthful Eyes," or composer Michel Legrand quoting his own end-of-summer score from *The Umbrellas of Cherbourg*. After a jubilantly absurd happy ending, Godard finally concludes his movie "like in a pulp novel, at that superb moment when nothing weakens, nothing wears away, nothing wanes." His new film is titled *Eloge de l'amour*, but after almost four decades, the gorgeous and undimmed *Band of Outsiders* may be his true elegy for love. (*Nashville Scene*, Jan. 24, 2002)

● ● ● ● ● ● ● ● ● ●

Two English Girls
Dir. François Truffaut
1971, R, 130 min.

The Man Who Loved Women

First loves are haunting, as much for the immediacy of the initial rush as for the inevitable mellowing and fading of memory. For me, the sensation of falling in love will always be associated with the movies of François Truffaut. I was 15 and a high-school sophomore when a local college professor let me attend her screening of Truffaut's 1960 crime-thriller reverie *Shoot the Piano Player*. It's an ideal movie to see when you're just starting to comprehend the vast possibilities of cinema: a fizzing brew of elevated technique and low comedy, lyrical tenderness and sudden violence. I came away with a lifelong love of movies and an awkward crush on the teacher in the bargain.

By that point, it was too late for me to grow up with Truffaut's movies in sequence, the way young cineastes had done in the 1960s. (The closest equivalent for movie geeks my age was Woody Allen, who caused similar feelings of affection and frustration that went beyond mere appraisal.) But by starting with his first feature, 1959's *The 400 Blows* — an autobiographical account of his delinquent childhood, made less than 10 years after the director was out of his own teens — cinephiles could've charted their development against that of Truffaut and his frequent leading man Jean-Pierre Léaud, who played the director's alter ego Antoine Doinel from adolescence (*The 400 Blows*) to adulthood (1979's *Love on the Run*).

Throughout those years, moviegoers could see their own romantic yearnings reflected in Truffaut's films. Disarming trifles such as the Doinel films *Stolen Kisses* and *Bed and Board* made sweet sport of callow passion and indecision, and no movie has ever captured the exhilaration of young love as piercingly as his 1961 classic *Jules and Jim*. Yet for all their beauty and lyricism, Truffaut's films are profoundly marked by a sense of the ultimate folly of romantic love. That he addressed this theme in some of the most stunningly romantic movies ever filmed — such as *Two English Girls* — is a fascinating paradox.

When released in 1971, 10 years after *Jules and Jim*, *Two English Girls* was treated as a holding pattern in Truffaut's career, as if the director were so starved for ideas that he felt a simple gender inversion of *Jules and Jim* would do the trick. The comparisons are certainly there. *Two English Girls* is based on the only other novel Henri-Pierre Roché published besides *Jules and Jim*, and indeed it too concerns a love triangle. And like *Jules and Jim*, it's a study of love among impulsive, artistic intellectuals in the years surrounding World War I — a love that ultimately ends in death and solitude.

Where *Jules* is among the most fleet and freewheeling of films, though, *Two English Girls* is a work of quiet, somber and devastating power. Like Hitchcock's *Marnie*, Kubrick's *Barry Lyndon* and Scorsese's *The King of Comedy*, it was unjustly slighted at the time it came out, in part because it didn't deliver what audiences expected of its maker. Truffaut did himself no favors by shearing it of 14 minutes, which could only have destroyed the movie's cumulative urgency. But the 130-minute version he restored just before his death in 1984 is a glorious thing: the ultimate expression of his theme that perfect love may be unattainable, but life without the attempt is untenable.

Two English Girls traces the lengthy relationship between a young French-man, Claude Roc (Léaud, more hesitant and birdlike than ever), and the Brown sisters, Anne (Kika Markham) and Muriel (Stacey Tendeter). During a visit to Claude's mother, Anne suggests that he visit their country home in Wales. Claude is taken by Anne, but she sees him more as a mate for Muriel, who spends most of her days protecting her fragile eyesight. Nevertheless, it's as a flirtatious, endlessly curious threesome that they're happiest — the sisters grill him about his experiences at a bordello, and he's charmingly shocked by their request that he take them sometime.

Once the girls' mother gets wind of their frank talks, though, she banishes Claude to a neighbor's house. As always in Truffaut, isolation and restriction are a can't-fail recipe for obsession. Suddenly Claude falls in love with Muriel, who rebuffs him. He courts her ardently by letter. Their mothers, flustered, agree to enforce a year's separation between the budding lovers; at the end of that time they can marry. In a wrenching passage, Truffaut contrasts the passing of months for Claude and Muriel. Back in Paris, his attentions have drifted elsewhere. She dwells in sleepless agony, driven to inexpressible rage and despair over his letters.

In time, Anne will become a sculptress, and Muriel will become a teacher. Claude will always love the two sisters, who represent intoxicating extremes of romantic possibility — free love and obsessive devotion. "To choose between two things, you must know both," Muriel tells him early on. "I can't choose vice or virtue knowing only virtue." But Claude will never be able to choose between Anne and Muriel. And none will love the other as much, at any given time, as he or she is loved.

As Antoine de Baecque and Serge Toubiana's biography of Truffaut observes, the director himself was haunted by two sisters: Catherine Deneuve, who had broken off a brief but intense relationship with Truffaut just before the filming of *Two English Girls*; and Françoise Dorleac, the star of his *The Soft Skin*, whose untimely death in a 1967 car accident saddened him. Whatever the cause, the movie has a sustained, sorrowful gravity that's rarely present in his early films. In *Jules and Jim*, Truffaut's whirling camera transmits the fleeting passions of his characters straight to the viewer, which makes the movie's closing tragedy a real shock. It's a young man's idea of the impending ravages of time: the suddenness of loss without the heaviness of loss.

In *Two English Girls*, the sense of impending grief, for loves that cannot last, is a lengthening shadow. Thanks to the breathless narration, read by Truffaut at the pace and pitch of an auctioneer, we're always told what the characters are thinking and feeling. With that knowledge, though, comes the awareness that their idyllic passions will inevitably fade. Throughout much of the film we're kept at a literal distance from the characters: The lovers are specks against the rolling hills and seascapes.

But Claude, Anne and especially the religious Muriel are also prisoners of the uncertainties of the time. *Two English Girls* is set in the period of transition near the end of the Victorian era and the birth of modernism. (As if to signify this clash, Truffaut uses compositions as formal as 19th-century landscape paintings alongside spanking-new techniques from the onset of silent cinema, like the irises that zero in to end scenes.) The period isn't repressive enough to stifle the characters' curiosity about sex, but it isn't permissive enough to let them live as a menage à trois, either. Yet even as we witness the contrast between 19th- and 20th-century values, the movie's intensity of feeling is inseparable from its period detail. It has a depth of emotion born of a world with fewer distractions, when the smallest of social gestures was endlessly parsed for hidden meaning.

When I was in my late teens, I adored *Jules and Jim* but couldn't make it through a chopped-up video of *Two English Girls*. I love them equally now. The speed and whirling beauty of the former makes the latter even more poignant; the sad, persistent ache of *Two English Girls* makes *Jules and Jim* seem even more buoyant. To choose between them would be to choose between your first and greatest loves — between the one that taught you how to feel, and the one that's all the richer and deeper for the memory of the other. Unlike Claude, we can choose them both. (*Nashville Scene*, June 8, 2000)

● ● ● ● ● ● ● ● ● ●

Private Fears in Public Places
Dir. Alain Resnais
2006, NR, 120 min.

Alone Again, Naturally

The ubiquitous snowfall that blankets Alain Resnais' *Private Fears in Public Places* is a king-sized box of Hollywood soapflakes. As glimpsed through plate-glass facades, postage-stamp windows and doorways that might as well be portals into the void, it's fake in a grand tradition of movie snow: the art-directed sifting that isolates Jane Wyman at last with Rock Hudson in *All That Heaven Allows*; the Yuletide blizzard that douses one set of romantic hopes and blesses another in the glorious finale of *The Umbrellas of Cherbourg*. What these movies share, besides fragile and hard-won happiness — and the raw material for a snowball fight — is the use of blatant artifice to engage our imaginations and empathy; to find, through stylized heightening, something more real than sense-deadening "realism."

And so the snow falls, in Resnais' exquisite comedy-drama, on a Paris of color-coded soundstage interiors, some without ceilings or even a fourth wall. Six characters, either nearing or passing middle age, combine and recombine into couples, seeking the warmth of human connection against the chill outside. A pair of public spaces — a glass-walled real-estate office and a wowsers space-age bachelor pad of a hotel bar — are the hubs they orbit before retreating to the pitched battlefields of home.

The sets are deliberately artificial; the longing and isolation they contain are genuine. Coming from a director who made some of the most challenging and form-breaking films of the Nouvelle Vague era — particularly the memory-as-shrapnel meditations *Hiroshima, Mon Amour* and *Last Year at Marienbad* — this quasi-farcical fugue on loneliness and the difficulty of forging new loves late in life seems almost quaint in its mixing of golden-age cinematic gloss and transparently theatrical design. But Resnais' mastery shows how avant-garde the movie equivalent of a well-made play can be.

That isn't a slap at the source material, a play by Alan Ayckbourn (who also provided Resnais with the Anglophilic diptych *Smoking/No Smoking*). Rather, it's a tribute to the pleasures of Ayckbourn's elegantly symmetrical construction and Resnais' nimble staging. In the office, timid agent Thierry (André Dussollier) shyly eyes his co-worker, a redheaded sprite named Charlotte (Sabine Azéma) whose devout faith doesn't rule out amateur porn. In the hotel, worldly barkeep Lionel (Pierre Arditi) dispenses Scotch and wisdom to Dan (Lambert Wilson), a disgraced ex-career officer turned midlife layabout. Lionel hires Charlotte to nurse his bedridden, curmudgeonly father, represented by Claude Rich's offscreen voice and several airborne projectiles. Meanwhile, Dan's frustrated girlfriend, Nicole (Laura Morante), tries to resuscitate their dying relationship by finding a new apartment, with Thierry's help.

Resnais' last two films, *Same Old Song* and *Not on the Lips* (which went all but unseen in the U.S.), experimented with musical conventions. *Private Fears in Public Places* resembles a Vincente Minnelli musical with the songs elided, leaving the persistent ache of unexpressed desires. Where Minnelli's characters would open their hearts and throats in confidence to the viewer — eking out, say, some sliver of personal space in the close quarters of *Meet Me in St. Louis* — Resnais draws a curtain. The snowy dissolves that punctuate each scene strand the characters (and the viewer) in mid-emotion — none more painfully than Thierry's lovelorn sister Gaëlle (a radiant Isabelle Carré), who pins a bold crimson flower to her lapel on a succession of luckless blind dates.

Visually and dramatically, the movie is partitioned into small sections. The script, adapted by Jean-Michel Ribes, consists mainly of brief two-character vignettes, some barely lasting a minute. No one — not Thierry, holed up in lust-struck thrall to a spicy VHS tape; not Lionel, secretly agonizing in a roomful of oblivious customers — keeps our company for very long. The effect, at times, is of channel-surfing among six stations of simulcast melancholy. Among Resnais' trash-TV referents here is the lowly soap opera, that boon companion to the lonely and housebound. (Every time a scene ends with a character staring wistfully into space, you may imagine an announcer's voice thanking Procter & Gamble for its sponsorship.)

But lowbrow plus highbrow does not equal middlebrow, and the breezy accessibility of *Private Fears in Public Places* does not make it any less a work of art than Resnais' more difficult early successes. The effervescence of his direction disguises its formal rigor: the horizontal stripes that recur from set to set, subdividing apartments into compartments and walling off characters; the blocking that equates physical barriers with mental minefields; the coolly precise camera movements that shift the emotional focus within a scene. (The ravishing camerawork by Eric Gautier, who serves nouvelle-nouvelle-vague directors as heroically as Raoul Coutard did Truffaut and Godard, charges every ion of the pristine 'Scope frame with tactile longing.) By the same token, Resnais' intellectual engagement in no way diminishes the charm of a flawless cast at work (veterans Dussollier, Arditi, Azéma and Wilson are particularly fine) or of the unfashionable virtues of what gets disparaged as "civilized entertainment." Alain Resnais is now 84 years old; perhaps it takes eight decades of living to make a movie this compassionate, this confident — and this young. (*Nashville Scene*, May 31, 2007)

• • • • • • • • • •

Notre Musique
Dir. Jean-Luc Godard
2004, NR, 79 min.

Slipping Into Darkness

There's no living filmmaker who compares to Jean-Luc Godard — at least not one whose oracular bent is supported by his stature, and by the decades of association we have with his earlier work. But another name does spring to mind. The gnomic personal mythology, the restless need to reinvent himself, the work composed of snatches of remembered culture — does anyone else hear the music of Bob Dylan's second coming (or third, or fourth) in the wintry splendor of late-period Godard?

Having shaken off most anyone who would still holler for the early stuff — except for those fans who cling to him like barnacles through each new shift in identity — Dylan now makes art out of scraps: ancient bromides, old Tin Pan Alley standards, Delta blues, passages and titles of arcane books now fractured in memory. Ask him to tell you the future, and he opens up the Old Testament and the 1905 *Farmer's Almanac*. For Godard, the world is a bombed-out library, a cinematheque in ruins. In his career's waning light, he's made elegiac, magisterially broken movies from the shards that rain from the sky.

I won't belabor the comparison by calling Godard's *Notre Musique* his *Time Out of Mind*. But if ever a filmmaker conjured the benumbed calm of "walking through streets that are dead," Godard does in his 90th (!) film, a threnody for peace, cinema and the voices of the vanquished. Like his previous feature, *In Praise of Love*, it's a patchwork of film clips, literary allusions and historical citations, fastened by dialogue that sometimes suggests the output of a random aphorism generator. And yet the severity of *In Praise of Love* gives way to something like serenity — or the stillness after a cannon blast.

Notre Musique is a kind of fugue on the theme of opposition: not just enmity, but the life-defining relationships between light and dark, reality and imagination, rubble and rebuilding. The film is divided into three segments, or "kingdoms." The first, "Hell," is a dialectical firefight between real slaughter and fake war drama that gives the writing and erasing of histories the force of tectonic upheaval. It acts as a prologue for the second section, "Purgatory," which convenes fictional characters and French and Palestinian authors playing themselves at a literary conference in ravaged Sarajevo. The city forms a way station of tentative reconciliation before the unearthly paradise of the sun-dappled final segment, "Heaven."

Stylistically as well as thematically, *Notre Musique* is a sustained movement from violence to calm. The editing rhythms in "Hell" recall the famous moment in Godard's *My Life to Live* that evokes machine-gun fire visually. It takes him roughly 10 minutes to encapsulate human warfare. An atrocity exhibition of 20th-century horrors (death-camp footage, Middle East bombings) vies for posterity with clips from *Zulu* and *Battleship Potemkin*, histories officially endorsed by the winners. The effect, immediate as calamity, is of deepening darkness — the fog of war.

The darkness relents, if not lifts, in the movie's longest section, "Purgatory." Though set at the epicenter of another of the 20th century's proliferating genocides, it's shot through with cautious optimism. Godard's modern-day Sarajevo is a common ground, not a killing ground, where the world's citizens try to neutralize the politics of victimization and oppression. In this no-man's-land, a Spanish author (novelist Juan Goytisolo as himself) meets with fictitious Native Americans in the ruins of a public library, far from the ghost of Columbus. An Israeli journalist (Sarah Adler) hopes to find "a place where reconciliation was possible," not another irresolvable West Bank, while her Russian-Israeli doppelganger (Nade Dieu) brings the movie's allusions to *Hamlet* to their despairing end: to be or not to be.

In the background is Godard himself, owlish and bespectacled, seen early on nursing a foot-long stogie he might've bummed off Samuel Fuller. His hopes for Middle East peace seem slim but faintly hopeful, though more hopeful than he seems to regard his continued relevance. The movie's centerpiece is a dazzling lecture in which Godard breaks down cinema (yet again) to its atoms of composition: "shot and reverse shot," Cary Grant and Rosalind Russell, the thing and its opposite, just like the celluloid negative that produces an image filled with light. "Go toward the light and shine it on our night," he commands his listeners, who sit bored and twittering. Somebody has a question: Will those little digital cameras save the movies? Godard sits silently in silhouette. Nostradamus gives an audience, and all anybody wants to know is who'll win tomorrow's football game.

As befits a movie (and a career) so obsessed with claiming equality of text and image, *Notre Musique* practically demands separate viewings — one for the bristling thicket of Godard's interlocked provocations, one for his still mesmerizing command of montage and movement. But that doesn't mean he'll get them. To converts won by the *Band of Outsiders* reissue, *In Praise of Love* resembled something smashed on the ground and imperfectly reassembled, no matter how beautiful and wounding its jagged pieces. *Notre Musique* is much more linear and thematically accessible — it's amusing to note how many reviews use the word "lucid" — but it's still hard to sort out the many unidentified literary figures, and there's no one person to serve as our guide or point of identification in Godard's democratic design. The movie won't placate critics who can't stand his use of characters as philosophical mouthpieces, or who don't have the time to unpack arguments as dense and spiraling as supernovas — even if those arguments can change the way you consider the world. People love a seer, until he starts to look beyond them.

We will not get back the man who made *A Woman Is a Woman* and *Masculin-Feminin*: He is no longer here. His characters will not sing out "*New York Herald Tribune!*" on the Paris streets again, or hand-jive an impromptu Madison. Instead, we have this stubborn soothsayer who is interested in the there and then only as it relates to the here and now. But if we listen close, he is making music as strong and passionate as that of his youth, *our* youth. Just like the guy a few years back who sang, "Well my sense of humanity has gone down the drain / Behind every beautiful thing there's been some kind of pain." In *Notre Musique* it's not dark yet, but it's getting there. (*Nashville Scene*, Jan. 13, 2005)

How the Western Won 2

Among the many objects vying for visual attention in Jim's office at the *Scene* was an envelope bearing this hand-scrawled message: "THAT'S WHAT I'VE GOT." The *what* was emphatically double-underlined in green Sharpie. The line comes from Howard Hawks' 1959 film *Rio Bravo*, in which John Wayne plays John T. Chance, a small-town sheriff who enlists two rather unlikely partners to help him beat the bad guys: a lawman with a drinking problem (Dean Martin) and a guy with a limp (Walter Brennan). At one point, a friend tells Chance what he thinks of his squad: "A game-legged old man and a drunk. That's all you got?" he says.

Chance responds tersely: "That's *what* I've got."

As *Scene* staff writer Steven Hale tells it, "Jim told me he had put that sign on his wall to remind him not to give in to the discouragement that could come from being short-staffed and under-resourced. . . . He made you believe that in a pickup game of journalism, with everyone on the field to choose from, he'd want you on his team."[1] If there's any genre that can inspire a belief that codes of honor and loyalty hold the key to surviving against all odds, it's the Western. This chapter collects some of Jim's best work on the Old West as presented in film.

One of cinema's most enduring archetypes, the Western is itself an amalgam of influences that has found ways to evolve and reinvent itself. In Jim's imagination, they all deserve a closer look, from the intimate "termite Westerns" of Sergio Corbucci to the immersive, off-kilter *McCabe & Mrs. Miller*, from the abrasive violence of *The Wild Bunch* to the grave restraint of *Meek's Cutoff*.

---

1   "Jim Ridley, 1965–2016."

● ● ● ● ● ● ● ● ● ●

Once Upon a Time in the West
Dir. Sergio Leone
1968, PG-13, 164 min.

Hot Leaded

"Once upon a time in Nazi-occupied France," reads the chapter heading that opens Quentin Tarantino's *Inglourious Basterds* — a commando mission in counter-mythmaking where a movie theater, a projector, a handy editing deck and a great big heap of flammable film stock (not to mention the climaxes of *Carrie* and *The Wizard of Oz* and the theme song from *Cat People*) team up to wipe out the Third Reich's high command. It's a movie about the power of movies to change history, in that celluloid parallel universe where memory and imagination stand off with the record.

How fitting that Tarantino's chapter heading tips its visor hat to the movies of Sergio Leone, an alternate history of America conjured up from gunsmoke and mirrors. The first time I saw *Once Upon a Time in the West*, I was a kid watching the WNGE "Award Movie" on Sunday afternoon, on the floor of my grandmother's living room. For lots of reasons, it was the worst possible way to watch one of the most visually striking movies ever made. But I can still see this image, burned into my mind's eye: a gaunt bald gunslinger standing impassively, staring into the camera, as a drip from the ceiling fills the wide brim of his hat with a thup! thup! thup!

Over the years, I've found something more to appreciate every time I've seen *Once Upon a Time in the West*. But every time, it leaves me feeling like an awestruck 10 year old. It has something to do with the scale of Leone's gloriously excessive 1968 Western. Every dusty street is a football field's width. Every grizzled face, shot in screen-filling close-up, looms like a head on Mount Rushmore. Every gunfight is a duel of the gods. A viewer becomes an HO-scale brakeman walking through a regular-sized trainyard. In this, the most elaborate and exhilarating of his grandiose pistol operas, Leone took the Western he envisioned as a child — an Old West of quick-triggered warriors, enormous open spaces and superheroic deeds — and transferred it to the screen with its mythic distortions intact.

Apart from the scale (and the title), there's nothing childlike about *Once Upon a Time in the West*. An inextricable mix of cynicism, violence and delicate lyricism — as voluptuous and perverse as you'd expect from a story dreamed up by Bernardo Bertolucci (*The Conformist*) and Dario Argento (*Suspiria*) — the movie was a critical and commercial failure when released here in

1969, as the genre's audience was either riding into the twilight with the Duke or grooving on the revisionist bloodbath of *The Wild Bunch*. It was not the time to be romanticizing manifest destiny, even if Leone's quasi-Marxist take equates business with bloodshed.

Over the years, though, a funny thing has happened. Leone's outsized rethink of the Western, an exaggerated pastiche of the John Ford films and gunfighter mythology he absorbed as a boy overseas, has gradually edged aside the John Wayne and Roy Rogers models in the popular imagination. You can see it when you close your eyes: the figures at opposite ends of a dust-blown street, the close-ups of "two beeg eyes" glaring edgily, the duster coats whirling like a bullfighter's cape. Thanks to Leone's invaluable collaborator, composer Ennio Morricone, you can hear it, too: the matadorial trumpets, the celestial female vocals, the trebly electric guitar that stabs and slashes.

Morricone's score clarifies a convoluted plot that concerns four main characters: a shadowy avenger (Charles Bronson); a prostitute, Jill (Claudia Cardinale), on her way to a blood-soaked wedding day; a scruffy outlaw named Cheyenne (Jason Robards); and a pale-eyed angel of death known only as Frank. He is played by Henry Fonda, who demolishes his decades of good-guy rectitude at the moment of his terrifying entrance. This is Tom Joad's evil doppelganger — a guy who's present wherever there's a fight so hungry people can eat, all right, but always working for those with a whip hand on the drawstrings of plenty.

Morricone composed the music before the movie even started shooting, and it is as much screenplay as score. Each character has a theme — Jill's motif is a soaring solo wail, Cheyenne's a pokey, halting clip-clop — and the composer interweaves them, stating the connections between characters without a word of dialogue. No one needs to state that Frank and his pursuer are bound; Morricone's menacing theme uses an ever-present harmonica to link them. Bronson's harmonica is literally an instrument of vengeance. It's the totem he wears around his neck, for a reason he means to explain to Frank at the point of death.

Oh, there's so much more. There's the tremendous opening sequence, in which Western icons Woody Strode and Jack Elam converge on a railway depot to the John Cage-like accompaniment of various squeaks and clatters. There's the hangdog decency of Robards' Cheyenne, the outlaw doomed by the suits moving West. And above all, there's the almost inhuman perfection of Leone's widescreen images, with their rhythmic alternation of flyspeck long shots and bulbous close-ups. Each frame has a painterly precision and clarity, as if the director had somehow eliminated anything standing between the screen and the image he had in his head. *Once Upon a Time in the West* is the kind of movie whose total intoxication with moviemaking can lead to a lifetime's love. (*Nashville Scene*, Aug. 27, 2009)

● ● ● ● ● ● ● ● ● ●

Dir. Sergio Corbucci
Navajo Joe
1966, NR, 93 min.

Django
1966, NR, 92 min.

The Great Silence
1968, NR, 105 min.

The Mercenary
1968, PG-13, 110 min.

To Sergio With Love

Back in the '70s, during his stints on *The Tonight Show*, Burt Reynolds spent a lot of time on Johnny Carson's couch recounting the bum assignments he'd taken as an up-and-comer. One of the worst, he said, was something called *Navajo Joe*. The spaghetti Westerns that made a star of Clint Eastwood, he explained, were directed by Sergio Leone — a genius, an artist, an auteur. No such luck for Reynolds. He got somebody named Sergio Corbucci.

The punchline brought down the house. But decades later, the late Corbucci may have the posthumous last laugh. On Christmas Day, one of the director's most ardent fans, Quentin Tarantino, releases *Django Unchained*, a down-South spaghetti Western variation that appropriates the title of Corbucci's biggest hit. Tarantino's hardly a Djohnny-come-lately on the subject of the Italian director: The *Kill Bill* saga borrows Ennio Morricone's *Navajo Joe* score for its climax, while *Inglourious Basterds* doffs a dagger to its forehead-carving revenge motif.

But you can go straight to the source, as the Belcourt offers a four-film introduction to Corbucci's savagely unsentimental West. Where the Hollywood Western traditionally concerned itself with the building and maintaining of civilization — the lawman facing down the gunslinger and his ilk in the street — the Italian-backed, Spanish-shot spaghetti Western cut the genre down to cold commerce. Deaths mean money, bodies mean money; killing is business, and business booms.

Even within that framework, the politically caustic Westerns of Corbucci — a former film critic who worked his way up the ranks of Italian cinema through sword-and-sandal programmers and the like — deliver a mule kick of unbridled cynicism. The zestfully vicious *Navajo Joe* opens by establishing scalps as currency; its villain is an upstanding town doctor who sells out his own kin to an outlaw gang for filthy lucre. "You can smell those dollars," the gang leader chortles, smacking his lips (which rarely match his dubbed dialogue).

Too bad they crossed Reynolds, an American Indian Terminator with a caveman coif and a skin tone that might be described as Burt Orange. At the end, Reynolds will reveal why he has racked up a double-digit body count — through a plot device maestro Leone reworked for his epic *Once Upon a Time in the West* — but not before dispatching the entire gang one by chopped, scattered and smothered one. It's a Western, all right (Reynolds' pony even comes by whistle), but its morally ambiguous hero's rejection of society and all it stands for — including its money — says we're a long way from John Ford's Monument Valley.

In 1966, *Navajo Joe*, co-scripted by *poliziotteschi* cult favorite Fernando Di Leo, was considered the most violent movie ever released by a major studio. With Morricone's banshee-cry theme doing its damnedest to scare every bird out of Spain, it anticipates the slasher movie at times in its stalk-and-kill single-mindedness, and torture porn in the hero's sadistic ordeal at the hands of captors, a ritual the spaghetti Westerns used to bear-prod the audience's bloodlust. (The mood must've been catching: The assistant director was future *Cannibal Holocaust* goremeister Ruggero Deodato.)

By comparison, Corbucci's acknowledged 1968 masterwork *The Great Silence* is more like sci-fi in its otherworldly bleakness. Here a mute gunslinger (the great Jean-Louis Trintignant, a possible Best Actor contender this year for Michael Haneke's *Amour*) tracks a lupine bounty hunter (Klaus Kinski at his most feral) through a blizzard-struck Chernobyl of a Mormon village. Unstinting in its brutal nihilism — try re-hinging your jaw after that ending — it's as ferocious as Morricone's jewel-box score is elegiac and haunting.

Leone has gotten the lion's share of critical attention over the years, perhaps because his epic yarns have an operatic grandiloquence and an element of myth-making almost absent from Corbucci's termite Westerns. That will make it all the more interesting to compare their takes on similar material —

such as Corbucci's 1968 *The Mercenary*, which pits turn-of-the-century Mexican firebrand Tony Musante and Polish gun-for-hire Franco Nero against another of the director's vengeance-warped villains, American angel of doom Jack Palance. It arrived ahead of Leone's own Mexican Revolution reverie *Duck, You Sucker!* by three years; by that time, Corbucci had already made his own partial remake, *Compañeros*, reuniting Nero and Palance.

No self-professed spaghetti-Western aficionado will want to miss Corbucci's best-known film and a touchstone of the genre, 1966's *Django* — not just to bone up for Tarantino's movie, but to see how the director handles the *Yojimbo/Red Harvest* setup Leone spun into gold in the genre-defining *A Fistful of Dollars*. Corbucci immediately establishes the tone of grimy surrealism with black-hatted gunslinger hero Nero clanking robotically into view . . . dragging a coffin. Meanwhile, a gang of banditos strips and flogs a maiden, only to have a rival ex-Confederate and his red-hooded Klansmen intervene — and claim the woman for their own.

Django's comic-book violence escalates to trick shots and outright machine-gunning, bookended by a nifty theme song that suggests being escorted through the Wild West by Andy Williams. Taken as a whole, these movies form a burlesque of manifest destiny as a carnival shooting gallery that falls to the biggest, fastest, coldest gun. Burt Reynolds may have been right that Sergio Corbucci would always play second fiddle in the spaghetti Western's atrocity orchestra. For as long as the ammo holds out in Corbucci's merciless West, though, as the title of the Belcourt's retro suggests, it's Leone's turn to be "the other Sergio." (*Nashville Scene*, Nov. 29, 2012)

• • • • • • • • •

McCabe & Mrs. Miller
Dir. Robert Altman
1971, R, 120 min.

How the West Was Lost

Long before anyone thought of handing audiences pushbuttons and joysticks to control the outcome of a work of art, Robert Altman was making interactive movies. A necessary step from the loose-limbed horseplay of 1970's *M.A.S.H.* toward the kaleidoscopic sprawl of 1975's *Nashville*, his 1971 Western *McCabe & Mrs. Miller* engages a viewer's attention in ways that make other movies seem narrow and stodgy — especially those controlled by pushbuttons and joysticks.

The movie's set in a frontier mining town just after the turn of the century, and the viewer enters it at the same time as a nameless man, who saunters into a shanty saloon and sets up a poker game. Eventually, among the clatter of voices and sounds, we overhear a conversation in which the man is identified as one "Pudgy" McCabe — Warren Beatty in a scruffy prospector's beard, his Popeye-like mutter serving as his own commentary track.

Before long, the bluff, big-talking McCabe has set up a rustic whorehouse with three scraggly hookers. He thinks big enough to hire a real madam, Mrs. Miller (Julie Christie), an unsentimental businesswoman who challenges him to open a proper sporting house. They become lovers, for cash up front, and their booming business draws the attention of a corporate syndicate. It will settle this matter of commerce in the ways of the coming century — a hostile takeover.

Working loosely from a script co-written by novelist Brian McKay, Altman created something new in American moviemaking: a genre piece in which the narrative emerges from the periphery — from the buzz of incidental voices, from actions that aren't always at the center of the screen. A viewer watching this for the first time is a stranger in town. When violence occurs, it's not the ritualized gunplay of *High Noon* or the balletic bloodshed of *The Wild Bunch*: It's ugly and clumsy and cruelly disruptive. There is uncommon horror in its bleak unfairness and finality — the fate that befalls Keith Carradine's lovably gawky cowpoke is more chilling even than its icy backdrop.

Yet the action, like Vilmos Zsigmond's yellowy, memory-clouded cinematography, gets clearer as the tale unfolds. By the ending's climactic shootout, Altman has fixed the town in our minds as a specific universe, and his piquant ensemble players (including Shelley Duvall, Rene Auberjonois and John Schuck) are its true landmarks. Leonard Cohen's opiate murmur on the soundtrack turns the movie's elegiac mood into melody — you recall the fragile songs with a pang of sadness.

Beatty, always good at finding unexpected dimensions in foolish characters, transforms the boastful McCabe into a tragicomic hero. And Christie was never more vivid a presence; she plays Mrs. Miller as a kind of starved animal who's frightened to feel anything other than hunger. See *McCabe & Mrs. Miller* today and marvel that it was ever released by a major studio, let alone made. (*Nashville Scene*, July 16, 2009)

• • • • • • • • • •

The Wild Bunch
Dir. Sam Peckinpah
1969, R, 135 min.

Forever Wild

A group of children stand laughing in a circle; we assume they are playing a game. They are. They have tossed scorpions into an ant colony. They smile, watching to see which creatures get killed first. This scene is intercut with two separate actions: a group of Texas Rangers riding into a small town, and a minister conducting a temperance meeting. A martial drumbeat is heard on the soundtrack; a solarized freeze-frame bearing a different credit ("William Holden") punctuates each drum roll.

Suddenly, a new element is introduced: A posse of gunmen gather on a rooftop above the town streets. The Rangers walk into a bank. The gunmen load their weapons. The temperance band begins to march. A brassy version of "Shall We Gather at the River" blares on the soundtrack. A heartbeat pounds in time. In a shattering instant, we realize how these elements are about to combine — and what follows is a massacre that, 25 years ago, obliterated all previous screen standards for violence. Bodies whirl in slow motion, cut apart by bullets. Gunshots open holes as wide as silver dollars in their victims. When the streets are filled with blood, the movie cuts back to the group of laughing children. They have tired of their game. They have set both the ants and the scorpions on fire.

When Sam Peckinpah's *The Wild Bunch* was first released in 1969, that brilliant opening scene — and the even more gruesome ones that follow — ignited a debate about screen bloodshed that has never been fully resolved. The movie was condemned as mindless mayhem, and its director's name became synonymous with gory violence. The outcry over the movie's still horrific killings often overshadowed the movie's artistry, its fearless and magisterial command of film technique.

Today, however, you can turn on a cable station and see sex and violence far more explicit than anything in *The Wild Bunch*. What seems shocking today about *The Wild Bunch* — which has just opened at the Belcourt for the first time in a newly restored director's cut — is its astonishing cinematic invention. Our senses have been so dulled by the gutless, carbon-copy mentality of contemporary major-studio filmmaking that *The Wild Bunch* stands out like a Faulkner first edition in a Danielle Steel boutique.

Like Peckinpah's marvelous 1962 debut, *Ride the High Country* — now there's a movie due for re-release — *The Wild Bunch* is an elegy not just for the West but for the Western itself, with its codes of honor and courage and manhood. Pike Bishop, the aged Texas Ranger–turned–bank robber played by William Holden, joins the gallery of Peckinpah heroes — Joel McCrea in *Ride the High Country*, Jason Robards Jr. in *The Ballad of Cable Hogue* — whose integrity and personal loyalty have no place in a world dominated by corporations, mechanization and modernization. His men — Ernest Borgnine, Ben Johnson, Warren Oates, Edmond O'Brien and Jaime Sanchez, the most formidable assemblage of character actors since the days of John Ford — ride with him because Pike's code of mutual support is all they have.

Pursued by a former associate, Deke Thornton (Robert Ryan), who feels more kinship with the outlaws he's hunting than the bloodthirsty scum in his posse, Pike and his men settle on one last score: hijacking a train (which itself will soon be obsolete) and delivering its shipment of guns to a sadistic Mexican general, Mapache (Emilio Fernandez), in exchange for gold. An alliance with Mapache, however, is too low even for them. In the movie's breathtaking conclusion, Pike and his men seek redemption in a final blaze of glory against Mapache's entire army.

Peckinpah establishes his major themes — the cruelty underneath the veneer of civilization, the sanctity of masculine loyalty and honor in a world without God — in the very first scene, and the rest of the movie is a virtual tone poem about masculinity in peril: women are madonnas *and* whores, and woe to the man who turns his back on them. In later Peckinpah films like *Straw Dogs*, where female characters are more central, this view would calcify into intractable macho nonsense; in a Western, it seems appropriately archaic coming from characters who are themselves becoming anachronisms.

The Wild Bunch was made at a time when Westerns were beginning a slow fade into oblivion, and the movie has a mile-wide sadness, a respect for vanishing space: With the peerless cinematographer Lucien Ballard, who dapples the screen in shadows and sifted light, Peckinpah uses his wide frame to show both the expanses surrounding his characters and the boundaries that will ultimately imprison them. For this reason, seeing the movie on a wide screen is imperative: Watching it on TV counts no more than viewing the middle section of a painting.

The most surprising thing about seeing *The Wild Bunch* after more than a quarter of a century, though, is how well Peckinpah's style has survived after decades of imitation. Working with editor Louis Lombardo, Peckinpah captured the rhythm of chaos like no other director, mixing slow-motion shots with quick cuts to heighten the sensation of violence. The use of slow motion, however, has another purpose: Like the passages in epic poetry when a particular death is eulogized for several lines, it permits a moment of reflection on the end of a human life. As with the famous Robert Capa photograph of a victim in the Spanish Civil War at the moment of death, or Goya's pitiless recordings of wartime atrocities, a chill of mortality passes through you whenever one of Peckinpah's countless corpses settles to the ground.

Former television directors like Peckinpah and Robert Altman, among others, viewed feature filmmaking as an explosion from captivity. They looked at the vast expanse of the movie-theater screen, and they saw visions that could not be confined within the restraints of a little black box. They tried editing tricks and wide-angle compositions that couldn't be used on TV; they explored subject matter, language and actions that would never pass a network censor. Today, when you watch a blank, futile mediocrity like *Bye Bye Love* or *Man of the House*, or even a clunky prestige picture like *Nell* or *Legends of the Fall*, you forget that you're not sitting at home clutching a remote control. Today there no escaping from TV.

There is no escaping the legions of imitators, also, who looked at Peckinpah's vision of hell on earth and saw only how cool violence looks in slow motion. Peckinpah himself never escaped the self-destroying creation that is *The Wild Bunch*; by the end of his career, he was the victim of his own macho mythmaking, a Hemingway killed by the burden of living up to his press, and he tricked out his familiar mannerisms until they became self-parody.

But I look at William Holden filling the billboard-sized screen once more at the Belcourt, his eyes like beacons, his deeply lined face like granite cut through by decades of wind and weather-beating, and I am reminded once more of greatness. When he slings on his holster to face Mapache, William Holden moves with the confidence and authority of someone who spent a lifetime commanding every inch of those giant screens. The little black box couldn't hold him any more than it could Sam Peckinpah or the movie that endures as his greatest creation. When *The Wild Bunch* leaves the screen, even after 25 years, it still leaves in flames of glory. (*Nashville Scene*, April 20, 1995)

● ● ● ● ● ● ● ● ● ●

The Ballad of Little Jo
Dir. Maggie Greenwald
1993, R, 121 min.

Go West, Young Woman

Maggie Greenwald's *The Ballad of Little Jo* is quite simply one of the year's best movies, one of those rare films like *McCabe & Mrs. Miller* that reimagine our past in fresh, invigorating ways. Inspired by a real life, it recounts the story of a woman named Josephine, who traveled the Old West alone after being disowned by her family back East. Finding the life of a single woman in a macho world unbearably cruel, she chose an unexpected solution: She took a razor to her pretty face, outlined herself in men's clothes and passed herself off as a frail miner named Jo.

In most movies, this situation would be played for ludicrous farce. Instead, writer-director Greenwald makes us understand that the motivations behind Little Jo's decision — fear of rape and murder, the intolerance and oppressive laws of the male society — are neither laughing matters nor passing threats. Even her closest friend in this society, a boisterous sheep rancher played unfussily and well by Bo Hopkins, makes a habit of attempting to kill any stranger who isn't white, male or heterosexual. As the years pass, and Little Jo strikes up a dangerous romance with someone in an even more precarious social position — a Chinese man called Tinman (David Chung) — the tension never slackens. To reveal her true nature means certain death.

Through Little Jo, who longs to be recognized as an individual, the movie shows that gender roles then (like now) were as damaging for men as they were for women. But *The Ballad of Little Jo* never dwells on the abstract; it focuses primarily on the minutiae of frontier life, from the problems of disentangling a woolly sheep to the proper way of smoking a pipe. We get a feel for the atmosphere and realities of Western living that puts the revisionist clichés of *Unforgiven* to shame.

As Little Jo, Suzy Amis gives one of the most remarkable performances of the year, regardless of whether you think she could pass for a man. (To these eyes, she looks uncannily like Eric Stoltz.) She keeps us constantly aware of the desperation behind the deception; the burden shows in her purposefully unreadable expression and restricted movements. Although she gives the movie its basic credibility, the film is helped immeasurably by Declan Quinn's marvelous cinematography, which uses naturalistic lighting to outstanding effect, and a pleasingly unobtrusive score by David Mansfield.

This excellent film deserves a wider audience than it will ever reach. (*Nashville Scene*, Oct. 28, 1993)

● ● ● ● ● ● ● ● ● ●

Meek's Cutoff
Dir. Kelly Reichardt
2010, PG, 104 min.

Meek Shall Not Inherit

Even good Westerns these days tend to look like pageants — excuses for people to dress up and go through ritualized motions of gunfights, shoot-outs and hard rides. To an extent, you can blame Sergio Leone's operatic spaghetti Westerns of the 1960s, glorious as they are, which fetishized every sidelong glance and reach for a pistol. Over time, the gestures in something like the *Young Guns* movies or *The Quick and the Dead* became more important than whatever motivated them, as if the gunslingers were assuming predetermined roles in a passion play.

Along comes Kelly Reichardt's *Meek's Cutoff*, a kind of anti-Leone Western, to reassert the virtues of economy, purpose and tight construction. The time and setting, established in the same breath as the title, is 1845 Oregon; a wagon fords a river, followed by several settlers. The crossing hews closely to real time — not because long takes are the rage these days in art movies, but because nothing for people headed west in 1845 would be hastened by modern convenience. Under Reichardt's scrutiny, each action takes on weight because of the time and effort behind it. You want a drink of water, you'll hoist that big wooden bucket; you want to wash that dish, you'll haul it down to the creek.

Those duties take on a different cast after the movie's early scenes — about the time we realize we're watching a settler laboriously carve a message into a downed tree: "LOST." (Even the speed of desperation has been slowed.) Three couples have hired a guide named Meek (an ideal Bruce Greenwood, less Rooster Cogburn than a boastful capon), whose main qualification seems to be his resemblance to a Wild West show ringmaster. His swaggering confidence passes for knowledge. As a skeptical settler (Michelle Williams) figures out what Meek is increasingly unable to hide — he doesn't know where the hell he's going — the trailblazer gets a break. He secures a convenient diversion: a lone American Indian captive (Rod Rondeaux) who provides a handy focus for the party's fears.

If Leone brought enormity to the Western genre — a mythic scale that made every dusty street into Monument Valley — Reichardt brings gravity. The cinematographer, Christopher Blauvelt, uses the same roughly square 1.33:1 aspect ratio that Anthony Mann filmed his early 1950s Westerns in, and Reichardt employs the boxy frame with similar skill. There's space all around the characters, but having no clear-cut path or destination makes it eerily claustrophobic — an effect heightened by the sci-fi desolation of lunar salt flats and empty plains.

Being lost in this landscape builds a steady, unrelieved tension, and the weight Reichardt gives all those mundane chores in the early scenes pays off when the situation calls for something as grave as a standoff with guns — a beloved genre convention whose urgency and underlying resolve is fully felt here. When you see how much trouble it takes to lock and load a rifle, you get a much stronger sense of the determination it takes to point one at somebody.

Meek's Cutoff, written by Jon Raymond with an admirable emphasis on action over language and exposition, has been read as a Bush II allegory of a corrupt leader guiding unquestioning followers into the abyss. The movie's much better than that. With Williams, an actress who projects a questing mind and hard head, as the movie's acting intelligence, it's more a story of misplaced faith and a populace starting to listen to its conscience. The ruthless manifest destiny Meek represents may be exposed as a con, but in the boldly unresolved ending, there are no guarantees the route the settlers choose will lead anywhere but a different doom. (*Nashville Scene*, May 19, 2011)

Heroes and Anti-Heroes 3

n the middle of a particularly tough week, when rumors swirled that the *Scene* might be sold, Jim called us into his office for an emergency meeting. Everyone was on edge, and none of us knew what was coming. When we were finally all packed in, Jim opened his mouth to speak, but he burst into tears instead. In a moment, he collected himself, punching his leg in anger at not being able to hold it together. In the end, the paper would be sold, and we would all lose our jobs before most of us got them back again. But what Jim didn't know, and what I wish I had told him, was that in that moment I was far more inspired by his raw honesty than I would have been by the cocksure old-school newspaperman he had hoped to conjure.

"Superman is who we would like to be," Jim writes, but it turns out we can't leap tall buildings after all. That doesn't mean we can't make a difference to the people who depend on us. This chapter considers the powerful characters we choose to stand in for our better selves — and sometimes our worst — while also problematizing the notion of the hero. Crusaders caped and otherwise coexist alongside the cold-blooded assassin of *Le Samouraï*; the fleet-fisted Bruce Lee, the good-hearted criminals Thelma and Louise. There's a tension between restoring order and imposing it, between violence as an instrument of justice and violence as a misguided purifying rite.

While these are murky territories, Jim always navigates them with a sense of a moral center. Jim's review of *Star Wars: Episode III* tracks the tragic story arc of a gifted young man seduced by power. It also discusses how Anakin Skywalker becomes Darth Vader. Elsewhere, Jim interrogates the question: What does "getting the hero treatment" mean? And is it a mixed blessing at best? Jim also raises other questions about the nature of our entertainments. He likens the success of *Star Wars* — or, more accurately, its transformation of the way movies are marketed — to a contaminant in the water supply. Jim is referring to Batman's alter ego, Bruce Wayne, when he writes, "He can't change what he's become, flaws and all." But he could be talking about anyone.

● ● ● ● ● ● ● ● ● ●

Batman Begins
Dir. Christopher Nolan
2005, PG-13, 141 min.

The Dark Knight Returns

The difference between DC's defining comic-book heroes comes down to this: Superman is who we would like to be, but Batman is who we are. Superman was born with the power to outrun locomotives and bend bars of steel; to fit in with the rest of us, as David Carradine's coldhearted bastard observes in *Kill Bill Vol. 2,* he has to dress like a four-eyed dork and pretend to fumble at simple tasks. Batman, by contrast, is a costume — a mask, a suit of armor and some wicked accessories. Its wearer, Bruce Wayne, is essentially what Superman must feign to be: flawed, vulnerable, human — one of us.

That crucial distinction came through in Tim Burton's 1989 *Batman,* the movie that completed the character's decade-long rehabilitation from campy irrelevance to renewed Caped Crusader. But subsequent sequels made him even sillier than Adam West's TV quip dispenser in tights. The character was supposed to be scary, an avenger who struck fear on sight. It's hard to fear a smirky poseur with sculpted nipples. Worse, the void that should have been a heroic presence was overrun with hammy celebrity villains. The villains did more damage than the weak central character, because they emptied the movies of genuine menace. Without a threat to counterbalance, Batman is just a Halloween getup.

Why take issue with the portrayal of a guy in a bat costume? The answer's in *Batman Begins,* Christopher Nolan's bracingly camp-free retelling of the Dark Knight origin story. It's a measure of the movie's care, as well as its limits, that it's easier to talk about what the movie doesn't do wrong than what it does right: It doesn't treat the material with condescension; it doesn't clutter the story with celebrity cameos; but it does restore the potency of the comics' resonant premise — an ordinary man armed against evil with the power of a symbol.

Nolan's Batman is neither the joker of the TV version nor the executioner of Frank Miller's *The Dark Knight Returns.* As played by Christian Bale, he's introduced as a scraggly, cold-eyed prisoner in a remote gulag — a training camp where he hones his fists on the scum of the earth. Orphaned by crime, the vengeful Bruce Wayne plots a payback in blood until he encounters a shadow society of true vigilantes. Under the tutelage of Liam Neeson's suavely severe instructor — a studly, ruthless Yoda — he learns what eye-for-an-eye justice is, but decides he wants no part. Instead, he returns to crime-ridden Gotham City to see if its good people can be protected and saved.

The story's been told before, but not with Nolan's painstaking attention to narrative construction and creating a believable world. As in his tricky *Memento*, Nolan shows a gift for placing flashbacks and revelations where they'll make the most impact, usually on character development. With co-screenwriter David S. Goyer, an ardent champion and translator of comics to film, he finds the story's emotional core, seizing upon Bruce Wayne's grief for his murdered father — an ache not dulled by his devoted butler Alfred (a wonderful turn by Michael Caine, less servile and more parental than previous incarnations).

Nolan also gives old gimmicks a new grounding in physical and psycho-logical plausibility. None (except maybe the rugged new Batmobile) gets more of an upgrade than the bat insignia — a symbol that, in this telling, fuses fear with a father's protection. Like the hero's gadgetry, the villains are properly scaled, and better for staying largely in the background. As aided by the nightmarish Scarecrow (Cillian Murphy, in a strangely effective feed-sack mask), their timely plot is to drive Gotham into a hallucinatory frenzy of fear, then let people tear each other to pieces — in the name of restoring order.

All the movie lacks is a spark of transformative vision. Many fans resented Tim Burton's black humor and morbid romanticism, but his Gotham City came alive as a city of vaults — a bat's nocturnal kingdom. Nolan's version, by comparison, seems cautious, and his action scenes are a mess of blurred torsos, disconnected limbs and unrecognizable bodies. That might not matter if there weren't so many of them, and if they didn't assume such dramatic weight in the plot. Batman's final showdown with his archenemy is especially anticlimactic. For the last stand of judicious heroism vs. blind vigilantism, I'd rather have one well-scripted duel of words than the same old CGI madhouse.

Maybe it speaks well of Nolan, though, that rendering a fistfight properly means less to him than connecting with the material's substance. (For the inverse, see *Mr. & Mrs. Smith* — a collection of superbly staged explosions and killings without a whisper of moral or emotional weight.) Christian Bale may not have the quicksilver temper Michael Keaton brought to the Burton film, but his overall aura of ill-defined hurt better suits this film. Newly bulked up, his sad, isolated Bruce Wayne still looks a little uncomfortable in his own skin. He can't change what he's become, flaws and all; he can only try to become something better. In other words, he's one of us. (*Nashville Scene*, June 16, 2005)

• • • • • • • • • •

Le Samouraï
Dir. Jean-Pierre Melville
1967, PG, 101 min.

This Gun for Hire

It may have been the Summer of Love, but 1967 has gone down in film history as the year of the postmodern gangster movie. It was the year John Boorman's brilliant, brutal *Point Blank* shattered its narrative like a jackboot stomping a weakling's glasses. It was the year Faye Dunaway's Bonnie and Warren Beatty's Clyde got gunned to pieces because they bought into their own outlaw mythology. And it was the year a stone-cold hit man adjusted his wide-brimmed fedora, walked into a crowded Parisian nightclub, and emptied his pistol into the owner. Why did you come here, the victim asks. "To kill you," the hit man replies. There is no emotion in his voice and none expected. This is just business. Bam. Bam. Bam.

Like *Point Blank* and *Bonnie & Clyde*, *Le Samouraï* is impossible to imagine without the influence of six decades of crime movies. It's the work of a French director, Jean-Pierre Melville, who grew up feasting on American pulp thrillers and glossy Hollywood dramas, which fueled his themes of loyalty, betrayal, and codes of honor and conduct among the criminal classes. And yet it's an amazing, one-of-a-kind movie — a slow, fanciful, ruminative character study seething with thuggish cool — that has led to some of the most over-the-top action movies of recent years.

If you go expecting the slam-bang bloodshed of the movies it inspired — chiefly *Reservoir Dogs* and *The Killer* — you'll probably fall asleep. (This influence is probably what got the movie re-released.) But if you love movies that change the way you see the world, that plant you in another person's consciousness for two hours, that allow you to pretend you're stalking the streets of Paris with steel-blue eyes and killer reflexes, you'll want to tell every hardcore movie nut you know about it — which I pretty much spent the weekend doing.

Le Samouraï opens with a great, unsettling shot of a big empty hotel room with a solitary figure laid out on the bed, wreathed in cigarette smoke. Using a famous trick employed by Hitchcock and countless other suspense directors, the camera simultaneously pulls backward and zooms forward, creating a disorienting warp in perspective — but cinematographer Henri Decae (*The 400 Blows*) staggers the zoom effect, making the room seem to bow and bend. That's how it feels to be master assassin Jef Costello, a cold-blooded loner whose sole companion is a bullfinch that chirps at the sign of danger (a neat touch). Alain Delon, his face as pale and impassive as a Kabuki mask, plays Jef; he was cast as much for his suave, blank pretty-boy looks as for his ability to look debauched and haunted all at once.

The movie follows Jef as his latest assignment turns into a nightmare of police lineups, constant surveillance and double crosses that must be repaid in blood. The police press his casual lover (Nathalie Delon) to rat him out; a mysterious cabaret singer (Caty Rosier) refuses to finger him, which is suspicious in itself. It dawns on him, and on us, that he has fulfilled his last contract. Nevertheless, he accepts one more job — one whose target, he learns, is much closer to home. He refuses to back out. He has, after all, accepted the money.

Jean-Pierre Melville (né Grumbach; he adopted the name of his favorite author) was a flamboyant tough guy and lifelong movie buff who fought in the French Resistance during World War II. His wartime experiences, like Samuel Fuller's, shaped a view of the world best expressed in tough, gut-level crime-dramas. (His fast, economical methods of working were an inspiration to the young Truffaut and Godard, the latter of whom cast the veteran director in a great cameo in *Breathless*.) Melville even dressed the part. He favored wide-belted Sam Spade trench coats, and he adopted a brash Stetson as his trademark.

It is no surprise, then, that he would understand the allure of gangster chic so well. His 1955 noir drama *Bob le Flambeur* unfolds in a kid's dress-up dream of a criminal underworld, and Melville loses himself so completely in its ambience that he doesn't even fool with the rat-a-tat requirements of action filmmaking. He's happy just to tag along with his fatalistic hero, savoring the streets and the feeling of owning them.

Le Samouraï, made 12 years later, is even more refined. Every movement has the heaviness of ritual. Crime is a formalized repetition of behavior: Jef performs every criminal act in the movie at least twice, in exactly the same methodical way, whether it's stealing a car with a ring of skeleton keys or acquiring a new set of plates. When Jef dons his fedora before leaving for a hit, he rubs his thumb along the brim as if he were crossing himself — a gun-slinger's rite of preparation. This isn't just a killer's natural caution, though; it's an acknowledgment of how much we movie junkies crave the conventions of gangster flicks. So potent is the gangster iconography that Melville sometimes obscures Jef's face completely. He knows the cocked hat and trench coat have power all by themselves.

Delon looks so perfect and moves with such stealth that the director follows him as if in a wish-fulfillment reverie. If you took out every scene of Jef stalking the city streets, the movie would be an hour shorter. But it wouldn't have its bizarre, unique mood of moving constantly without going anywhere, the mood captured in the very first shot. And it wouldn't have its overwhelming sense of place. We're always aware of city life at its different levels, in every sense of the word. The action takes place in apartments, on the street, and underground, sometimes simultaneously, and there's a strong sense of criminals, civilians, and police coexisting uneasily in the same world. As lit by Decae, that world is all hard, matte-finish surfaces, as cold and grayish-blue as gunmetal. Even the glass interior of the nightclub seems confining — part prism, part prison.

There are plenty of cool assassin movies, many of them influenced by this one. But *Le Samouraï* imagines more vividly than any other what it would be like to stand in a killer's shoes — not just during bursts of violence, but throughout every agonizing second of existential dread, insecurity and elation. The movie's glacial pace makes you feel the weight of Jef's every small decision — which is appropriate, since his life rides on every one. It's easy to see why generations of movie fanatics, from the Nouvelle Vague to Martin Scorsese to John Woo and Quentin Tarantino, fell in love with the icy glamour of Jean-Pierre Melville's movie-fed fantasies of underworld life. To see *Le Samouraï* on a big screen is to remember pointing toy guns as a kid and reenacting scenes from the late show — only with Melville's adult awareness that the stuff of cinematic fantasy draws real blood. (*Nashville Scene*, June 12, 1997)

• • • • • • • • • •

Dragon: The Bruce Lee Story
Dir. Rob Cohen
1993, PG-13, 120 min.

A Hero's Welcome

At a Chinese nightclub in the 1960s, a rowdy gang of Australian gobs barge into a local dance and begin terrorizing the couples, manhandling the women and humiliating the men. As the sailors harass the Chinese women, pawing them roughly and stinging them with lewd comments, the Chinese men stand mortified — except for a small, neatly dressed, bespectacled youth who walks up to a massive goon and asks if he can cut in. The sailor shoves him away rudely and resumes his casual molestation, completely unmindful of the unwavering gaze and underlying fierceness of the young man — whose name happens to be Bruce Lee.

If you grew up in the early 1970s, when the martial-arts hero's likeness adorned the walls of many a Caucasian youngster's room, the first scene of *Dragon: The Bruce Lee Story* carries an undeniable thrill. For the kids of my generation, Bruce Lee was the patron saint of the underdog: a slender, relatively short man who did not seek violence but would dismantle an entire army with his bare hands if pushed to the breaking point. (As a respected but controversial martial-arts trainer, Lee probably did more than anyone else to turn legions of second graders into budding Zen masters.) Lee was never allowed to show much range as an actor, but in his best films — especially the mind-boggling *Enter the Dragon*, which came out the same year he died tragically of a swelling of the brain — his breathtaking skill and intense focus represent some ideal union of body, mind and spirit.

No martial arts star has ever matched Lee's combination of charisma, sex appeal and wit, which makes *Dragon*'s task even more daunting. Finding an interesting action hero is difficult enough without having to fill the shoes of a legend. However, from the moment the camera catches its first glimpse of Bruce Lee in the Chinese dance hall, *Dragon* pulls off this incredible feat. As Lee sizes up the menace from Down Under, neither his wary smile nor his glasses can disguise the playful ferocity glittering in his eyes; we recognize the expression from the classic fight scenes that would follow in his milestone action films. It's a terrific introduction — not just to Lee the character, but also to Jason Scott Lee, the terrific young newcomer who plays him.

The slam-bang opening, an expert, fanciful blend of sublime action choreography and slapstick, immediately establishes the tone and attitude of *Dragon*, a slight but thoroughly entertaining biopic that paints the late cult hero in broad, vivid strokes. Based on a biography by his former wife, Linda Lee Cadwell, here portrayed by a relentlessly spunky Lauren Holly, *Dragon* traces Lee's life from his Hong Kong childhood to his early years in Hollywood as a trainer and bit player. The film concludes just before his death in 1973 with the triumphant filming of *Enter the Dragon*.

Despite some ill-advised forays into pop psychology — the movie has Lee physically hounded by his fears, which manifest themselves as a sort of walking pagoda — *Dragon* succeeds by transforming Lee's life into the big-budget movie Hollywood never gave him. Although we don't learn much about Bruce Lee, who (according to the movie) was motivated by a desire to reconcile Asian and American culture through his inventive *jeet kune do* teachings, the young actor Jason Scott Lee (currently starring in Vincent Ward's romantic adventure *Map of the Human Heart*) gives the role some complexity, allowing us to see the ambition and the furious desire to assimilate that the movie says fueled Lee's career.

Wisely, Jason Scott Lee doesn't try to do a Bruce Lee imitation. He's so compelling in his own right that he blends into our memory of Lee. He's a better actor, which makes his fight scenes doubly exciting — he keeps us aware of the frailties that the late hero concealed so artfully in his screen appearances. (He also has Lee's sensual magnetism; when, in one scene, the actor flexes so intently that his flawless body bursts through his shirt, the two women sitting next to me literally moaned.) With his intelligence and charisma, he's definitely a talent to watch.

While the script (by Edward Khmara, John Raffo and director Rob Cohen, who stages the action scenes with crisp vitality) traffics in the lamest pop biography clichés — down to the headache that signals the hero's oncoming demise — Jason Scott Lee's riveting performance more than holds our attention. He single-handedly transforms this TV-caliber tribute into something more than an exploitation of Bruce Lee the pop icon. By enshrining the legendary martial artist in this most conventional of movie vehicles, *Dragon* ironically grants the wish that, for the most part, the American film industry never accorded the real Bruce Lee during his life. It tries to turn him into a standard Hollywood hero, with all the double-edged glory that implies. In restoring to the late actor the mystery and complexity the rest of the movie denies him, Jason Scott Lee rescues Bruce Lee from Hollywood blandness — and himself in the process. (*Nashville Scene*, May 20, 1993)

● ● ● ● ● ● ● ● ● ●

Bonnie and Clyde
Dir. Arthur Penn
1967, NR, 111 min.

Gun Crazy

Gangster movies are a law-abiding citizen's version of porn — a film-looped ritual that endlessly spools out fantasies of rebellion, of brute force and money, of death. The Code-era gangster classics of the '30s hid behind a moral smoke screen to deliver doses of lowdown thrills. You still got to see lawbreakers raise hell and bang bang bang, and as long as justice prevailed before "The End," your appetite for destruction was sated, not challenged. *Bonnie and Clyde* calls into question just what the hell we find so thrilling.

Bonnie and Clyde is quintessentially the product of a country where guns are props in the national playhouse, from the time a kid is old enough to play cops-and-robbers. At the same time, the movie is shrewd enough to wonder what kind of impact that has on our notions of reality and fiction, law and order, right and wrong. As such, *Bonnie and Clyde* may not be the greatest American movie — let's not even play that parlor game — but you could certainly make a case for it as the great American movie, the one that best represents our character and our cinema, warts and all. Even after 31 years, after countless imitations and the numbing escalation of movie violence, its basic contradictions remain more pertinent than ever. How can we demonize crime as citizens and romanticize criminals as moviegoers?

First and foremost, *Bonnie and Clyde* is a great gangster movie about two people who imagine themselves as the stars of a gangster movie. Everything in it calls to mind the outlaw classics of the 1930s, only fonder and dreamier. No Little Caesar or Scarface ever looked as flawlessly handsome as Warren Beatty's Clyde Barrow; no moll ever gave off anything like the heat of Faye Dunaway's Bonnie Parker. The gleaming roadsters, the vintage fashions (which sparked a short-lived craze) — Burnett Guffey's camera polishes them all to a stylized gloss that evokes the world through a celluloid curtain. Car chases cut from real cars to obviously fake process shots; the fleeing robbers see themselves riding to glory against a back-projection screen. A scene in a movie theater captures the disparity between the movie world and their life of crime. Onscreen, dancing chorines sing "We're in the Money" in a Busby Berkeley production number. In the audience, Clyde fatmouths about killing a bank guard — the first of many killings to come.

What isn't stylized is the violence. It isn't poetic, as in *The Wild Bunch*; it's blunt and ugly. The director, Arthur Penn, undercuts the rollicking tone of the early scenes with ominous hints: credits that fade to blood red, a splash of ketchup on Bonnie's blouse. A clerk with a cleaver bolts into the frame behind Clyde as he holds up a grocery, deliberately violating the lighthearted mood, and from then on the violence is sudden, disruptive, and as harsh as the rest of *Bonnie and Clyde*'s world is idealized. The outlaws pose for photos with guns and write their own ballad, but the grubby reality constantly undermines the glamour — matinee-idol Clyde is an impotent coward, beautiful Bonnie is a vicious crook, and the people they kill look like us. We start out admiring the outlaws, and they respond by shoving their shiny guns back in our faces. In the notorious ending, a masterpiece of montage in editor Dede Allen's hands, a firing squad brutally punctures their delusions with a hail of machine-gun fire.

Ironically enough, it was the seriousness of the violence that infuriated reviewers when *Bonnie and Clyde* was released in 1967. (Many of them turned about-face when the movie became a blockbuster and a critical cause célèbre.) The blood was nothing new, and neither was the brutality. Herschell Gordon Lewis' far grislier cheapies had been playing drive-ins for years, and one of the biggest hits the same year was Robert Aldrich's *The Dirty Dozen*, which tossed in a near-rape and several beatings along with a substantially higher body count.

But those movies didn't explode their cartoonish use of bloodshed as entertainment the way *Bonnie and Clyde* did. *Bonnie and Clyde* jumbled humor and horror in ways that recalled the groundbreaking thriller pastiches of the French New Wave — whose leading lights, Jean-Luc Godard and François Truffaut, were initially offered the David Newman–Robert Benton script by producer Beatty. (A lyrical slow-motion shot of a child tumbling down a hill, an homage to Truffaut's *Shoot the Piano Player*, gives a glimpse of the film that might've been.) The movie's moral ambiguity isn't about killing; it's about bank-robbing. The movie immerses us so deeply in the delusions of its bank-robber heroes that it makes banks deserving targets, stick-ups fun and lawmen bloodthirsty bullies. It takes bullets to snap us out of it.

The many caper movies that followed *Bonnie and Clyde* abandoned subjective subtleties altogether. The movie's careful ironic remove gave way to an easy cynicism that made heroes of criminals, patsies of working stiffs and villains of lawmen. By the time you get to something as corrupt as the recent *Set It Off*, in which the filmmakers' casual exploitation of economic troubles winds up glorifying armed robbery, you see violence reduced to window dressing, to affectless spectacle that leaves an audience feeling numb. As even a cursory look shows today, that's one crime nobody can pin on *Bonnie and Clyde*. (*Nashville Scene*, April 23, 1998)

● ● ● ● ● ● ● ● ● ●

Thelma & Louise
Dir. Ridley Scott
1991, R, 130 min.

Traveling Companions

Feminist writers such as Adrienne Rich have attempted to destroy language they feel excludes women — a noble idea, except that writers are always stuck with the same words, the same connotations. You can destroy the totems of communication, but you always have to rebuild with the splinters, the words themselves. Ultimately, as long as words carry the same associations, any attempt at changing language will be useless.

The same goes in spades for movies. Simply casting women in the formulaic roles usually occupied by men accomplishes nothing. You'd hardly call *La Femme Nikita* revolutionary: Anne Parillaud may play a tough woman torn between love and a career, but when she shoots up a restaurant, she doesn't transform the scene into anything new. She's just an unusually pretty Clint Eastwood. (Not exactly progress, although at least she doesn't curl up and whimper.)

But if you really want to shake things up, you have to hit society where it lives — its myths. You have to create new myths that steal the old ones' thunder. And where better to start than with the dominant archetypes in American literature, Huck Finn and Jim, outcasts and brothers of the road, the very symbols of lost innocence and gained experience. If you truly wanted to subvert the old myths, you could place Huck and Jim in a souped-up T-bird convertible, send them rocketing West and rename them Thelma and Louise.

Thelma (Geena Davis) is Huck reborn as a miserable housewife, stuck in a stifling home with a blustering creep of a husband. She hasn't got a clue about human nature; she's drawn almost instinctively to the worst men imaginable. Her Jim, a hard-bitten waitress named Louise (Susan Sarandon), wants her to wise up, but she'll settle for a brief vacation from their woes — a weekend fishing trip where both can let their hair down.

On the road in Louise's dreamy T-bird, Thelma spots a bar and wants to start the celebration early. Several margaritas and shots of Wild Turkey later, Thelma, to Louise's dismay, is whisked onto the dance floor by an oily good-ol'-boy. After a couple of close, steamy dances, the cowboy leads the drunken Thelma to the parking lot and comes on to her. When she turns him down, he responds by beating her savagely; he slams her face down on the hood of a truck and prepares to rape her.

The only thing that stops him is the pistol Louise presses to his neck. Even then, he's hardly apologetic: He tells Louise he should have continued, and he invites her to take Thelma's place.

That's when the myths explode.

The ensuing scene absolutely polarizes audiences. It engenders both snorts of derision (mainly from men) and cheers of satisfaction (mainly from women). As overwhelming as that moment is, however, at that point *Thelma & Louise* isn't much different politically from *Death Wish*. You fear it's going to become just another dreary vigilante picture — a real comedown from the promise of its amusing, prickly beginning.

But that doesn't happen, and revealing more would ruin the pleasure of watching this weird, enthralling road movie unwind. The less you know about *Thelma & Louise*, the more this buzzing skyrocket of a movie flares in your imagination. Without giving away too much, *Thelma & Louise* is the story of two women who would prefer anything to dealing with lecherous bosses, loutish husbands and lying charmers. Fed up to here with the world of men, the waitress heroine refuses to take any more orders.

The screenplay, by former Nashvillian Callie Khouri, is an unusually assured piece of writing, a wild, ambitious scrambling of genres and moods. It's the road movie to end all road movies. Khouri consciously sets her heroines on the road because it's the center of our psychic landscape, the symbol of all human possibility. Just as consciously, she makes their road a literal dead end. Thelma and Louise's world allows them only so much possibility, and that's only one of the ways Khouri subverts our most cherished myths of opportunity.

With the exception of a kind detective (Harvey Keitel, in his second great understated performance this year) and a decent boyfriend, the men Thelma and Louise encounter are scum distinguished only by levels of intimidation. After one bad experience too many, they aren't intimidated any longer. No matter how large the men loom — and a state trooper is photographed to appear larger than an Arizona mesa — they end up being steamrollered by Thelma and Louise. What the two women learn on the road isn't that they have to follow men's rules and rejoin a male-dominated society. What they learn is how stupid they were for ever following them in the first place. They become smart — and honest — through a life of crime.

The sight of Thelma and Louise standing in their convertible, brandishing handguns, could become part of our secret iconography, along with such exemplars of scuzzy Americana as *Repo Man* and *Bonnie and Clyde*. With the voluptuous Sarandon and the statuesque Davis in the leads, we're always aware of their physical presence, and they appear to grow as we watch them.

By the film's end, they look like true warrior queens, and they're smarter than the average martyr. The burden of acting larger-than-life saps most performers. It energizes Sarandon and Davis. *Thelma & Louise* is the sixth film by the British director Ridley Scott, who specializes in such otherworldly ambience exercises as *Alien* and *Blade Runner*. Working on a smaller scale than usual, Scott does his best work to date, never sacrificing the actors or the story for his distinctively smoky, unsettling images. The movie's dusty, sun-baked look gives the comic scenes an edge of menace that hints at things to come.

With assistance from the fine cinematographer Adrian Biddle, who distinguishes the many hues of orange and blue in the panoramic Southwest, Scott emphasizes gigantic rock formations, in proportion to his heroines, to show the enormity of what they're up against.

The images of the gleaming convertible hurtling down a desert highway have a genuinely seductive gloss. Autoerotica, indeed!

Thelma & Louise, the most original and entertaining movie so far this year, ticks along to twangy rock 'n' roll on the soundtrack, with excellent use of Marianne Faithfull's definitive "Ballad of Lucy Jordan." And just when you think the movie can't go any higher, it culminates in a brilliant ending that enriches everything that has come before.

Get used to seeing the last shot in your mind for days after the movie ends. (*Nashville Scene*, May 30, 1991)

● ● ● ● ● ● ● ● ●

Star Wars: Episode III — Revenge of the Sith
Dir. George Lucas
2005, PG-13, 140 min.

Lost in the Stars

Watching *Star Wars: Episode III — Revenge of the Sith*, a viewer who saw the original *Star Wars* in 1977 feels like *Memento*'s Leonard Shelby, going forward into the past to get someplace he's already been. Twenty-eight years ago, did anyone think he'd be here three decades later, still playing with the same set of action figures? Did anyone think the Force would still be with him? Did George Lucas?

At the time, we couldn't read the warning signs. *Star Wars* was a shiny pop novelty — a thieving-magpie space opera that played as if its maker couldn't distinguish Joseph Campbell from Flash Gordon or *Triumph of the Will* from *The Wizard of Oz*. Every sixth grader in my class had seen it twice or more; every adult I knew was bored stiff. From Lucas, it was a mixed blessing: a technological leap forward from his 1974 left-field smash *American Graffiti*, but a stumble backward in almost every human element — character, dialogue, performances. Since then, Lucas has yet to make another movie outside the *Star Wars* saga. The sad truth is that the best movie in the series — the one with dire human consequences, unresolved emotions and a believable romance — is one he neither wrote nor directed.

If *Star Wars* had arrested only George Lucas' development, that would be bad enough. But its blockbuster success triggered an irreversible change in the movie industry, like a pollutant whose dire consequences aren't known until somebody catches a three-eyed fish. In his book *The Big Picture*, Edward Jay Epstein compares 10 movies since 1999 that have earned $1 billion worldwide (two of them being Lucas'), then finds their common formula: a fairy-tale setting; a weak young protagonist who achieves power; strictly platonic romance; incidental characters suitable for toys or action figures; room for sequels; and, above all, plentiful violence that is nevertheless inconsequential enough not to waver a PG-13 rating. Sound familiar? After 28 years, *Star Wars* remains the movies' dominant business model — and as a result, American movies remain dominated by business models.

Thus the climactic *Revenge of the Sith* amounts to a progress report on the past three decades of mainstream American filmmaking. Technologically, financially, the movies have come of age. Morally, emotionally, politically and intellectually, they're sucking on Nuks. When the screen went black — and the *Star Wars* logo appeared with that orchestral "bampff!" — I felt my heart in my throat. And that was pretty much the last emotional connection I had to anything onscreen. You'll hear a lot in coming weeks — trust me — about the "darkness" of Lucas' vision, and it's true that in this concluding film the director does dip his toes in the Dark Side, at least as much as his afternoon-matinee contraption will allow. "Dark," for Lucas, means PG-13 instead of PG.

But it's the supposedly heavy *Revenge of the Sith* that shows how insubstantial that vision is, down to the usual weightless megaviolence in service of cornball good-and-evil absolutes. Not yet the Mattel-issue Ming the Merciless he'll become in the '77 *Star Wars*, the renegade Jedi-in-training Anakin Skywalker (Hayden Christiansen) is intended here as a tragic hero — a regal warrior whose fate is to become the monstrous Darth Vader. Plagued by visions of his beloved Padmé (Natalie Portman) in peril, he earns only stony silence from the indifferent Jedi council. (In Lucas' boys club, love only clouds the mind.) As the gnomic Yoda would say, there to console him the Dark Side is.

As visual spectacle, *Revenge of the Sith* is astonishing, a tremendous achievement: a biosphere created out of thin air and pixels. Stammering robots, giant mosquitoes, impossibly vast cityscapes — thanks to Lucas' ILM dream team and their digital backlot, most every voluminous establishing shot in *Episode III* has the equivalent of five of the original film's hologram chessboards. (And that's what everybody really remembers, right — the props, the cantina scene, the stuff on the edges?) It's in the movie's obsessively detailed settings that one sees the Lucas of *American Graffiti*, that densely textured ode to the minutiae of a gearhead's SoCal adolescence. Everything that popped into

Lucas' head, he managed to doodle here into the margins of the frame. I can't remember watching another movie and looking less at the center of the screen.

Or having less reason to look. In the coloring book of Lucas' imagination, only the backgrounds get any ink. Actors, in the recent *Star Wars* movies, are props to be posed center frame at a careful remove. They're what the special-effects team has to draw around. In the earlier films, the wooden performances were almost a comic annoyance. Here, in a movie that supposedly hinges on grand passions — heartbreak and hubris and betrayal — they're disastrous. The actors don't have the gravitas to fill in these cardboard characters — and when you have Padmé explaining away Anakin Skywalker's turn to the Dark Side by saying, "He's been under a lot of stress lately," you need something more than Portman's mallrat simper or Christiansen's pouty petulance to put it across. Lucas gets exactly the performances he wants — ones that mesh perfectly with their digitized, mechanized surroundings. But apart from Ewan McGregor, as welcome an actorly presence as Alec Guinness was in the original, the director reduces even electrifying talents to coat racks. Poor Samuel L. Jackson: Under Lucas' tender care, his performance is like something you'd order from IKEA.

Revenge of the Sith is straitjacketed by its place in the series — both as the missing puzzle piece that connects the two trilogies, and as the colossally downbeat story of the triumphant rise of the universe's biggest fascist. You can see the grand design: The story of Anakin's emergence as Darth Vader should give *Episodes IV* to *VI* a tragic depth, while a viewer's knowledge of the later episodes should resonate throughout this one. It doesn't work that way. Because we've known since 1977 how this story is going to play out, we're aware at every juncture of how it's being rigged to get us there. Anakin's premonitions, like his love for Padmé, function only as a convenience that gets *Episode II* to *Episode IV*. Whatever significance the images and characters have — including the movie's one moment of operatic grandeur, the Frankenstein stagger of the newly formed Darth Vader — comes from the other films. More than anything, *Revenge of the Sith* just seems . . . obligatory.

It's a curious thing, this matched set of trilogies — and not just because the effects worsen dramatically as the tale moves *forward*. See *Episodes I* through *VI* in sequential order, and the first three appear the long windup to a sprightly tale of adventure, resistance and the defeat of a ruthless despot. This is the yarn the Reagan administration co-opted to sell its Star Wars missile-defense system, not to mention its entire foreign policy of blows against the "evil empire." (Somehow *Revenge*, with its executive-branch power plays and homeland-security smokescreen, better suits the current White House.)

View the movies in order of release, though, and they tell a different, more depressing story. This way, the entire *Star Wars* series ends not with a bang but the whimper of countless casualties, as a noble knight turned galactic tyrant learns to stop worrying and build the Death Star. At the same time, there's Lucas, an early admirer of experimental and world cinema, who went from his dystopian sci-fi debut *THX-1138* — a despairing vision of dehumanized technology — to becoming the biggest technocrat and toy-pusher on Planet Hollywood. The question is: How far apart are these two stories of men who gain unrestricted power over their worlds and in the process become everything they seem to hate?

With his unprecedented clout and unlimited bankroll, George Lucas may be the only truly independent filmmaker at work today. This is freedom? Lucas has been the prisoner of his creation for 28 years. The creative recklessness and confusion of early '70s Hollywood enabled him to gamble (and fail) with *THX-1138*; ironically enough, the success of *Star Wars* slammed the door on scruffy, marginal studio fare, ensuring the terminal adolescence, effects-driven monotony and emotional atrophy of mainstream American movies for decades to come. It must be said that Lucas aspires to a vast, mythic scale no other filmmaker has dared, and he's committed his entire career to it. But peers such as Spielberg and De Palma have managed to move beyond their gadget-freak obsessions, or at least explore them in provocative, grown-up films. Lucas, meanwhile, can't even stop futzing around digitally with his earlier work. The dude in the black helmet couldn't have struck a more lucrative devil's deal.

But if Lucas is now finally free of the Force — if his next movie can reclaim the observant warmth of *American Graffiti*, or the experimental spirit and cautious humanism of *THX* — then this saga may have a redemptive ending after all. Maybe, in keeping with the screwy chronology of Lucas' visually magnificent but developmentally stunted trilogies, this closing chapter is really the one that promises *A New Hope* — for its audience, as well as its maker. (*Nashville Scene*, May 19, 2005)

Shorts 4

L imitations, like deadlines, can spur creativity, and the restrictions of physical space inherent in writing for print helped hone Jim's skill at economy, a notable and consistent quality of his work. As a reminder, he kept a placard in his office that read, "Can you say it as plain as Hank Williams?"

Think of this selection of Jim's capsule reviews like a program of short films that might precede a feature attraction at a festival. They echo the themes and motifs of the surrounding chapters, contextualizing references or expanding them, while demonstrating how much can fit into a small space. These micro-reviews can be deceptive in their brevity. To paraphrase the French philosopher Blaise Pascal, sometimes film reviews are long because the writer didn't have time to make them short.

● ● ● ● ● ● ● ● ● ●

Rio Bravo

"A game-legged old man and a drunk — that's all you've got?" asks an incredulous trail boss, hearing that outmanned sheriff John Wayne is under siege by desperadoes. Wayne corrects him: "That's *what* I've got." That's *Rio Bravo* in four words. After the big-budget thud of *Land of the Pharaohs*, Howard Hawks emerged from a three-year sabbatical, including a stay in Paris and a purposeful study of TV drama, to create this 1959 rifle opera: a laid-back yet hard-headed response to the sanctimonious *High Noon* — which pissed off the director because no lawman worth his badge would ask civilians to risk their hides doing his job. The result is an irresistible ode to loyalty, cool under fire and masculine honor — which in the Hawks universe extends even to Angie Dickinson's stand-up saloon gal. From the French, Hawks said, he learned that audiences cared less about plot points than about all the pleasures in between: the comedy, the camaraderie, the stray bits of business. (The French probably got this notion from Hawks' own meta-movie *The Big Sleep*.) Genre thus became a kind of backdrop, a set of agreed-upon conventions that cleared the stage for the good stuff — in this case, for the casual interactions between Wayne's Sheriff John T. Chance and the ragtag volunteers seeking his respect. While the plot cools its heels in the hoosegow — along with its bad-egg McGuffin, an outlaw (Claude Akins) whose powerful gang means to spring him from Chance's lock-up — Hawks serves up a movable feast of contrasting charisma. The director butts Wayne's relaxed machismo up against Dean Martin's drunk act, Ricky Nelson's teen idolatry and Walter Brennan's maternal crustiness, often within the same frame. Martin comes through with an aching, career-best performance that wins the only currency worth anything in this boisterous meritocracy — a nod of approval from the Duke. Perhaps the most purely enjoyable Western ever made, *Rio Bravo* only deepens with age and repeated viewing, right down to the genial juxtaposition of Martin's slouch and Wayne's saunter. It's doubtful another American movie has ever taken so much interest in the way its characters walk — or understood why it matters. (*Nashville Scene*, Nov. 2, 2006)

● ● ● ● ●

Meet Me in St. Louis

I can't put it any plainer: This belongs near or at the top of anyone's list of the great American movies, and the chance to see it on the big screen (especially at Christmas) is a gift in itself. The honey-dipped heartland Americana of Vincente Minnelli's musical looks as corny today as it must have in 1944 — at first. Even in the '40s, the movie's turn-of-the-century "simpler time" was distant, and Arthur Freed's fabled MGM production unit burnished it to a nostalgic glow for heartsick wartime audiences. But the emotional intensity, fondness and empathy of Minnelli's direction make the movie anything but sappy: This is a beautiful, bittersweet imagining of a collectively dreamed past. The setting is St. Louis in the seasons leading up to the 1904 World's Fair; its promise consumes the entire Smith family until patriarch Alonzo (Leon Ames) suddenly announces that they're moving to New York. To evoke public, private and inner space, Minnelli varies the depth of the frame for expressive effect, isolating characters within the household's bustle or embracing them fully into the fold. His emotional palette is keyed to a pair of stunning performances: Judy Garland as the lovestruck daughter Esther, singing "The Boy Next Door" and "The Trolley Song" with a desperate torrent of feeling that's just this side of neurosis; and Margaret O'Brien as little Tootie, who gives full vent to a range of childhood terrors. These fears culminate in the most disconsolate Yuletide song ever: "Have Yourself a Merry Little Christmas," sung by Esther to Tootie, one breaking heart to another. It all ends happily, of course, but with the lingering poignance of a snapshot moment frozen in time — which, unbeknownst to the subjects, will eventually yellow and fade. (*Nashville Scene*, Dec. 6, 2007)

• • • • •

Point Blank

A betrayed hood's feverish search-and-destroy mission through a purgatorial Los Angeles, John Boorman's hallucinatory 1967 pulp thriller *Point Blank* is a gauntlet of sharp angles, eruptive violence and jagged editing strategies. It's either a dying man's fantasy of the Big Payback, or a dead man's lumbering swath through the world of the semi-living. Either way, it looks like it was made tomorrow.

Lee Marvin is Walker, the hood, gunned down by his best bud (wormy John Vernon) and faithless wife (Sharon Acker) in the bowels of deserted Alcatraz over a measly $93,000. The money will grease Vernon's way back into "the Organization," a literal Murder, Inc., run like any dehumanized bureaucracy. Two years later, the reanimated Walker makes a relentless Frankenstein stagger through LAX (click clack), his footsteps on the soundtrack a metronome of coming doom (click clack) as his ex gets ominously dolled up in a beauty salon (click clack). She comes home and barely manages to shut the door (clack CLACK) when Walker busts through it, emptying his pistol into her tainted bed. She doesn't have his money? He'll have to find who does, even if it means wiping out the Organization one middle-manager at a time.

The dense flash-forwards and associative flashbacks (triggered by sounds, colors, thoughts) may be borrowed from Alain Resnais' fragmented memory films of the Nouvelle Vague era, but *Point Blank* seems at once of its time and beyond it. As mod as the previous year's *Blow-up* in its décor and desiccated chic — dig that nightclub fight bathed in psychedelic gels — Boorman's film has a less gimmicky sense of the unreal. Early on, Walker is framed against straight lines that point his way like an arrow to hell; the Los Angeles he enters is a mosaic of shattered glass — reflective surfaces that splinter in every direction.

It's the marvelous Marvin, simian and sardonically deadpan, who lifts *Point Blank* into the realm of the timeless. Numb and remote, his Walker is unaffected by anyone else in the frame: not his perhaps imaginary guide (Keenan Wynn); not his wife's sister (magma-hot Angie Dickinson), even when, in the movie's most memorable scene, she beats the impassive lug until she collapses. He gives the scandalous brutality its vicious authority, whether he's delivering one of the movies' first and most savagely effective nut-shots or reducing a corrupt car salesman's pricey sedan to scrap metal. Even after 40 years, with Marvin as its blunt weapon of choice, *Point Blank* remains one cold hard shot to the head. (*Nashville Scene*, Feb. 21, 2008)

● ● ● ● ●

Taxi Driver

Exhibit A for the deification of '70s Hollywood, *Taxi Driver*, Martin Scorsese's 1976 vision of hell as New York nightlife, holds up remarkably well as a portrait of a uniquely American brand of rage and resentment. Maybe too well. Whenever creepy loners practice their death strikes in front of the mirror, from Bernhard Goetz to John Hinckley, it's Robert De Niro's wiry angel of doom they see staring back. Forget that scowling, mugging, grumpy dude from the Fockers movies: This hails from the period when De Niro was the most electrifying actor in movies, a live wire whose every improvisatory impulse crackled with threat.

De Niro's cabbie-as-warped-crusader, Travis Bickle, roams a festering city of night-shuttling scum and preteen whores (the latter represented by 12-year-old Jodie Foster, whose ease in the role still produces unease in viewers). Imagining himself as God's angry man, the scourging rain that will wash the streets, Travis is a corroded urban descendant of the lone Westerner who lives outside society and above the law, like John Wayne's deranged tracker in *The Searchers*.

Working from a serrated Paul Schrader script soaked in coke and flop sweat, Scorsese prowls the zone where the rugged individualism of such a man morphs into the I-stand-alone fury of America's lunatic fringe — its ticking human bombs, its assassins. In the process, he stakes his claim as the movies' poet of suffocation. With cinematographer Michael Chapman and composer Bernard Herrmann, whose downbeat score (his last) mixes jazzy melancholia and psychotic-break blares, he creates a richly toxic atmosphere of steam, noir shadowscapes and barely suppressed savagery.

Schrader's screenplay was influenced equally by Bresson's *Pickpocket* and by the diaries of George Wallace's assassin Arthur Bremer. Between those spiritual extremes, the movie finds no redemption, only catharsis — and a temporary one at that. Those who read the movie as a celebration of gun worship and vigilantism miss the point of the ironic climax: The difference between being a murderer and a hero, in such a culture, is killing the right person. The message isn't lost on the movie's mad-dog cult following — and it wasn't lost on Goetz, either. (*Nashville Scene*, May 19, 2011)

• • • • •
The Devil's Rejects

This astonishing genre mashup from director Rob Zombie isn't a connoisseur's smorgasbord of grindhouse revivalism like the *Kill Bill* movies: It's real-deal rotgut that pushes an audience's buttons too hard and too far, then keeps on pushing. Not so much a sequel as an epic expansion of the splatter-rock impresario's *House of 1,000 Corpses*, it turns the original's claustrophobic *Texas Chainsaw* tribute into a combination road movie, revenge thriller, outlaw saga and balls-out horror show. The movie picks up after the first film's bloodbath in '78, as the (thermo)nuclear family of psycho doll Baby (Sheri Moon Zombie), Mansonesque mass murderer Otis P. Driftwood (Bill Moseley) and killer clown Captain Spaulding (Sid Haig) escape a police ambush to carve a bloody swath through the Southwest. Zombie stages head-on collisions of hellish cruelty, macho brinkmanship, and unwatchable sadism — along with (I'm not making this up) a garrulous Gene Shalit wannabe deconstructing the career of Otto Preminger. But the effect isn't the weightless only-a-movie snarkiness of the *Scream* pictures: It's authentically and savagely nihilistic, as the "heroes" call out a God who won't lift a hand against them. And Zombie plays his audiences' taboos and sympathies like a pinball machine. Anyone who gets off on the insane clown posse's mid-film torture of some luckless innocents — a sequence sicker than anything in the entire Tarantino oeuvre — gets strapped into the victim's chair later as a Bible-thumping lawman (a mesmerizingly rabid William Forsythe) delivers a payback so protracted it thwarts the audience's ample bloodlust. Because Zombie owns up to his taste for hard candy without ironic distancing, *The Devil's Rejects* will strike a lot of people (perhaps justly) as indefensible. But it's also irreducible: beholden to no conventions, complex in tone and texture, fearless in its rejection of mass-marketed good taste and timidity. If this sounds like artless, irredeemable yahoo bait, let it be said that Zombie manages to create and detail an entire world around his characters; that Phil Parmet's gloriously grainy Super 16 cinematography nails the look of '70s drive-in movies right down to the grubby optics; that Zombie's cast of Carter Administration cult faves amounts to a midnight-movie dream team; and that the auteur's amazing soundtrack of vintage Southern rock does for the overplayed "Free Bird" what *Breaking the Waves* did for David Bowie's "Life on Mars." If you need convincing after the title, "Sid Haig," and "A Rob Zombie Film," you're not tall enough for this ride. (*City Pages*, July 22, 2005)

• • • • •

20 Million Miles to Earth
First Men in the Moon
Earth vs. the Flying Saucers
It Came From Beneath the Sea

Ray Harryhausen may be the only auteur in the history of movies who never directed, wrote, or acted in any of his films. A special-effects wizard whose credits belie his influence, Harryhausen worked throughout his career with weak scripts and journeyman directors. But the vision behind classic fantasies such as *Jason and the Argonauts* is unmistakably his; by the time of 1981's *Clash of the Titans*, his name on a picture still carried more weight than the director's or any of the stars'. As part of its fun "Summer Camp" sci-fi retrospective, the Watkins Belcourt shows four of his films, offering contemporary viewers a rare big-screen look at the fantasy master's work.

A cult hero to postwar, preteen movie geeks — many of whom now run Hollywood's biggest effects houses — Harryhausen saw *King Kong* when he was 13 and was transfixed. He later worked as an assistant to *King Kong*'s pioneering stop-motion animation expert, Willis O'Brien, on 1949's *Mighty Joe Young*. With O'Brien, Harryhausen shared a sympathy with monstrous misfits; he also loved the spectacle of these beasts in collision with outsize manmade monuments.

His 1957 thriller *20 Million Miles to Earth*, which plays on a double bill with his 1964 *First Men in the Moon*, features one of his niftiest creations, the Ymir, a reptilian humanoid from Venus that grows huge after landing on Earth. (It has something to do with sodium.) Flicking its scaly tail, the Ymir battles an elephant before defying bazookas and artillery atop the Colosseum. Yet the creature, not astronaut William Hopper, is clearly the hero: As animated, he has wit and charisma, and like many Harryhausen monsters, he's more a baffled outsider than a hell-bent conqueror.

Not that Harryhausen couldn't do those too. Neither *Independence Day* nor *Mars Attacks* could top the low-tech grandeur and streamlined design of the marauding alien warships in 1956's *Earth vs. the Flying Saucers*, which still contains the movies' most convincing destruction of Washington, D.C. And the octopus that dismantles the Golden Gate Bridge in 1955's *It Came From Beneath the Sea* is nearly as impressive even if Harryhausen had to trim two tentacles to save bucks.

Computer-generated effects have made creature movement and large-scale destruction more seamless since Harryhausen's reign. But the effects in

Godzilla and *ID4* have no weight: There's no sense of physical mass or three-dimensional space in their photographic mayhem, and precious little wonder. By moving his sculptured beasts and skeletons one frame at a time to create the illusion of motion, Ray Harryhausen breathed life into inanimate objects; he made steel move like sinew and rubber move like skin. In so doing, he made movie-making into something very much like magic. (*Nashville Scene*, July 30, 1998)

• • • • •

Point Break

A battle of wits between Keanu Reeves and Patrick Swayze is a mighty clash indeed. But for all its preposterous plotting and hilarious dudespeak, this 1991 yarn about an FBI agent (Reeves) who joins Zen thrill-seeker Swayze and his robber gang of presidential-masked surfers — believe me, you ain't heard nothing yet — has the momentum and velocity of a runaway jet. Thank *Near Dark* director Kathryn Bigelow, one of Hollywood's greatest and most underused action specialists, who stages foot chases and free falls with dizzying kinetic verve. Bigelow's currently getting the best reviews of her career for the Iraq War thriller *The Hurt Locker*, another study of men inching their way through a pressure-cooker situation — but it doesn't offer the chance to watch the Red Hot Chili Peppers' Anthony Kiedis suffer. You know you want it. (*Nashville Scene*, July 2, 2009)

• • • • •

The Warriors

The *ne plus ultra* of comic-book cinema isn't a comic-book adaptation: it's Walter Hill's exhilarating 1978 re-imagining of *The Odyssey* set in untamed pre-Giuliani New York, where a gang framed for the murder of a charismatic would-be ruler must bop its way home to Coney Island across miles of hostile territory. (Back in '78, my friends and I thought Michael Beck's Swan was the last word in big-screen badassery — and next thing we knew, he was roller-skating with Olivia Newton-John and a bunch of cartoon fish in *Xanadu*.) In this immersive fantasy of urban peril — a template for 30 subsequent years of video games; it's basically *Grand Theft Auto* on foot — the city is one big interstitial interrupted by boldly stylized encounters with mythic foes: the siren-like Lizzies, the skinhead Turnbull AC's and, best of all, the glam-rock, bat-swinging Baseball Furies. Hill, the movies' poet of the cleanly thrown punch, stages every beatdown and bust-up with such exultance in motion you can practically feel the swoosh of whizzing fists. I love this movie. (*Nashville Scene*, Sept. 25, 2008)

• • • • •
Rock 'n' Roll High School

A pack of cartoon '50s hubcap thieves time-warped to the hedonistic '70s, the Ramones were so stunningly out of step with the glitzy mainstream that they made uncoolness cool. Their gawky diffidence spawned what's known as punk, and yet the youth-culture swamis at Roger Corman's New World Pictures were sharp enough to see that their three-chord Bowery beatdown had more in common with the prior decade's bubblegum pop than with the Class of '77's safety-pinned sloganeers. As a result, this tailor-made vehicle from 1979 — a celebration of pizza, mild petting and the iconic power of leather jackets draped over scrawny frames — is more AIP beach-party flick than rock 'n' roll swindle, a loving send-up of Corman's drive-in delinquency epics and don't-knock-the-rock B movies.

Despite the end-of-the-'70s setting, the sensibility is pure Eisenhower era right down to the costumes and the PG-rated sex. Our peppy punkette heroine Riff Randell (P. J. Soles) dresses and acts like a *Happy Days* carhop even as she wages culture war on the Ramones' behalf against stern Miss Togar (Mary Woronov), the new principal at Vince Lombardi High ("where winning is better than losing"). The corny Frank Tashlin–esque jokes, concocted by three credited screenwriters (including Joseph McBride, now a noted film historian), miss at least as often as they connect: Some of the best ones go to Paul Bartel's tweedy music teacher and to Clint Howard as an amiable fixer who literally keeps office hours in the boys' room. But director Allan Arkush maintains a sugar-rush energy level, aided by the blitzkrieg bopping of '70s sexpot Soles and the deliciously butch villainy of former Warhol trouper Woronov.

Best of all, the movie gives ample screen time to the Ramones in all their rip-kneed, splay-legged glory — a poignant sight now that Joey, Johnny and Dee Dee Ramone are rock 'n' roll phantoms. To see the eternally young Joey sing "She's the One" — propped against a mike stand with graceless grace — is to realize the irrelevance of the fine line in rock between brilliant and stoopid. (*Pith in the Wind*, July 22, 2011)

• • • • •
The Big Lebowski

Set at the time of the Gulf War, the Coen Brothers' meandering homage to Raymond Chandler baffled most audiences upon release in 1998. But as the full suckitude of the sucky decade to come revealed itself, suddenly it looked less like a rangy goof and more like a pretty sensible design for living in a world of senseless hostility: mix up a White Russian, fire up another doob and go bowling. Jeff Bridges' abiding Dude was the perfect hero for the Bush II years, cosmically unfazed by the looming menace of Saddam Hussein (who proved to be about as big a threat in real life as he is here). A decade later, though, the figure that seems most prophetic is John Goodman's Walter Sobchak, the original teabagger, a wellspring of apoplectic rage and bad information. All we can hope is that 2019 isn't the Year of Jesus Quintana. (*Nashville Scene*, Sept. 24, 2009)

• • • • •

300

A manly saga of manly manliness, in which the swarming masses of the world's largest army are held off by 300 tribesmen of the Village People's Indian. As relentlessly computer-generated from the Frank Miller–Lynn Varley graphic novel retelling the Battle of Thermopylae, it's the movie version of a Molly Hatchet album cover: Buff Spartans with spears and shields perforate the faceless Persian hordes and send their inked-in blood spewing and splattering, while brawny King Leonidas (Gerald Butler) shepherds them to slaughter and glory against their epicene foes. (Apart from the shirts-and-skins battles, you can tell the good guys from the bad guys even in the sack: Leonidas has wholesome softcore sex with his queen, Lena Headey, while Rodrigo Santoro's bad ol' Persian king Xerxes lolls around watching stunt teams of deformed lesbians — the 5th-century-B.C. equivalent of Spike TV.)

Directed with obvious if misplaced care by Zack Snyder, who made the sharp *Dawn of the Dead* remake, this should have been a rousing spectacle of rugged physicality: a live-action Greek-mythology comic book full of graphic snap and gusto. Instead, the sickly digitized imagery manages the trick of being at once ponderous and weightless. The Spartans are fighting to the death for their land, but their devotion means little when Sparta's fakey fields look like something airbrushed on the side of a van. There are impressive sequences of anime-like mayhem — there hasn't been a movie yet that wasn't improved by battle elephants — and stirring shots of a hail of whizzing arrows blotting out the sun. But whenever the characters bellow their staggeringly stupid dialogue, the war-poetry effect is ruined. The only Homer the movie evokes is the one that worships donuts.

Even so, the oppressive recruiting-commercial solemnity and the onslaught of pixel-on-pixel violence still shushed my audience into reverent silence. At least on DVD, the inevitable home drinking game where you take a shot every time someone hollers "Spar-TAH!" should take care of that. (*Pith in the Wind*, March 21, 2007)

● ● ● ● ●

Swept from the Sea

In a British coastal village, gruff doctor Ian McKellan and dying patient Kathy Bates reconstruct the tragic romance of outcast Rachel Weisz and shipwrecked gypsy Vincent Perez. Awful writing turns this into a *Masterpiece Theatre* rendition of *Edward Scissorhands*, with shearless Perez filling the part of the outsider too noble and delicate for our uncouth world. McKellan and Bates are customarily good; Weisz is lovely and does a lot of heavy breathing; Perez's Ukrainian accent sounds like a man with a head cold speaking through a mouthful of blintzes. Notwithstanding Dick Pope's starkly handsome cinematography, this is a dismal two-hour slog through miserably predictable events in a grubby village outfitted with the usual orthodontically impaired squires and harridans. For masochistic Anglophiles only. (*Nashville Scene*, April 9, 1998)

● ● ● ● ●

The Order of Myths

The Order of Myths is one of those extraordinary docs, like *The King of Kong* or *Hands on a Hardbody*, where the scope, detail and characters make contemporary fiction filmmaking seem pale and wan by comparison. It may be one of the best films ever made about the paradoxes and complexities of the postwar South.

The director, Margaret Brown, chronicles the weeks leading up to the 2007 Mardi Gras celebrations in Mobile, Ala. — a tradition that predates Mardi Gras in New Orleans, dating back more than 300 years. But the city's festivities are cleaved in two, straight down racial lines. There's a black coronation ball and parade and a white coronation ball and parade, and questions about integrating the parties are generally dismissed by the city's landed gentry with the classic segregationist dodge: "They like it that way."

Do they? The beauty of Brown's film is that the answer isn't a clear-cut yes or no. The city may be frozen in a kind of pre–Civil Rights limbo, but the traditions unique to each festival are cultural treasures: Is it possible to bring them together without sacrificing their character? The movie follows the royal court on both sides as they make the first tentative steps across the color line in three centuries — a social event that, in the immutable terms of Mobile society, takes on the significance of a moonwalk.

Brown, a Mobile native, watches the rituals leading up to Mardi Gras (dress fittings, float negotiations, ceremonial luncheons) with amused curiosity but without judgment or condescension. (That's her own kin onscreen, we learn late in the film, and she accords all her subjects the same clear-eyed courtesy.) If racism is an unspoken fact, at a sweeping social level, so is a mutual respect and goodwill between individuals. However separate the races remain as a group, they interact one-to-one in the Mardi Gras economy — whether a black crew chief is renting a white crew's float, or a black dressmaker is putting the finishing touches on the white queen's horizon-long train.

Mostly, though, *The Order of Myths* is hugely entertaining: sharply detailed, laugh-out-loud funny, possessed of a cast of characters Brown was smart enough to realize she couldn't make up. There is no more surefire recipe for a movie than viewing the world through the fixations of a narrow subculture or prism; most every street scene, crowd shot or place setting brought back my own Southern childhood in a flash. Brown has suggested her surrogate might be the Mobile debutante and self-professed liberal we see in the movie — who reluctantly takes her place in the white celebration, only to get caught up in the tide of tradition. (*Pith in the Wind*, Oct. 21, 2008)

• • • • •

I Like It Like That

The new comedy-drama *I Like It Like That* snuck into a single Nashville theater last week with virtually no notice, and it would be a shame if audiences missed out on one of the year's most vibrant, upbeat and original movies. Writer-director Darnell Martin's extraordinarily assured debut stakes out familiar territory — domestic strife in the inner city — yet fleshes out the characters, the situation and the locale with such good humor, perception and gritty common sense that we feel we're seeing a slice of American life the movies haven't shown us before.

At the movie's center is a young couple, Lisette (Lauren Vélez) and Chino (Jon Seda), struggling to raise three kids in the Bronx on a slim income. When Chino goes to jail, Lisette is forced to support the family by any means possible until she finds a job at a record company — a job that enhances her self-confidence and pride as much as it bruises Chino's The partners clash; the marriage crumbles, affairs and bitter recriminations occur on both sides.

What the above description doesn't convey is Martin's love and hope for her characters, who screw up and say things they don't mean and have the sense to learn from the experience. Although the despair Martin portrays is very real, even the youngest characters grow from their mistakes instead of wallowing in the hopeless nihilism portrayed in most recent urban dramas.

As the resourceful Lisette and her thin-skinned Chino, Vélez and Seda radiate tenderness, sensuality and unspoken regard: They seem so natural together, so attuned to each other's quirks and temperaments, that it's hard to believe we're not watching a real married couple. Martin's direction is as sinuous and energizing as the irresistible salsa music on the soundtrack — the whole movie has a sexy, impudent forthrightness. Darnell Martin is the first African-American woman ever to direct a major-studio release; once you see *I Like It Like That*, you'll be thrilled she got a chance to share her voice — even as you wonder about the other voices that have never been heard. (*Nashville Scene*, Nov. 10, 1994)

● ● ● ● ●

Sugar Hill

At first glance, *Sugar Hill* looks like another entry in the new wave of blaxploitation movies, which use a lot of flashy, glamorized drug dealing and violence to show the futility of drug dealing and violence. Look closer and you'll find a sobering drama that owes more to *Long Day's Journey Into Night* than to *The Mack*. Wesley Snipes plays Roemello Harris, a former honor student who turned his back on school to become an expert pusher. Disgusted by the casual murder and wasted lives around him, he decides to turn his back on the 'hood and relinquish the business to his loose-cannon brother (Michael Wright).

Of course, leaving is tougher than Roemello realizes, but *Sugar Hill* does more than just rehash *Superfly* or *Carlito's Way*. The movie paints a powerful portrait of a circle of sickness: Roemello's trade infects everyone around him, and no one emerges unscathed. When violence occurs, it's usually protracted just long enough to smother any hopes of kicky thrills. Director Leon Ichaso, working from a tough, ambitious script by columnist Barry Michael Cooper (*New Jack City*), creates a stifling, airless urban landscape incapable of sustaining life: The apartment where Roemello desperately tries to mold his brother and his junkie father into a nuclear family has an atmosphere of sadness and evil no shaft of sunlight could pierce.

While Snipes broods attractively, the film's unforgettable performance belongs to Clarence Williams III as the elder Harris, whose eyes blaze like coals with a lifetime of regrets. By the time he makes the final confession that will seal his family's fate forever, *Sugar Hill* has transcended its exploitative elements to become something truly worthwhile: a drama that addresses a public problem without losing sight of the private tragedy at its center. (*Nashville Scene*, March 24, 1994)

• • • • •
Tony Takitani

Reading a novel or short story by Japanese author Haruki Murakami is like picking at a thread that eventually threatens to unravel the world. The movie version of *Tony Takitani*, a 2002 Murakami story that appeared in the *New Yorker*, evokes the same sense of disarming simplicity as a gateway to extraordinary depths. In 75 unwasted minutes, director Jun Ichikawa etches the life of an emotionally crippled illustrator (Issei Ogawa) who finds new love, and with it a new terror of his former loneliness. As if to underscore the isolation of Tony and his passively troubled bride (Rie Miyazawa), an offscreen narrator does most of the talking; the characters sometimes finish his sentences, as if desperate to make themselves known. When combined with Ryuichi Sakamoto's delicate piano score and the tidy, rigidly composed images, which the camera scans from left to right like a photocopier of the memory, the effect reminded me of graphic novelist Chris Ware's achingly plaintive *Jimmy Corrigan* series — or the understated desperation of good ol' Charlie Brown. The movie is an exquisite miniature. If you have ever watched your sleeping lover and felt the helpless vulnerability that adoration brings, its slow fade of an ending is a punch to the heart. (*Nashville Scene*, Oct. 20, 2005)

• • • • •
The Scent of Green Papaya

Certain movies force us to abandon our over-reliance on narrative filmmaking techniques; they unfold in startling, unconventional ways that reward our attention with a privileged glimpse of another way of life. *The Scent of Green Papaya*, a magnificent, entrancing new movie by the young Vietnamese filmmaker Tran Anh Hung, is just such a film. The film opens in 1951 with the arrival of a young servant girl, Mui, in the home of a patrician Saigon family. At first the family seems secure and stable, but tiny details inside the home indicate otherwise. Mui, however, is drawn more to the sensual world outside that they ignore, the home of frogs, crickets and ants, with whom she shares a solemn kinship.

As in *The Remains of the Day*, servitude serves as a metaphor for mental or emotional imprisonment. Mui's salvation, however, lies in her spiritual affinity with the living things around her — even the ants her employers' children crush without a moment's thought. When the film jumps forward 10 years, and Mui is suddenly faced with an opportunity to develop her own freedom, *The Scent of Green Papaya* becomes a strange, exquisite variation on the story of Cinderella — a story that involves special slippers, a handsome prince and a splendid moment of self-transformation.

The Scent of Green Papaya has been criticized in some circles for refusing to address the political upheaval or war in Vietnam. Yet it is precisely our knowledge of the horrors to come that gives this film its piercing poignancy. The lush world Hung shows us, with its delicate partitions, aesthetic obsessions, and careful balance of man and nature, seems hopelessly fragile — we know it will blow away. The hushed, dazzling tableaux Hung creates allow us to see both the rigorous class structures of the household and the casual order of the natural world; neither will last. What we are left with, though, is the hope expressed in Mui's smile — a radiant vision that endures, among the many extraordinary images in this film, like a flower pressed in a book of lace. (*Nashville Scene*, April 7, 1994)

● ● ● ● ●

Ikiru

The difference between seeing Akira Kurosawa's film early and later in life is the difference between looking at a window and a mirror. It's the kind of benedictory statement one would expect at the end of a director's career, but Kurosawa's 1952 drama preceded his massive international success *Seven Samurai* and another 45-plus years of filmmaking. After 30 years of futile paper-pushing, an aging bureaucrat learns he has a short time to live. He seeks escape in drinking and gambling, but they don't help. He tries reconciliation with his grown son, but it doesn't work. Eventually, he decides that before he dies he will accomplish one worthwhile task. It is the beauty of Kurosawa's film, and the measure of his clear-eyed compassion, that this act is shown in flashbacks, after the ailing Mr. Watanabe (Takashi Shimura) has been laid to rest, while the mourners at his memorial service grapple with his selfless example.

In Kurosawa's *Rashomon*, made two years earlier, the X variable of human nature lies within the movie's conflicting views of the same event. Here, the differing viewpoints suggest that a man's life is measured twice: by himself, in the present, during whatever time he has on Earth; and by others, in the future, when his deeds are the only legacy he leaves. In Shimura's staggering performance — if you've seen *Seven Samurai* or *Stray Dog*, you may not believe you're seeing the same actor — his salaryman's stoop takes on a heroic cast, like Don Quixote's ratty armor. The movie makes an appropriate conclusion to the Belcourt's summer-long Kurosawa centenary celebration: In this marvelous film, with its indelible closing image of earthly satisfaction, the director penned an epitaph any man would be proud to claim. (*Nashville Scene*, Aug. 12, 2010)

Twin Cinema / Double Visions 5

A s we have seen, one side effect of writing for a weekly print publication is by necessity honing one's skill at saying a lot in a small amount of space. Another is that sometimes the only way to get two movies into one edition of the paper is to find a way to write about them both at the same time. This can make for strange bedfellows — *Boys Don't Cry* and *Fight Club*, for example, don't seem like an obvious pairing at first glance. But these dual reviews can also conjure refreshing insights from the sheer dumb luck of timing; these movies just so happen to be showing in this city at the same time, but here's how they connect to each other.

In the it-just-so-happens mold, Jim uses *Chicago* as a way into 1952's *Singin' in the Rain*, which by chance was touring the country for its 50th anniversary in 2003. In a remarkably brisk few paragraphs, Jim sets out some genre basics, delineates what makes each movie tick, and differentiates how each of them deals with the inherent artifice of the musical. In so doing, he defends the joys that artifice is uniquely capable of creating. Think of this section like a twin cinema: There's a different movie showing in either theater, and Jim's out in the lobby to talk about what they have in common.

This chapter is itself a double feature. After the side-by-side treatments, it moves on to reviews that explore doubles within the movies themselves: mirror images, doppelgangers, alter egos, parallel realities and dual versions of the same film. There's also a fun call-back to the genre-cribbing tactics of the Nouvelle Vague, in a review of the American remake of a French movie that imitates American movies. And, fitting for a chapter about doubles, there are two films by Brian De Palma, one of Jim's favorite directors, and one he went to great lengths to defend. There might also be two films by David Lynch, but they're both inside the same film.

• • • • • • • • • •

Full Frontal
Dir. Steven Soderbergh
2002, R, 106 min.

Signs
Dir. M. Night Shyamalan
2002, PG-13, 120 min.

Caught on Video

Thirteen years ago, in his debut film *sex, lies and videotape*, Steven Soderbergh posited video over film as the medium of ragged truth. Never mind that video can be doctored with far greater ease than celluloid. The big diff, back in 1989, was that video footage looked so awful it had to be real. When the characters confessed before James Spader's bulky camera, the contrast between the gray noise and the surrounding 35mm gave the video footage a grimy authenticity. Who'd fake something that looked like *that*?

It's a straight line from Soderbergh to Dogme 95, *The Blair Witch Project* and the coming hi-def/DV revolution, which threatens to supplant celluloid with pixels. But as video becomes more ubiquitous in feature filmmaking, will it lose the illusion of veracity (if in fact it ever existed)? It's illuminating to compare how video figures in two current films: M. Night Shyamalan's *Signs*, which deploys TV footage to enlist our belief in the story, and Soderbergh's own *Full Frontal*, which wonders why we buy fake grubbiness any more than fake glamour.

Apart from a fashionably tricky narrative structure, the two movies don't have much in common. *Signs* is a canny mix of classic invasion sci-fi, millenarian fear, and trembling and unease about strikes at America's heartland, while *Full Frontal*, a spiky Hollywood comedy, alternates a glossy 35mm sudser with a digital meander through several interlocked stories. But the use of video in both films is strikingly similar. *Signs* and *Full Frontal* exploit video for the illusion of caught-on-tape realism — of breaking news, of supposedly unstaged emotion. Shyamalan uses it to say, "This is really happening!" Soderbergh uses it to ask, "Is anything *really* happening?"

Signs ingeniously views an impending apocalypse through the narrowest of windows: an Iowa farmhouse connected to the outside world mainly by TV. (At this point, I should deliver the obligatory warning in every review of a Shyamalan film — the one in which you are cautioned to stop reading if you haven't seen the movie, as surprises will be spoiled, wild pigs will devour your gonads, etc.) The hero, a former priest (Mel Gibson) who has lost his faith, awakens to find crop circles flattened in his cornfield. His little girl flips on the tube and mentions, in a deadpan voice, that there's nothing to watch — the same thing is on every channel. All over the world, the circles are multiplying.

An alien invasion is imminent, but special effects aren't. A gifted tease of a storyteller, Shyamalan limits the global attack to whatever trickles of blurry, jiggly video the characters witness on TV — exactly what you or I would see on CNN if the Martians were landing. He gets more chills from a constellation of indistinct dots over a televised Mexico City than *Independence Day* managed with a sky full of CGI saucers. What's scary isn't the footage; it's the suggestion that everyone else on earth is watching incomplete snatches of a mass trauma. Shyamalan uses video the way Orson Welles used radio newsflash interruptions in *The War of the Worlds*: to rattle our certainty about what is fake with something we're accustomed to thinking is real.

The movie's less successful with its heavy-handed religious subtext, which basically uses a restoration of faith as another of Shyamalan's patented last-minute whammies. Gibson's fallen minister says at one point that there are two kinds of people: those who see only blind chance, and those who see coincidences as the mark of God's hand. Shyamalan's own heavy mitts don't leave much room for doubt. He plants narrative clues so blatantly that even a dimwit can tell they'll pay off later, then presents his own contrived setups as a divine plan. You'd think God sat around all day watching *The Usual Suspects*. The gimmickry undermines Shyamalan's undeniable gifts: his patience in laying out a story, his expert manipulation of offscreen sound and space, his intimate understanding of what makes genres work.

Like Shyamalan, Steven Soderbergh seems fascinated by the ticking machinery of genre films and commercial filmmaking in general. Where Shyamalan merely wants to build a better mousetrap, though, Soderbergh's actively curious why we keep taking the cheese. His caper comedy *Ocean's Eleven* didn't spend a second asking anyone to consider its plausibility: It operated in a helium-headed atmosphere of celebrity camaraderie and cinematic sleight-of-hand, reveling in its own breezy artifice. In interviews, Soderbergh said he was intrigued by making a movie that the audience was never supposed to consider "real." *Full Frontal* carries that idea even further: How much does the appearance of reality factor into enjoying a movie?

Full Frontal inverts *sex, lies and videotape* by cutting back and forth between a 35mm commercial film — a piece of froth called *Rendezvous*, about the romance between a celebrity journalist (Julia Roberts) and her actor subject (Blair Underwood) — and a jerky digital-verité character study. The "real" movie concerns the failing marriage of neurotic insiders David Hyde-Pierce and Catherine Keener, the travails of Keener's massage-therapist sister (Mary McCormack), and a circle of L.A. fringies that includes a stage actor playing Hitler (a hilarious Nicky Katt) in an abomination called *The Sound and the Führer*. The plots converge on the 40th birthday party of producer David Duchovny, where the cast of *Rendezvous* boldly ventures into the grainy digital world.

Acting as his own cinematographer, Soderbergh doesn't try to camouflage the cruddiness of DV camerawork — on the contrary, his color-saturated images are so fuzzed-out they approach pointillism. But he's after something more complex than a merit badge of indie honor. If anything, he's kidding the illusory chasm between indie and studio filmmaking, between the supposed veracity of video and the falseness of film. The split sections of *Full Frontal* have the same star power, the same heightened dialogue and emphasis on entertainment value, only in cosmetically different packages. The celluloid sellout and the digital gabfest turn out to be part of the same cinematic universe, each playing on a different set of conditioned viewer responses.

Billed as "a movie about movies for people who love movies," *Full Frontal* is nine innings of insider baseball, filled with crisscrossing in-jokes, cameos and deadpan riffs. What saves it from empty tail-chasing, or at least keeps its indulgences engaging, is that Soderbergh is a moviemaker who thinks like a moviegoer. With screenwriter Coleman Hough, he closes *Full Frontal* with the hokiest of Hollywood conventions, happy endings all around, and acknowledges that they require the mutual suspension of disbelief between maker and watcher. Video has seldom seemed less remote. (*Nashville Scene*, Aug. 8, 2002)

• • • • • • • • •
Singin' in the Rain
Dir. Stanley Donen and Gene Kelly
1952, NR, 103 min.

Chicago
Dir. Rob Marshall
2001, PG-13, 113 min.

Fear of Musicals

Of all the praise that has been heaped upon the movie *Chicago*, the strangest is something I've heard a dozen times now. "I loved it!" someone will enthuse. Their eyes gleam, and a song bubbles on their lips, then comes the inevitable kicker: "And I usually hate musicals."

The funny thing is, most everyone who claims to hate musicals has an exception, a song-and-dance spectacular they adore. Maybe it's *West Side Story*, maybe it's *Purple Rain*. Usually, these movies have either the trappings of realism (like the locations in *West Side Story*) or a stage setting that keeps music separate from "life" (as in *Purple Rain*). *Chicago* has both, and that seems to be part of its appeal; to people who can't abide sugar-sweet sing-a-thons, its tart cynicism doesn't taste like corn.

By contrast, 1952's *Singin' in the Rain*, now touring the country in an eye-popping 50th-anniversary print, has little of either. When people say they dislike musicals — the lovestruck duets, the splashy production numbers, the characters who burst into song because that's how they feel — *Singin' in the Rain* is apparently the movie they mean. And yet Gene Kelly and Stanley Donen's evergreen crowd-pleaser subverts those pet peeves as shrewdly as *Chicago*, if not more so. Where *Chicago* draws a clear line between its musical numbers and actual life — too clear — *Singin' in the Rain* sneaks its stylization past the viewer intact.

It does so by whisking us behind the scenes in Hollywood, masking one kind of illusion by unmasking another. *Singin' in the Rain* opens with Tinseltown in turmoil as the talkies hit. For heartthrob Don Lockwood (Kelly), who sings and dances, leaving the silents is no big deal. For his leading lady, Lina Lamont (Jean Hagen) — whose voice sounds like a balloon deflating — it's curtains. The solution is to dub Lina's voice with fresh-faced ingenue Kathy Selden (Debbie Reynolds), who loves Don. But bitchy Lina insists on keeping Kathy hidden, lest her own career burst. Ironically, it's the illusion of Hollywood — of how movies are made, and how stars behave — that *Singin' in the*

Rain punctures to construct another fantasy: a world where people sing as if saying good morning, and nobody blinks.

The common gripe against musicals is something like, "People don't just go around singing and dancing all the time." Exactly. So to get an audience to play ball, the form depends on one of two approaches: Either expressing oneself through song is a natural part of the movie's universe — in other words, people do just go around singing and dancing — or it's an aberration that has to be confined somehow.

In the intermittently dazzling *Chicago*, it's the latter. Musical numbers are initially restricted to the nightclub stage, then to the imagination of the baby-faced murderess Roxie Hart (Renee Zellweger); they're intercut with a grubby "real world" of courtrooms and prison cells. It's a softening of the corrosive sensibility that the late Bob Fosse brought to the stage version of *Chicago*, where showbiz, crime and corruption are indivisible. By making the numbers imaginary, the movie's framing device dampens some of the play's tawdry sizzle.

This is a trick *Singin' in the Rain* finesses. As Don and Lina film their first talkie, the movie throws in great gags about the shift to sound and the perils of hidden microphones: The tools of moviemaking are out in the open, lying on the workbench, but the characters still break into song as casually as conversation. The fake realism of exposed mics and lights is the anchor that allows the illusion to float. By the time Kelly takes his famous stroll in the rain, only a literal-minded chump would scoff at a world that permits such soaring release of pent-up feeling.

And that's exactly what makes musicals so wonderful: They don't have to cling to tethers of realism. If anything, it's our world that could use a dose of their exuberant conventions. One of my fondest moviegoing memories was about 20 years ago, when a midnight screening of *Singin' in the Rain* emptied into an unexpected downpour. A passerby would have seen 30 people splashing through puddles, singing and twirling umbrellas. With any luck, when *Singin' in the Rain* opens this weekend, we'll have stormy weather. (*Nashville Scene*, Feb. 6, 2003)

• • • • • • • • •
Darwin's Nightmare
Dir. Hubert Sauper
2005, NR, 107 min.

Grizzly Man
Dir. Werner Herzog
2005, R, 103 min.

Natural Facts

As if we needed any more proof of how fragile and illusory is man's dominion over nature, two sobering new documentaries arrive to put us in our place. *Darwin's Nightmare*, directed by Hubert Sauper, offers dispatches from an environmental catastrophe: the hostile takeover of Lake Victoria by the Nile perch. A non-native species introduced some 40 years ago, the monstrous fish is now the sole export of the Tanzanian villages on the shore. It's also a ravenous predator wiping out the lake's native species. When there's nothing left, the perch will eventually turn on its young and eat itself into oblivion.

What Sauper records, in intimate, glaring video, is a perfect storm of ecological and economic disaster. Too expensive for the starving locals, the precious flesh ships out daily for Europe, on planes that carry out the region's food and bring back guns. What the fish does to the lake, the ravages of global commerce accomplish on shore. Sauper's enraging film is less a methodically constructed narrative than a lobster pot of scalding ironies: homeless kids left with nothing but a cheap high from huffing discarded fish containers; a prostitute whose living turns out to be her death. Each scene finds a fresh new hell.

Man's folly, in *Darwin's Nightmare*, is to treat the world as his laboratory and expect nature to sweep up. In Werner Herzog's *Grizzly Man*, a work of serene and severe greatness, it's his attempt to impose any kind of anthropomorphic design on the wild. The film's subject, Timothy Treadwell, spent 13 years in the Alaskan wilderness, returning to civilization with minor celebrity as an activist on behalf of grizzly bears. With mostly a camera for company, he remained convinced that he knew how to live amongst the bears as an equal — until one devoured him and his girlfriend in 2003. From his copious footage, Treadwell, an ex-actor, often emerges as a painfully sincere show-off. Addressing the grizzlies by cute names, genuflecting before bear poo, he resembles Andy Dick with an L. L. Bean catalog. He would not be the first filmmaker to think that just because he has a camera, the outdoors is his backlot. But in his deluded quest to have the bears return his love, and his genuine obsession with the wild, Herzog seems to recognize a kindred visionary.

Tempering Treadwell's manic optimism with his own dour narration, Herzog turns what could have been a Discovery Channel snuff movie into an eerie contemplation of nature's unknowable depths. *Grizzly Man* ends with a haunting shot of Treadwell receding into the wild, followed close behind by two ambling grizzlies. Nature does not have motives, both films suggest; it simply is. But if you turn your back on it, it will devour you. (*Nashville Scene*, Sept. 8, 2005)

● ● ● ● ● ● ● ● ● ●

Boys Don't Cry
Dir. Kimberly Peirce
1999, R, 114 min.

Fight Club
Dir. David Fincher
1999, R, 139 min.

A Man's Man's World

It's tough to be a guy these days, and tougher still to be a white guy. At least that's the impression I'm getting from the news and from pop culture. Whenever somebody "goes postal," the perpetrator is inevitably white and inevitably male. A stockbroker goes on a killing spree in Atlanta; blank-looking dudes go up on unthinkable murder trials in Texas and Wyoming — in one case, for dragging a black man behind a truck until his body separated; in the other, for virtually crucifying a gay college student on a fence in bone-chilling cold.

A friend of mine argues it's the pressure of privilege — the fear of losing dominance — that's created the phenomenon of going postal. Gotta watch out for the damn minorities; gotta watch out for the women. Especially the women. As a result, there's a backlash brewing that makes the one Susan Faludi described look like a NOW meeting. On TV, multiple channels of pro wrestling swap viewers with the woman-haters of *The Man Show*. The enemy now isn't just feminism; it's femininity, period.

If angry white guys can take comfort in one thing, it's that Elizabeth Dole has fallen to Dubya, the frat-party candidate, and "reformists" can align behind their choice of Donald Trump, Pat Buchanan or Jesse Ventura. But that won't lessen the sense that men have to stick together against women — that masculinity can only be defined by stomping out the other. For men who no longer see how they fit into a changing social order, being a guy means belonging to an exclusive club. Two fascinating new movies deal with what it takes to be a member, and how swiftly and brutally your membership can be terminated.

On the surface, the docudrama *Boys Don't Cry* and the apocalyptic satire *Fight Club* seem radically dissimilar, in content as well as style. Yet as an examination of men's terror that they're being pushed aside — a fear that specifically involves women — the two movies fit together in startling ways. *Fight Club* tells the fictitious story of an insider: a guy who helps create a violent underground men's movement that he ultimately can't escape. *Boys Don't Cry* tells the true story of an outsider: a woman who attempted to join the company of men disguised as a peer — and was ultimately destroyed for trying.

Kimberly Peirce's shattering *Boys Don't Cry* is based on an infamous 1993 murder case in which two ex-cons, John Lotter and Thomas Nissen, killed three people at a Falls City, Neb., farmhouse. The case made national headlines when one of the victims was identified as Teena Brandon, a woman from nearby Lincoln. What attracted the media was that Teena Brandon had been known in Falls City as a boy named Brandon — a boy who even had several girlfriends. A transgender man who couldn't afford gender reassignment surgery, Brandon had been accepted as a guy by his buddies John and Tom until the local paper printed his/her actual name as part of an arrest record. Feeling betrayed, they gang-raped him, then killed him and two companions after he defied them and filed a police report.

The crime doesn't interest Peirce as much as the issues Brandon's story raises about the flimsiness of identity — the roles of men and women in particular. In a subtle, brilliant early scene, Brandon ventures into a roller rink as a boy for the first time. Giddy with excitement at going undercover, he starts to appropriate gestures from the guys around him, and he's so good at it he starts to transform before our eyes. That's as much because of Hilary Swank, the remarkable actress who plays Brandon, as because of the alert, unobtrusive way Peirce lays out the scene.

That thrill deepens when he's accepted as a guy by the people who will eventually kill him. According to the movie, what initially draws John (Peter Sarsgaard) and Tom (Brendan Sexton III) to Brandon is his foolhardy willingness to punch a hulking bully in a beer hall. Nothing separates boys from girls like a senseless beating. John and Tom may treat all the women around them as subordinates or groupies, but they welcome Brandon as an adoring kid brother, initiating him into macho rituals of drinking, lawbreaking and tailgate rodeos.

It's clear to John's girlfriend Lana (a deeply felt performance by Chloë Sevigny) that Brandon is somehow more sensitive than the other guys. But to John and Tom, there's a world of difference between being a guy, however bewilderingly soft, and being a woman — there's no androgynous in-between. This black-and-white sense of gender becomes a prison for Brandon. In a powerful scene that makes the metaphor explicit, he's forced to define himself to fit either a man's or woman's jail cell. John and Tom end Brandon's charade with the only tools they know — rape and violence — only to find they lead to the same prison.

Class is an unspoken issue in *Boys Don't Cry*. We're always aware that the women work in factories, the men blow off steam and the lack of options is an oppressive fact of life, but the movie never scores easy points off its heartland milieu — when Lana and Brandon fall in love, Falls City becomes a stylized fairy-tale idyll. In *Fight Club*, however, the setting is an unnamed urban jungle, stylization is rampant and overwhelming, and the rumbling corporate underclass is magma waiting to erupt. Where *Boys Don't Cry* is specific and perfectly focused, *Fight Club* is grandiose and free-swinging — so much so that it compromises some of its satirical points. But in its overwrought way, it's just as effective a portrayal of the male psyche in siege mode.

In a performance that strikes just the right note of ironic detachment, Edward Norton plays an insomniac corporate drudge drowning at home in consumer goods. Unable to feel anything, he starts to sample vicariously the suffering at support groups for cancer victims. But he doesn't snap out of his torpor until he encounters Tyler Durden (Brad Pitt), an anarchic soap sales-man who hips him to the empowering catharsis of a good fistfight. The pair's recreational beatings tap into some nameless, voiceless hostility and soon spawn an underground "fight club" network where disaffected waiters and wage slaves pound each other into meat — until they develop more militaristic aims.

Adapted by Jim Uhls from a cult novel by Chuck Palahniuk, *Fight Club* is never keener than when it's skewering the reactionary, tribalistic terror of the men's movement. What is Fight Club, after all, but a 12-step program for guys who'd tell you 12-step programs are for wusses? The difference between it and some kaffeeklatsch of Oprah's book clubbers is that it's legitimized by macho brutality.

From inside Norton's warped mind, the movie carries misogyny to deliberately cartoonish extremes: It doesn't just hate women, it holds up for ridicule everything even remotely associated with femininity. (As in *American Beauty*, the fall's other men-in-peril satire, women are directly linked to an emasculating consumer culture.) The harshest yuks are directed at Meat Loaf as Bob, a weightlifter whose steroid abuse led to testicular cancer — and to a massive pair of "bitch tits" that envelop Norton in sweaty embraces.

Because of this satirical viciousness, and director David Fincher's obvious relish in staging the yahoo mayhem he's supposedly condemning, *Fight Club* has been willfully misread as a celebration of fascist might. Like Kubrick's *A Clockwork Orange*, an obvious inspiration, its biggest liability as a satire is that it doesn't seem underpinned by any values of its own. When Norton expresses his contempt for a dying cancer victim, the woman is presented so cruelly that we feel invited to laugh at her. But the movie has the guts to follow the deranging effects of misogyny right over the brink. Once unleashed, the movie's id threatens even the celluloid itself.

Of the two movies, *Boys Don't Cry* seems far superior. It treats its subjects as people, not state-of-the-art abstractions, which doesn't give us the comfort of distancing us from its darkest truths. But both *Boys Don't Cry* and *Fight Club* face up to the rage that results from blind fear of the other. Though one's based in fact and the other in furious fantasy, their conclusions are the same: It's the other that should be afraid. (*Nashville Scene*, Oct. 28, 1999)

● ● ● ● ● ● ● ● ●

Femme Fatale
Dir. Brian De Palma
2002, R, 110 min.

Double Vision

A witty, subversive gadget freak with a telescopic sight for an eye and a yen for conspiracy scenarios, Brian De Palma is the second gunman overlooking the grassy knoll of American movies. He's also the wiseguy who caught the whole crime on film, only to find out nobody will listen. These two figures — the conspirator and the voyeur — recur like countermelodies in the elegant suspense thrillers De Palma has made his domain since the mid-1970s. Within the scope of these two perspectives, you'll find the sensibility of the guy who made paranoid fever dreams like *Blow Out* and *Dressed to Kill*: movies where everyone is watching and everyone is being watched.

To his many haters, De Palma's an irrelevant show-off who only makes movies about the movies he's seen. I would argue that he makes movies about a world alternately besotted, lulled, hoodwinked and alienated by a century of passive voyeurism — and that he doesn't exempt himself. Eyesight itself depends on two fields of view adjusted into one: It's the principle of binocular vision, in which the mind reconciles the twin views on either side of the nose to perceive depth and space. Something crazily similar is going on in the split screens, multiple perspectives and shifting vantage points of De Palma's movies, which prevent us from placing too much trust in any single image. The proof is in his latest film, a diversion with the collar-grabbing title *Femme Fatale.*

On one viewing, *Femme Fatale* appears a deliberately excessive caper thriller, a triumph of high style and visual command over cheerfully unhinged plotting. Look closer, though, and you'll find an intricate symbolic order that shows De Palma has more in mind than pretty surfaces and a game of Spot That Reference. On one level, it's absolutely about the ways we respond to movies and the sometimes contradictory things we want from entertainment. But it's also a morality play of disarming conviction, one that finds De Palma using his split screens and visual fragmentation to evoke the yearnings of a divided self.

Doubles figure extensively in *Femme Fatale*, starting with the image of Barbara Stanwyck in *Double Indemnity* on a hotel-room TV. The movie isn't about her, though: It's about the indistinct blur reflected in the screen, which is gradually revealed to us as a woman named Laure (played by Rebecca Romijn-Stamos). The TV screen functions as a mirror, but it isn't just Stanwyck reflected back at Laure: It's also Fred MacMurray's lovestruck patsy. In this one shot, De Palma shows us the reflection of a woman who sees in herself both the cold-blooded mankiller and the compromised but wised-up good guy.

Laure is joined by an accomplice, the sinister Black Tie (Eriq Ebouaney), who briefly goes over a scheme to steal a $10 million jewelry set during a gala at the nearby Cannes Film Festival. This sets up the first of De Palma's elaborate, beautifully organized set pieces, as the action switches to the festival's red carpet. Disguised as a photographer, Laure bewitches the jewelry model into a ladies-room tryst. The resulting caper cuts amusingly among several different sets of voyeurs: an audience in a movie theater, a thief with a serpentine camera extension, a roomful of surveillance technicians hooting at starlets on the security monitors. The only person who isn't peeping is Black Tie; his eyes are on the jewels.

There is a double cross, and Laure escapes with the loot. Thanks to the contrivances of the plotting — something De Palma breezes past with amusing flippancy — it turns out that she has an exact double, a woman whose identity she slips into with alarming ease. What the director does at this point is so breathtaking in its audacity and complexity that a second viewing is essential. On one level, he gives us two narratives to satisfy our contradictory desires as moviegoers: one that indulges our curiosity about how naughty Laure can be, and one that engineers the happy ending that we generally want for the main character in a light entertainment. On a deeper level — and this is far trickier — he immerses a character in a dream-like parallel destiny, as her waking conscience and consciousness try to alert her to an alternate path.

That certainly explains the movie's many scenes involving churches and crosses. It also explains the split screens, which suggest that even the darkest of lives has unexplored options. Laure is the latest De Palma hero, like telekinetic Carrie White or the gangster bound by thug life in *Carlito's Way*, whose very skill resigns her to a life she doesn't want. In this regard, it's tempting to see her as a reflection of her creator, who has complained that his wise-guy rep and showman's flair keep people from seeing anything but cheap thrills in his movies. The giddy flourish that closes *Femme Fatale* — a slow-motion showstopper that metes out redemption and retribution in a brilliantly executed montage — grants them both a future they've earned. (*Nashville Scene*, Nov. 14, 2002)

● ● ● ● ● ● ● ● ● ●

Point of No Return
Dir. John Badham
1993, R, 109 min.

Transatlantic Stalemate

For years, American and French directors have played a weird game of ping-ponging influences, with the B movie as the court of battle. When the young critics of the seminal French film magazine *Cahiers du Cinema* first began to champion American movies in the 1950s, they responded to the gut-level pulp thrillers of Don Siegel and Robert Aldrich, movies whose brutal immediacy betrayed not a moment's introspection. These movies were violent, they were garish, and their nightmarish who-gives-a-damn vision of the world made perfect sense to French intellectuals who embraced postwar existentialism.

When those same young critics (among them Truffaut and Godard) made their own *hommages* to American thrillers, in such ground-breaking films as *Shoot the Piano Player* and *Breathless*, they created a new language of film partly by trying to recreate the slam-bang junk movies they adored. Much of the fun of their films comes from seeing our own cultural obsessions — guns, gangsters, pulp movies — imitated and worshipped in this strange, lyrical, off-kilter way.

That's one reason Luc Besson's thriller *La Femme Nikita* became a huge and unexpected hit in this country a couple of years ago. Feverish, frantic and oddly playful, *La Femme Nikita* was a French movie any redneck could enjoy, a nitro-powered shoot-'em-up that reimagined B-movie conventions in punky, amusing ways. What made the movie so much fun, though, was Besson's over-the-top conception of what an American action movie should be: The characters' emotions are heightened to the point of lunacy; the tone lurches from lurid to sentimental in the blink of an eye; and the camera practically does handsprings in a riotous imitation of James Cameron and George Miller movies. Yet the result had a hypnotic, insistent, neon-drenched mood all its own. Besson was slammed for wearing his influences on his sleeve, but American audiences got off on its seductive nihilism the way French audiences got off on the unapologetic viciousness of old B movies.

So with the new thriller *Point of No Return*, a direct scene-for-scene remake of *La Femme Nikita*, we have the bizarre spectacle of an American movie remaking a French movie made as a tribute to American movies — a sort of cinematic "I'm My Own Grandpa."

The plot remains the same: A drugged-out punk murders a policeman and is sentenced to the chair. Instead of being killed, however, she is whisked away to a top-secret government training camp, where a smooth-talking operative named Bob (Gabriel Byrne) gives her a new identity and an ultimatum: Either become a high-level assassin or become a corpse. Once outside, she discovers that she no longer wants to kill — especially when she falls in love with a gentle, adoring man, J.P. (Dermot Mulroney), who represents a life of caring she has never experienced. As the government hands her increasingly risky assignments, and J.P. demands to know more about her past, the woman, code-named Nina, finds herself on the verge of a deadly breakdown.

The combination of women and guns has a tremendous erotic allure only Freud could have guessed at, and the success of *La Femme Nikita* had much to do with the image of sultry French actress Anne Parillaud in a clingy miniskirt wielding various implements of destruction. As la femme Nina, the exquisite Bridget Fonda gives *Point of No Return* the same volatile erotic charge. Fonda doesn't have Parillaud's unique killer-marionette panache, but she brings the role a balletic, coiled physicality that suggests a combination of animal instinct and mechanized response. After a string of good but somewhat anonymous performances, Fonda is starting to develop a strong screen personality. She carries the whole show here, and her mixture of savage grace and alluring vulnerability sustains your interest through the movie's silliest contrivances.

Among a strong supporting cast, the real standout is Harvey Keitel, whose brief appearance as the cold-blooded "cleaner" adds an element of true menace. An underrated comic actor, Keitel peers out here from behind inch-thick lenses and cocks his head like a rapt machine. His inhuman, horrifyingly funny unflappability makes him a perfect adversary for the emotionally shaken Nina.

The strangest thing about *Point of No Return* is that while it doesn't have anything new to add to *La Femme Nikita*, that really doesn't matter. In translating the movie from France to America, the movie loses some of its style. The director, John Badham, never finds a unifying look like the cold, steely sheen that held the original together. Yet if you've seen the first film, you start to look forward to seeing the same scenes played out with these actors.

People who complain that *Point of No Return* is some kind of travesty are missing the point. *La Femme Nikita* was no boldly original masterpiece: It was a slick, dazzling junk movie — the same kind of slick, dazzling junk movie director Besson appropriated from American filmmakers. By remaking Besson's *hommage*, the filmmakers have truly brought it all back home. They have reclaimed the trashy material and given it the technical gloss that serves as America's most identifiable contribution to the movies.

Godard once said that the best way to criticize a movie was to make a movie. Given that these two movies are virtually identical, I can only assume that *Point of No Return* was made because some Hollywood yahoo decided in a jingoistic fit that Americans could make a better trash movie out of *La Femme Nikita* than those Frenchies, by God. I'm not sure that's much of a reason to make a movie, but I enjoyed *Point of No Return* about as much as I enjoyed *La Femme Nikita*, which suggests a tie for the moment in this transatlantic tennis game. And until the French return the salvo with a remake of *Point of No Return*, the ball is in their court. (*Nashville Scene*, March 25, 1993)

● ● ● ● ● ● ● ● ●

A History of Violence
Dir. David Cronenberg
2005, R, 96 min.

Warring Impulses

David Cronenberg's *A History of Violence* is a gripping, hot-blooded contemporary Western about the terrible necessity of violent response in the face of direct threat. It is a chilling critique of America's obsession with the outlaw, a mythic figure whose status as hero or psycho depends on killing the right person. Since seeing the movie a few weeks ago, I've heard people argue either side with equal passion. At different levels — and this testifies to the movie's effectiveness as a thriller as well as Cronenberg's skill as a subversive artist — they're both right.

A devious thriller about divided nature, A History of Violence is itself a radically conflicted work, not so much schizoid but inextricably tangled and unresolved. (The trailer already gives away too much, but if you haven't seen the movie, you should stop reading anyway.) The title alone has a double meaning — a specific personal case and an epic overview of conflict — and the reactions Cronenberg incites are compatible with both. The movie treats violence as a makeup of our individual and national identity. To its credit, it could only be unthinkingly embraced as either a pacifist or a reactionary work.

The setup is as two-dimensional as the movie's graphic-novel source: a Midwestern family man, Tom Stall (played by Viggo Mortensen), thwarts a robbery in his diner by quickly and efficiently shooting the stickup men. The men are stone killers, and the violence is provoked: CNN hails Tom as a hero. Then a business-suited hood (a delectably nasty Ed Harris) sits down at the diner's counter and removes his sunglasses to reveal one working eye. He thinks that Tom is really Crazy Joey Cusack, a Philadelphia mobster who flipped on his crime family and disappeared into witness protection. Crazy Joey Cusack was not a hero. Crazy Joey was a bad man.

Are Tom's actions in the diner any different because they were carried out by a former mad-dog killer instead of a peace-abiding family man? The question cuts to the heart of a nation. Does it matter why the U.S. went to war in the Gulf, so long as Saddam Hussein was removed from power? Answer yes, and you're left to consider a murderous despot still in power: evil unchecked. Answer no, and you've got a dangerous precedent for willful bloodshed: evil unleashed. Cronenberg takes such absolutes in A History of Violence and turns them into ambiguities: his directorial emphasis suggests there's no either-or.

As the vengeance melodrama plays out, the details of small-town life are weirdly artificial, either stylized to the point of pulp abstraction or distorted with sinister low angles or a desolate atmosphere that produces a hollow effect. Not so the violence, which is jarringly realistic and cathartic as hell: my audience cheered as Tom/Joey blasted the jaw off a creep in close-up. It makes the idea of a peaceful life — of civilization — look delusional. The exhilaration of Cronenberg's violence leaves doubt that a force so uncontrollable could restore order. And yet that's just what the movie's many instances of justified carnage do — whether they're being committed by Tom or Joey.

I'm convinced another filmmaker would have taken the same feverish Josh Olson script, a model of taut construction, and made either a crackerjack revenge Western or an anti-violence screed. But I can't imagine anyone but

Cronenberg doing both simultaneously to undercut each other. Cronenberg started his career making movies of ideas for horror audiences: I remember sitting through a drive-in double feature in 1982 just to see his sublime *The Brood*, still the most potent depiction in movies of a failed marriage's psychic devastation. He used gory, gooey genre pieces like *Videodrome* and the underrated *eXistenZ* to wonder what effect our sweet tooth for disembodied thrills — and his — had on actual minds and bodies.

In *A History of Violence*, he's still watching our responses with a clinician's fascination. The movie registers our many contradictory attitudes toward violence through Tom's wife Edie, played with raw emotional conviction by Maria Bello. As Tom's identity morphs from husband to dark stranger, Edie's responses shift from pride to curiosity and fear. Their relationship is measured in two bracketed sex scenes of remarkable power: with Tom, a role-playing fantasy that is almost quaint in its suburban kinkiness; with Joey, a hot and hostile hate-fuck in which his violent unknowability comes almost against her will as a turn-on. Sex and violence, allure and repulsion, the rifle-toting homesteader and the killer — they all nestle somewhere to varying degrees in human nature, just as they do in Mortensen's haunting performance. People who say *A History of Violence* is either a yahoo vigilante celebration or an anti-violence tract are only seeing what they want to see. Peering into the mirror that Cronenberg holds up, we might think we're all Tom Stalls. The director suggests that if we don't look away, we might see Crazy Joey Cusack staring back. (*Nashville Scene*, Sept. 29, 2005)

● ● ● ● ● ● ● ● ●

Summer of Sam
Dir. Spike Lee
1999, R, 142 min.

White Heat

The first reviewer who says how different Spike Lee's *Summer of Sam* is from his other movies deserves a conk upside the head. OK, his cast is primarily white, not black; his setting is the Bronx, not Brooklyn; and he works in a dynamic style that's bold-faced and all caps, even for him. Thematically, though, Lee's snapshot of the summer of 1977 is the soulmate to his indelible portrait of the summer of '89, *Do the Right Thing*. Lee may have shifted from Public Enemy to punk, but he retains his focus on the ways that provincialism, prejudice, and, above all, heat bring a city's underlying conflicts and character to a boil.

If *Do the Right Thing* had the urgency of breaking news, *Summer of Sam* is history written in tabloid thunder. Appropriately, the movie is introduced by Jimmy Breslin, the *Daily News* columnist whose sparring with the serial killer dubbed "Son of Sam" gripped New York in '77. "There are 8 million stories in the naked city," intones Breslin, "and this is one of them." The quote connects *Summer of Sam* to the gritty, location-shot Mark Hellinger melodramas of the late 1940s, which helped fuse New York and crime in the public imagination.

Lee aims for that kind of pulpy immediacy in *Summer of Sam*, which recreates the sweltering summer that punk, disco, Reggie Jackson, riots, mass murder, mass media and temperatures in the 100s converged to ignite the city's tensions. Shot in tints as hot and livid as lipstick by Ellen Kuras, *Summer of Sam* focuses on a single Italian-American neighborhood in the Bronx, where the killer's threat has turned brunettes blond and turned anyone offbeat into a suspect. To the fellas who hang out with Joey T. (Michael Rispoli) by the Dead End sign, Suspect No. 1 is Ritchie, a punk who dares to wear spiked hair and dog collars.

Ritchie's buddy Vinny (John Leguizamo) starts out sticking up for him, but he's got problems of his own — he's convinced his womanizing ways have made him Son of Sam's next target, and his trusting disco-dolly wife Dionna (an astonishing Mira Sorvino) is wising up. As the heat, the hostility and the body count rise, so does the vigilante fervor in the neighborhood — and with it the pressure on Vinny to side against his friend with the freaky 'do.

Lee's movies have been accused of a narrow, provincial worldview. But his films have a lot of sympathy for misfits who long to escape peer pressure, ingrained racism, and a world the size of a city block — even if they often take a beating for their curiosity. It's no accident here that his villain, gunman David Berkowitz (Michael Badalucco), is a shut-in who stews in his room until he pops — while the hero, Ritchie, played with scruffy gallantry by Adrien Brody, is the character most willing to explore life outside the 'hood.

Ritchie, like *Do the Right Thing*'s Radio Raheem, is also a scary-looking outsider who turns out to be a lot less threatening than the normal folks around him — normal folks like the thuggish Joey T. and bland, doughy Berkowitz. To Lee, there's nothing more dangerous than always being normal; he repeatedly forces his neighborhood boys into situations where they get to be "the other" for a change, whether ogled by Bowery punks or snubbed by disco patrons.

Working with a brilliant cast and a juicy, sprawling script co-written with actors Victor Colicchio and Michael Imperioli, Lee creates a tapestry of city life in which mobsters share meals with cops, drug dealers appoint themselves crime fighters, and overheated restaurant workers take turns in a meat freezer. From greasy spoons to glittery Studio 54, the movie's portrait of New York 1977 is as double-edged and multifaceted as its characters, who worry about the warring sides of their personalities and assume different identities with wigs and accents.

The movie's worst scenes, oddly enough, involve Berkowitz: They're shot in a hammy green-tinted horror-movie style that ranges from tasteless to ludicrous. I don't buy the contention that making the movie is an automatic affront to the victims' families, but there's no denying the shootings are photographed for grisly frissons: When one victim holds a book in front of her face, you just know Lee can't resist showing the bullet blasting through the cover. When he stoops to dubbing the words "Help me!" over a fly in Berkowitz's apartment, maybe it's time for Lee to start making movies instead of "joints."

However, if Lee handles the killer and the killings with gratuitous ugliness, he treats Mira Sorvino's wronged wife and Jennifer Esposito's promiscuous punk-in-training with a tenderness and empathy all but unseen in his female characters. And if the wall-to-wall score of '70s tunes resorts sometimes to cheap irony, it also conveys the vortex of passions and events swirling around the movie's many characters.

Despite its violence, the film's affection for the city remains intact. Lee's visual rock 'n' roll culminates in two electrifying montages of mayhem set to Who classics; even so, the closing sweep of Frank Sinatra's "New York, New York" seems anything but ambiguous. In *Summer of Sam*, as in *Do the Right Thing*, Spike Lee shows his love for the urban melting pot, even when it turns into a pressure cooker. (*Nashville Scene*, July 1, 1999

● ● ● ● ● ● ● ● ●

Passion
Dir. Brian De Palma
2012, R, 102 min.

Eyes Without a Face

Passion is a Brian De Palma movie for a world chilled by narcissism and held rapt by its own reflection. The director has devoted his career to the warping impact of surveillance culture, where everyone is a watcher or passive voyeur — in front of the big screen, the TV, the computer monitor — and conversely, everyone is watched. Long before the laptop, the iPhone and Skype, there was De Palma Nation, a place where everybody was either on camera or behind one. Because of the bulky, prohibitively expensive equipment, the latter group was limited — either to professionals, like John Travolta's sound engineer in *Blow Out*, or obsessives, like Keith Gordon's gadget-prone amateur sleuth in *Dressed to Kill*.

But technology has surpassed the spycam society forecast in early De Palma classics like *Hi, Mom!* and *Sisters*. Anyone with a cellphone can be both star and director of his own YouTube-documented life, which sounds like nothing so much as the setup for one of De Palma's loopy, sinuous erotic thrillers. In fact, it's a pretty apt description of *Passion*, a wickedly funny exercise in the audience misdirection and technocratic hoodwinkery that's been this filmmaker's stock in trade for nearly five decades. Its corporate milieu is an orchard of gleaming little trademark Apples, most of them concealing worms.

De Palma borrows the hothouse plot of Alain Corneau's 2010 French thriller *Love Crime* — its co-writer, Natalie Carter, gets a dialogue credit here — but gives it a cold-to-the-touch sheen and a clammy metallic palette that's at ironic odds with the title. (It was shot on 35mm but transferred to digital, which mutes the steamy lushness that marks De Palma's thrillers.) When color bleeds through this sterile environment, it's typically the siren-red lipstick worn by Christine (Rachel McAdams), a coolly kinky executive at a Berlin advertising agency where the glass planes and slashing angles suggest the Apple Store of Dr. Caligari.

So self-obsessed she likes her lovers to wear a doll-mask facsimile of her own features, Christine is grooming an avid protégé, Isabelle (Noomi Rapace), who covets her boss' power and modernist digs down to the upholstery on her sofa. De Palma poses them in the frame like mirror images, and Christine can't help but try shaping her underling into a human selfie. "You need some color," she coos to Isabelle, applying her lipstick as well as her lips.

But Isabelle isn't such an eager apprentice once Christine hogs the credit for her viral smartphone ad campaign — a spot that only looks like an updating of the reality-TV "Peeping Toms" gag that opens De Palma's 1973 *Sisters*, but is in fact a replica of an actual guerrilla YouTube ad. The ad mixes the director's favorite ingredients, sex and spying — and so does the mad soap-opera-on-steroids revenge fantasy that follows, as Isabelle sleeps with Christine's shady colleague-lover (Paul Anderson) and her boss rigs a nasty public payback.

Each step of this battle is registered on screens, even screens within screens, creating a hall of mirrors that fires the gaze back at the gazer: the "ass cam" that secretly films leering gawkers, the sex tape where the parties stare into each other's eyes only when they watch themselves on a monitor. Imagine what this plethora of recording devices means to the man who once called film 24 lies a second. De Palma plays this mediated alienation for queasy-funny effect, as when Isabelle lies in bed with her hands in masturbatory position — only they're poised over her laptop rather than her lap. The two women's fight is personal, all right, but so much of it is waged on a digital playing field that they might as well be video-game avatars. But some things you still have to do the old-fashioned way. That's when a knife comes in handy.

Shot by Almodovar's longtime cinematographer José Luis Alcaine — the Spanish director's resolutely De Palma-esque melodrama *The Skin I Live In* was good practice — *Passion* shows De Palma reveling in the blatant craziness of his contrivances. (This features perhaps the quintessential De Palma line of dialogue: "You have a twin sister?") Rapace's Edvard Munch cheekbones and startled eyes do the heavy lifting of her performance, but McAdams, firmly back in *Mean Girls* mode, delivers her vicious lines with venomous zest. De Palma introduces more and more variables into the scenario, leading to a split-screen showstopper where high art and low crime compete for the viewer's attention. Guess what wins.

In *Passion*'s brightest moments — almost all of them in its booby-trapped second half — art and lowbrow kicks strut the runway in stiletto heels, hand in hand. If *Passion* isn't quite as much fun as De Palma's feverish 2000 rocket ride *Femme Fatale*, it's in part because of the risky long con the director is working here. For the movie's naughty surprises to pay off, he makes viewers wade through long stretches of the stuff DVD watchers generally skip: bad actors delivering bad exposition. It's a test of patience, and some viewers may set down their pencils.

But De Palma isn't just anticipating our annoyance, he's counting on it. The justly famous centerpiece of *Blow Out* has Travolta reconstructing a sequence we've already watched using magazine stills, adding elements of cinema — sound, editing, projection — to reveal a crime that took place right before our eyes. The underlying theme of his movies is that people are so accustomed to looking that they've forgotten how to see. A viewer's impatience with *Passion*'s dull police procedural all but guarantees he'll be blindsided by the elaborate trap the director is laying in plain sight.

When De Palma springs it, in a denouement of spiraling delirium that deploys tropes from across his career, the laughter it produces is eruptive — part giddiness at watching the dominoes topple, part amused acknowledgement of how thoroughly we've been suckered. But in some ways, the altered media landscape De Palma sends up has the last laugh. The first new film in six years by the movies' most extravagantly gifted visual artist made its arrival via video on demand — consigned to TV and the tiniest of portals except in relatively few cities, of which Nashville is one. Pace Norma Desmond, the picture is big; it's the screens that have gotten small. But this portability has a side effect. It means this devious little gem can be passed around forever — like a secret, like a virus, like a clip you've just gotta share. (*Nashville Scene*, Sept. 5, 2013)

● ● ● ● ● ● ● ● ● ●

Touch of Evil
Dir. Orson Welles
1958, PG-13, 95 min.

The Greater of Two Evils

Orson Welles suffered from the career equivalent of progenia, the disease that prematurely accelerates the aging process. As a two year old in Kenosha, Wisc., he was pronounced a genius. At age 16, he was drawing ovations in adult roles at Dublin's Gate Theater. By the time Welles made *Citizen Kane* 10 years later in 1941, he had already achieved renown as a stage actor, a director, the founder of a theater company, and a radio star. Yet each new triumph only seemed to bring greater risks — of failure, of disappointment. Radio was considered a lesser medium than theater, the site of Welles' early successes, and movies were regarded as essentially flashy and shallow. It's telling that when Welles made his film debut, as a young man of 26, he was already playing a fallen giant whose greatest years lay behind him.

Far too early in a brilliant career, Kane became a self-fulfilling prophecy. Welles' subsequent films were butchered (*The Magnificent Ambersons*), panned (*The Lady from Shanghai*), or hampered by lack of financing (*Othello*); he left a legacy of unproduced scripts and unfinished projects. By the late 1950s, Welles couldn't get funding for his own infrequent films outside Europe; in Hollywood he could only get work as an actor, mostly in glorified cameos, a seasoning in other director's stews. Yet in 1957, when Charlton Heston was offered a role opposite Welles in a low-budget thriller for Universal, he accepted on the condition Welles be allowed to direct.

The resulting film, *Touch of Evil*, was taken out of the director's hands in the editing room, after Universal execs took a sneak peek at his footage and panicked. In place of the socko B movie they'd commissioned, they found a baroque, expressionistic miasma of tilted angles and bleeding neon and unrelenting tawdriness. (The tawdriness wasn't the problem — the producer, Albert Zugsmith, followed up *Touch of Evil* with passion-pit fodder like *Sex Kittens Go to College*.) Several heated exchanges ensued. Welles, somewhat self-destructively, distanced himself from the film's editing, and a new director, Harry Keller, was brought in to shoot four "clarifying" scenes.

The day after seeing the studio's finished cut in 1958, Welles dashed off a 58-page memo to Universal studio chief Ed Muhl. The memo addressed aspects ranging from the movie's sound design to its narrative structure; it proposed some 50 changes in Universal's edit. "I am passing on to you a reaction based not on my conviction as to what my picture ought to be," Welles reasoned, "but only what here strikes me as significantly mistaken in your picture." Instead, the studio hacked an additional 15 minutes from the film after bad test screenings; it wound up literally the B picture on a double bill with Keller's *Female Animal*, starring Hedy Lamarr. Welles claimed never to have seen his movie again.

This year, a team led by film editor and sound wizard Walter Murch set about re-editing *Touch of Evil* according to the specifications in Welles' memo. There's no restored footage: no outtakes could be found. Most of the changes are so subtle that if you watch the two editions side by side, you'll have a hard time finding the individual trims, shifts, and remixes. And yet they have an undeniable cumulative effect. If you haven't seen this lurid jewel in recent years, you'll be surprised by the new edition's texture, narrative force, and suspense.

Touch of Evil's origins are as disreputable as the inhabitants of its grubby locale, Los Robles, the proverbial border town where human life is cheap. According to David Thomson's biography *Rosebud*, Welles adapted (and kept pieces of) an existing Paul Monash script, which was taken from a Whit Masterson penny dreadful called *Badge of Evil*. Welles didn't even try to disguise the movie's genesis as hard-boiled drugstore-paperback pulp; if anything, he enhanced it. From the justly celebrated opening — which ticks off, in one unbroken shot, the minutes leading to a fatal car-bombing — *Touch of Evil* immerses us in extravagant degradation, a hothouse of Latin jazz and sweaty shadows and windows that open onto darkness.

Welles deliberately played up the sleaziness of the locale, the better to measure the fall of his detective villain, Hank Quinlan. In theory, Quinlan isn't the intended focus of the movie: the purported heroes are Mexican narcotics cop Mike Vargas (Heston, playing the unlikeliest Latino since Robby Benson in *Walk Proud*) and his new bride Susie (Janet Leigh). It's their honeymoon that is shattered by the bombing, which separates the couple; it's their unwanted arrival that sets in motion the plot's skittering trajectory.

But it's Quinlan who dominates the film from the moment he enters, filling the frame like a fleshy balloon. Quinlan is Welles' worst vision of himself: a kind of reverse vanity may have prompted Welles, though already large, to assume rubbery jowls and pounds of padding. But the corrupt, once idealistic lawman is right in keeping with the fallen Charles Foster Kane and the tragic heroes of Welles' Shakespeare adaptations. Welles, after all, chose to play Othello on film, not Hamlet; he played Falstaff, the broken-hearted old wit consigned to insignificance, not bonny Prince Hal.

We're told Hank Quinlan was a great detective once; now he's stuck in seedy nowheresville, fat and sloppy drunk, planting evidence to convict men whose guilt he already knows. His scenes with Marlene Dietrich's fortune-telling madam, Tana, his former lover, are suffused with a resigned self-loathing that grows sadder every time you see the movie. "Wish I'd gotten fat off your chili," he mumbles, taking a joyless, mulish chomp out of his ever-present candy bar.

In the restored version, Murch's editing more evenly crosscuts the scenes of Vargas' investigation and of Susie's siege at an isolated motel, one of the creepiest set pieces in movie history. (Leigh always had lousy luck with room service.) By doing so, though, Murch leaves Quinlan to become the movie's center. Thus, the love story that resonates in the new version isn't between Mike and Susie; it's between Quinlan and his loyal sidekick Menzies (Joseph Calleia), the one man who knows his past greatness — and who ultimately betrays him.

Even in its studio-tampered form, *Touch of Evil* is remarkable, and some viewers might even miss its drugged, somnambular quality. The most stunning differences, however, are in the opening sequence and the sound design. The re-editing team removed the titles Universal plastered over the astonishing first shot, which starts off with a close-up of a hand setting a time bomb — three minutes, 20 seconds — then wanders in real time through the streets of the town. Russell Metty's camera cranes around a building, then moseys past revelers to catch up with Mike and Susie. Suddenly, there's that damn car again with the bomb in the trunk. Check your watch — the couple inside has a minute to live. Bear in mind that everything in the extremely complicated shot has been timed to coincide with the camera's movement. Then watch it all end in flames.

Without the credits or Henry Mancini's admittedly cool samba-jazz theme, the town immediately comes to life as a locale, not a movie set — it has three-dimensional space as well as a wealth of incidental sounds. (Those sounds aren't accidental either — check out the way the doomed car's arrival is heralded by the song crackling on its radio.) The emphasis on space through-out is crucial to Welles' conception. Notice how many times the director has action take place on opposite sides of a window, or how often he crowds large people into small rooms in diagonal formations that indicate their relative significance at the moment. The town's twisted alleys and gnarled angles could be the corridors of Quinlan's mind: Vargas briefly loses his way in them, but Quinlan's the one who finally sinks into the quagmire. Then Dietrich has the last word — "Adios" — and the movie follows her into the shadows.

Welles went on to a career that was no doubt as frustrating for him as it was for his admirers. Without discriminating, he took bit parts in historical pageants and trashy spectacles and unworthy horror cheapies. He appeared on talk shows and spun outrageous lies about his life and work, as if he had to make up claims for fame. One of the saddest artifacts of Welles' later years is an oft-bootlegged outtake from a pea commercial, in which he harangues the director about the proper inflection and wording of the voiceover. What's sad isn't that someone of Welles' talent was reduced to such a task; what's sad is that he was right about each of his points. He had a showman's sense of what people want from a story and an artist's sense of how best to arrange it, and all too often we were denied the benefit of those gifts. The restored *Touch of Evil* clears away all the planted evidence; what's left is proof of greatness enough for any man. (*Nashville Scene*, Oct. 15, 1998)

• • • • • • • • •

Actress
Dir. Stanley Kwan
1992, NR, 119 min.

Imitation of Life

Three years ago, *Film Comment* magazine triggered a movie-geek avalanche when it polled a roster of film programmers, distributors, and critics on a simple question: What were the best movies of the 1990s that hadn't been released in America? To make things simpler, or so they thought, the editors ruled out English-language or American films, figuring those had a better shot at distribution. Even so, the respondents came up with a list of 150 movies that were all but unseen by American audiences. The article sparked (or shamed) distributors into picking up several films on the list, but tracking down most of the films became a sort of rotisserie sport for hardcore movie nuts — the way baseball-card fanatics or comic-book collectors keep checklists of obscure players or series.

The idea of glassy-eyed cinephiles trolling the aisles of Asian grocery stores or back-alley bootleggers is pretty funny. What keeps this quest from becoming another exercise in geeky one-upmanship is the quality of the movies. Of the top 20 films, I've only managed to find about six. But those six were diverse and exciting enough to juice me with the collector's bug: Finding these movies (which included John Woo's Vietnam epic *Bullet in the Head* and Leos Carax's *Les Amants du Pont Neuf*) adds a thrill of discovery that makes them that much more precious. At the same time, their very obscurity raises a troubling afterthought: If something this good can get discarded in the year-to-year, decade-to-decade shuffle of movies, what else out there is lost?

One such MIA movie is *Actress*, a 1992 biopic by Hong Kong director Stanley Kwan. On the *Film Comment* list, ranked by vote, *Actress* clocks in at No. 19. Yet its lost-in-the-supermarket status deepens its mysterious poignancy. A hard-to-describe hybrid of documentary, biography and costume drama, *Actress* is as much about the vanishing of the early 20th century as about the irretrievable loss of the era's photographic records. For the movie itself to be outside the reach of most viewers, so comparatively soon after its making, is a cruel irony.

Actress, at its most basic level, is a screen biography of Ruan Ling-yu, a stunning film star of the 1930s who was dubbed "the Greta Garbo of Chinese cinema." Molded by male directors, Ruan made her mark playing glamorous "noble" roles; even though her own upbringing was humble, she had to beg to play the prostitutes and working-class heroines of the Shanghai film industry's evolving slate of socially conscious films. But her eventual success in those roles didn't shield her from the gutter press, which pounced on the possibility that she was having an adulterous affair. In 1935, she committed suicide at the height of her beauty and fame. She was 25 years old.

If *Actress* had simply filled in the sketchy details of Ruan's life — a doomed marriage to a cheating, gambling wastrel (Tony Leung Ka Fai), an affair with a mogul that eventually claimed her career and reputation — it would've made an engrossing high-gloss soap. Instead, director Kwan had the inspiration to present the fragments of Ruan's life in fragments. The movie thus alternates black-and-white Super 8 interviews of Ruan's contemporaries with sumptuous, color-saturated depictions of the tango bars and steamy backrooms of 1930s Shanghai. The effect, as the *Chicago Reader*'s Jonathan Rosenbaum points out, makes the imagined past more vivid than the grainy present.

Adding to the poetic displacement of past and present is the casting of Maggie Cheung as Ruan. Cheung, a former beauty queen, started out as an ingenue in Jackie Chan's mid-1980s Hong Kong action epics (Chan co-produced *Actress*); she's perhaps best known to American audiences for the astounding martial-arts fantasy *The Heroic Trio*. Despite getting parts in early films by Kwan and Wong Kar-wai, though, she had a hard time breaking out of glossy, frivolous roles: According to Rosenbaum, she was a last-minute replacement in *Actress* for the less "lightweight" Mainland actress Anita Mui. The movie opens with a series of Ruan's production stills, over which Kwan describes the way she was typecast and held back as an actress. When he cuts to Cheung, the modern-day actress wryly observes, "Isn't she a replica of myself?"

Well, yes and no. The difference between Cheung and the real-life Ruan is part of the movie's complex, multileveled depiction of the relationship between the past and the present. Cheung's luminous full-moon face and cool contemporary poise don't match the "real" Ruan, who's shown in silvery scraps from her 1930s films. Instead of downplaying the difference, though, Kwan uses it to convey how little we know about Ruan apart from her film image: Just because we know how she looks doesn't mean we know her. Tellingly, Cheung is introduced not as Ruan but as herself discussing the role with Kwan. We're never meant to think of her as a substitute for the real person, just a thoughtful approximation.

That extends to Kwan's recreations of Ruan's films, many of which have been lost forever. In one scene, he cuts from Cheung as Ruan preparing for her role in 1930's *Wayside Flowers* to Cheung as Ruan reenacting the film. To emphasize the difference between the two actresses, and between present and past, he cuts from a close-up of Cheung's gorgeous suffering face to a shot of the actual Ruan receding into the shadows; it's as if the Chinese Garbo were refusing to let us see any more of her, wanting to be alone. When Kwan stages reenactments of the early films, only to stamp them with the legend "Film no longer available," he mourns more than just the loss of the celluloid; he commemorates another piece of our past that will forever remain a mystery.

So much of our sense of the immediate and distant past comes from the imaginings of filmmakers. We hear Woodward and Bernstein; we think Redford and Hoffman. We picture the Reconstruction era in the grainy images of D. W. Griffith, and the parting of the Red Sea in run-of-DeMille Technicolor. In some cases, as newsreels and silent films crumble into dust every year, the vestiges of remembered images are all that's left. Watching the awkwardly "reconstructed" four-hour cut of Erich von Stroheim's mutilated *Greed* on TCM last year, you were left with a glimpse of artistic glory that might have been — and the fistfuls of dust that represent an evaporated, unrecoverable past. *Actress* tantalizes us with pieces of that past and the sense of what we've lost. Ironically, the print that will show in Nashville is already significantly shorter than the 166-minute Asian version; the cut scenes reportedly show discussions between Maggie Cheung and Stanley Kwan — precisely the kind of archival footage we'll never see of Ruan Ling-yu. Yet even this version is worth seeing — while you have the chance, before it too is gone. (*Nashville Scene,* July 13, 2000)

● ● ● ● ● ● ● ● ● ●

Mulholland Drive
Dir. David Lynch
2001, R, 146 min.

A Mystery Wrapped in an Enigma

This is a story about two movies. The first movie is called *Mulholland Drive.* Perhaps you saw it last year, after it won a prize at Cannes, got salivating reviews and arrived in local theaters bearing millstones of hype. More likely, given its lackluster gross and brief stay, you didn't. If you did, though, you probably haven't stopped thinking about it — which is why it's worth seeing again.

The first movie is about a woman named Betty who meets a waitress named Diane, and a woman named Diane who meets a waitress named Betty. More about them later. The other movie is the movie within the movie. It is being shot on a Hollywood soundstage. It seems to be set in the 1950s and shows glossy babes lip-synching to pop tunes and whatnot. It is hard to tell what this movie is about. Some people say that about the first movie.

This is a story about two directors. The maker of the movie within the movie is Adam (Justin Theroux), a bespectacled, unshaven wonder boy. He is the director, which is not to say he is in charge. The people in charge include a quaking mogul, a dwarf in a secret cell and two fussy mobsters. This is "the industry."

The maker of *Mulholland Drive* is David Lynch. He made it originally three years ago as a TV pilot for ABC, which had great success with his surrealist soap *Twin Peaks.* ABC turned down *Mulholland Drive* — perhaps because the story seemed too freaky for tender primetime eyes, perhaps because a dwarf in a secret cell said so. At any rate, Lynch was given money by French backers to shoot new scenes and expand the movie into a feature. He did so mainly by supplementing the pilot's premise — a naïve blonde, Betty (Naomi Watts), helping an amnesiac brunette (Laura Elena Harring) navigate the underbelly of Tinseltown after a car crash on L.A.'s Mulholland Drive — with a daring half-hour coda that reshuffles and recontextualizes all that came before.

In some ways, Lynch is riffing on the kind of narrative disruption that sometimes only episodic network TV will dare. Think of shows like *Dallas*, *St. Elsewhere* or even *Newhart*, whose wiggy wind-ups cast their week-to-week runs retroactively in a baffling new light. The fascinating thing about what Lynch has done is that his coda makes it impossible for the viewer to discern what his original motives were for the pilot. Imagine that an artist paints a portrait of a fluffy kitten, stashes it in the attic, then exhibits it years later in a frame made of desiccated cat carcasses. Was the sinister intent there all along? Did the artist paint the original knowing that an altered context would bring out its hidden meanings, or is the frame just an inspired salvage job? Either way, does it matter?

Lynch, whose best movies seethe with nightmare imagery that follows a sort of private logic of imperiled innocence and sexual dread, tends to dismiss attempts to explain his movies. After years of critical blather-bait like *Blue Velvet*, *Lost Highway* and *Eraserhead*, he may have set the ultimate booby-trap for anyone who pretends to know what his movies are "about."

This is a story about two dreams. One is the dream of Betty, a heartland waif with aspirations of stardom. The screen fills with whirling jitterbuggers, the soundtrack with swing music. The blonde woman's superimposed face is irradiated, lit with a hope like the surge of power that shatters a lightbulb. The other dream is darker. It is the dream of a woman named Diane who loves the prettiest, hottest actress in Hollywood, the person every Betty wants to be. Diane's dream involves sinister cowboys, string-pullers who turn the cranks of Hollywood's dream machinery and killing the things you love. It also involves Betty. It may even be the same dream.

The hinge that links these dreams is Rita, a woman who has no identity, save what she gleans from a movie poster. She's a film-noir dress-up doll, replete with accessories such as the key to a mysterious box and $50,000 cash. With Betty, she embarks on a search to find out who she is — a harrowing journey that eventually takes them to the eerie Club Silencio. The singer onstage collapses, even as her song continues. Afterward, the mysterious box opens and sucks the movie into its darkness.

The coda, which is preceded by a ghostly command to "wake up" (just as the pilot is preceded by a point-of-view shot sinking into a pillow), recasts the previous 100 minutes as a mutant strain of wish-fulfillment fantasy. Betty comes back to us, only she is no longer called Betty, and she never was. As actors reappear from the first section in significantly changed roles, the tone edges closer and closer to horror — not because these new characters are unfamiliar, but because our identification with them means something scarily different.

That makes a second viewing essential, because the first time through we don't even know what we're watching for the first two-thirds of the movie. Betty's innocence, which seems so syrupy and fake the first time around, is heartbreaking the second time. In part, that's because it's something that only exists in movies, and it has power only as long as we sustain the illusion. In the pilot, the parallel of Betty and Rita's search for identity and the shaping of Adam's movie isn't just a self-reflexive plot gimmick: It suggests two different approaches to dreams and art, from the outside and inside, which connect at the common point where people try to see themselves in the picture. The coda turns *Mulholland Drive* into a different movie than just the sum of its two sections. It makes the movie a dream about the killing of dreams and a movie about the killing of movies, as they flare into being and snuff out simultaneously. It isn't until the movie ends that the movie begins. (*Nashville Scene*, March 7, 2002)

Phoners & Shoe Leather 6

A nother distinction to consider, besides the difference between a film reviewer and a film critic, is the difference
between a critic and a journalist. By and large, journalism
concerns the world as it exists, and not as represented in works of
art. It involves collecting and presenting evidence to make the case
that this is how things really happened. In its best examples, journalism, like criticism, situates its subjects in broader social and historical
contexts, and conveys a sense of why this story matters. This chapter
offers two selections from Jim's journalistic work, each a master class
in its own right.

It begins with an epic 4,500-word feature on Robert Altman's
Nashville, published on occasion of its 20th anniversary in 1995. Jim
reconstructs the fable of the movie's gala premiere in Nashville and
traces the origins of the movie, in part through an interview with
screenwriter Joan Tewkesbury, while also situating the production
within the roiling politics, both national and musical, of the mid-
1970s. At the same time he lays out why some Nashvillians hated
it, alongside an assessment of its artistry and legacy. (Worth noting
here: a "king-size three-way" refers to chili from the famed Nashville restaurant Varallo's; the "three-way" means beans, tamales and
spaghetti.)

The second piece is no less a landmark piece of work, and an
example of what alt-weekly types mean when they talk about journalism with a point of view: the story that challenged Nashville to save
the Belcourt Theatre from extinction — and did just that.

Look Back in Anger
Robert Altman's *Nashville,* 20 Years Later

Even by Nashville standards, the scene outside the Martin 100 Oaks Theater on Aug. 8, 1975, qualified as a spectacle. On a hot, gusty Friday night, more than 4,000 people crowded behind police barricades. Some of them had stood in line for five hours. The Tennessee Twirlers, a platoon of star-spangled majorettes equipped with flags and rifles, stood at attention. Atop a 40-foot flatbed truck festooned with red, white and blue bunting, a band called the Silver Spurs reeled off country tunes. The white-hot beams of searchlights swept the sky.

It could have well been some sort of grandiose political rally. But the elections were over. Just the day before, U.S. Rep. Richard Fulton had won a landslide victory over Earl Hawkins to become the second mayor in Metro Nashville history. And here was Fulton, smiling and waving to the crowd, along with incumbent Mayor Beverly Briley.

The steel arm of a construction crane had lifted a 60-by-80-foot American flag into the sunset. But by 6 p.m. the flag was coming down. The hot August wind was snapping the massive flag like a locker-room towel, and, with the festivities barely under way, a decision was made to rescue the flag and fold it away. The last thing the makers of the movie *Nashville* wanted was to cap the film's local premiere with an image of Old Glory lying in the dust.

The gala premiere of *Nashville* was the most eagerly anticipated event of the summer. During the previous year, ever since the production company had finished shooting its local footage, curiosity about the film had reached fever pitch. The previous March, the *New Yorker*'s influential film critic, Pauline Kael, had pronounced a barely finished three-hour cut of *Nashville* "the funniest epic vision of America ever to reach the screen." Kael's review alone had triggered waves of controversy, mostly from other reviewers, who were angered that they hadn't been invited to the private screening. By the time the movie had finally opened in New York in June, it had become a cause célèbre. Its studio, Paramount, had confidently booked *Nashville* into two adjacent screens on the East Side. It filled both theaters daily. In every major national publication, critics and editorial columnists debated the movie's merits; gossips speculated about the lead characters' real-life counterparts, identifying everyone from Loretta Lynn and Tammy Wynette to Roy Acuff and Hank Snow. In its cover story for June 30, 1975, *Newsweek* proclaimed that *Nashville* was director Robert Altman's "epic of Opryland" and "everything a work of social art ought to be but seldom is — immensely moving yet terribly funny, chastening yet ultimately exhilarating."

Back in Nashville, however, the locals were getting nervous. According to some critics, among them Robert Mazzocco in the *New York Review of Books*, the movie portrayed Nashvillians as gullible rubes at best and heartless automatons at worst. Others, including syndicated reviewer Rex Reed, agreed, but declared that Nashvillians deserved what they got. "[The film] floats like navel lint into the vulgar Vegas of country and western music, that plunking, planking citadel of bad taste called Nashville, Tenn.," wrote the former star of *Myra Breckinridge*.

Even the most positive advance reviews carried an implicit — and sometimes explicit — condescension toward Music City in general and country music in particular. "Country-and-western basically dresses up folk music in rhinestones and spangles, making hay out of Americana," Jay Cocks wrote in *Time*. Despite an unequivocal rave from the *Tennessean*'s Eugene Wyatt, who declared himself "a Nashvillian who loves his city and wishes it well," word still filtered back that the movie was anti-American, anti-country — and anti-Nashville.

With a mixture of anxiety and dread, musicians, producers, music-industry personnel and civic boosters alike had awaited the film's local premiere. Hardly anybody, though, had any intention of missing it. As the 7:15 p.m. show time neared, long lines of limousines snaked down Powell Drive toward the Martin. While flashbulbs popped and fans applauded, dozens of celebrities and local dignitaries emerged from their vehicles, crossed a red carpet and ducked inside the theater.

The audience, half of whom were invited guests, formed a cross section of the city as broad and colorful as any Altman could have devised. On hand from the music industry were established hitmakers Dottie West, Brenda Lee and Billie Jo Spears; Opry veterans Roy Acuff (who left before the movie started), Minnie Pearl and Del Wood; new country superstar Ronnie Milsap; producer Billy Sherrill; and the great Webb Pierce, whose raw honky-tonk sound was fading in popularity. Sheriff Fate Thomas was there to appoint cast members as honorary deputies. Tennessee First Lady Betty Blanton represented the governor. While Altman himself was busy shooting his next film, stars Ronee Blakley, Henry Gibson, Keith Carradine and Dave Peel represented the film's makers.

Outside, while the Rutherford County Square Dancers clogged, the celebrity-studded crowd slowly disappeared into the Martin's auditorium. The few remaining tickets for the performance were sold to eager patrons, who had begun lining up outside the box office shortly after noon. Once the theater's 741 seats were filled, at approximately 7:40 p.m., the lights in the theater dimmed, and the words "A Robert Altman Film" flashed on the screen.

What followed was a visual and aural cacophony, a credit sequence modeled on the commercials used to sell repackages of country hits on late-night TV. As a pitchman hawked the names of the movie's 24 principal actors, their representative "hits" scrolled beside a painting of the entire cast. In the center of the Panavision screen, one word in bold, tilted type overwhelmed everything else — the word "NASHVILLE." The applause for the title was loud, long and appreciative.

Two hours and 39 minutes later, the crowd that remained outside behind the police barricades saw the audience begin to emerge from the theater. The ensuing madhouse made the front pages of both daily newspapers. It made all three evening news broadcasts and was carried in columns from Atlanta to Italy. Exiting audience members were ambushed by print, TV and radio reporters anxious for comment. Some audience members, among them Buddy Killen, then executive vice president of Tree International, had enjoyed the movie. "I loved it," Killen told the papers. "I was not offended in any way. It was a great piece of work." Others were guarded. Dottie West said she liked it OK, although she expressed concern that the movie's only redhead did a strip number. "It was very interesting," Minnie Pearl told the *Banner's* Bill Hance — and then, with uniquely Southern diplomacy, she concluded, "Sure is good to see you tonight."

The majority of the Music Row insiders, however, were not quite so reserved. "I've seen a lot of movies in my day," Ronnie Milsap told Hance, "and this is one of them." Brenda Lee said that she had "one word" that would describe the movie, and her husband, Ronnie Shacklett, begged her not to say it. "The only way it will be a big movie is for it to play a long time in the North," Lee told Hance. "That's what the people up there think we look like anyway." Producer Buzz Cason commented, "It was so bad, it was different."

The harshest remarks came from Billy Sherrill, who, when asked by a journalist what he thought of the music, retorted, "What music?" Asked what he liked best about the story, Sherrill snapped, "I'll tell you what I liked about the film — when they shot that miserable excuse for a country music singer."

Twenty years have passed since Nashville's premiere, and opinions about the movie remain as divided now as they were in 1975. "I can't tell you how many people whose opinions I respect place it among the top 10 movies of all time," insists Gene Wyatt, who believes now, as he did then, that Altman's film is "one of the landmark efforts of the art." In direct contrast, music executive Charlie Monk, who attended the 1975 premiere, remembers *Nashville* as "just bad," an insult perpetrated "by people with no knowledge of the blue-collar-folk idiom."

Banner editor Eddie Jones, who in 1975 was executive vice president of the Nashville Chamber of Commerce, sounds a note of moderation. "The civic leadership–type people felt it was not representative of the city," Jones recalls. "Honestly, I don't think anybody paid a hell of a lot of attention. It just kind of tippy-toed into town and tippy-toed out."

This weekend, a 20th anniversary tribute to *Nashville* headlines the 26th annual Sinking Creek Film/Video Festival on the Vanderbilt University campus. One of the people most responsible for the movie's vision of Music City, screenwriter Joan Tewkesbury, will return to Nashville for the first time in years to host the Saturday-afternoon screening. A new generation of Nashvillians will gaze into Robert Altman's funhouse mirror of America. To many of them, his vision will hardly seem distorted at all.

● ● ● ● ●

In 1974, Robert Altman had been approached by a studio executive with an original screenplay called *The Great Southern Amusement Company*, a musical set in the world of country music. The director was less than enthusiastic about the script — "I didn't like it," he flatly told *Newsweek*'s Charles Michener, stating that it was "just a fake, a script" — but he proposed another feature in its place, one with a similar country-music setting.

At the time, Altman told interviewers that he knew little about country music. To get the project under way, he contacted Tewkesbury.

The two were frequent collaborators. Joan Tewkesbury had first worked with Altman as a script supervisor on his 1971 Western *McCabe & Mrs. Miller*. When Altman was dissatisfied with Calder Willingham's script for *Thieves Like Us*, he had called in Tewkesbury to assemble a new one. Tewkesbury was well acquainted with Altman's painterly approach, and the director dispatched her to Nashville to soak up material for a script.

Her first week-long trip to Nashville consisted mainly of historical sites and visitor-approved tourist attractions. "I got the docent's tour of the museum," said Tewkesbury last week, speaking from her home in California. For her next trip, she "very quietly went around on my own" and hit some of the clubs on Lower Broad, then home to some of Nashville's finest unrenovated honky-tonks.

"I asked some of the musicians at Tootsie's Orchid Lounge where I should go," Tewkesbury remembers. They steered her to funky little restaurants and pickin' parlors off the beaten path. She took in the Grand Ole Opry, then in its last days at the Ryman Auditorium. "I loved the Ryman so much — it made accessibility to the performers so natural," she recalls. She sat in unobtrusively at some of Loretta Lynn's recording sessions, where, she says, banter flowed and all the session musicians "had a barnyard animal's name." (In Tewkesbury's finished script, a country star gripes that he wants "Pig" — the famed Nashville session pianist Hargus "Pig" Robbins — for his recording sessions. Instead, he has to settle for a second-stringer named Frog.)

Tewkesbury enjoyed the city, she says, because it reminded her of Hollywood in the 1940s, "when everybody wanted to be a star and all these glamorous girls sat around on drugstore stools waiting to be discovered." As she returned more frequently to Nashville, though, she noted a subtle change in the city's mood. "Everybody was losing their innocence," she explains. "The country was losing its innocence."

In the spring of 1974, while Tewkesbury was completing her screenplay, the national news was dominated by the Watergate hearings. Consumers were plagued by the first signs of economic inflation, as well as the threats of an energy crisis triggered by unease in the Middle East. Many Americans were numbed by the prolonged tension and unrest of the Vietnam conflict and the Civil Rights struggle. Viewers no longer flinched as extreme brutality and bloodshed became a regular part of TV news coverage.

The violence had even reached Nashville and the seemingly peaceful music industry. On Nov. 11, 1973, the popular Grand Ole Opry comedian David "Stringbean" Akeman and his wife, Estelle, returned to their farm on Bakers Station Road after finishing an Opry show. They arrived just as three robbers were ransacking the house. One of the intruders murdered both Akeman and his wife. Tewkesbury witnessed the impact the murders had on Nashville. "[There] was a whole aspect of Nashville that got tighter and tighter, and people got scared," she told the *Tennessean* just before the movie's release. "It had been so open the first time I came, and as I kept going back things became tighter and tighter."

All of Tewkesbury's observations found their way into the patchwork of the screenplay's crazy quilt. As evidence of the Watergate conspiracy inched ever closer to the White House, the cloud of disillusionment seeped into the script — most poignantly in the character of Sueleen Gay, a talentless would-be country singer whose dreams of stardom are cruelly exploited. Altman's only initial instruction to Tewkesbury was to end the script with someone's death. In the original draft, the sacrificial lamb was Sueleen, who responded to her humiliation by taking a bottle of pills.

By the time Tewkesbury turned in her script, she notes wryly, Altman had decided that "there should be larger issues at stake." Instead of Sueleen's personal tragedy, the director devised a plot thread involving a political candidate planning a Nashville rally, which would climax with an assassination attempt. By the time filming commenced in Nashville in the summer of 1974, the political subplot had become the unifying device holding together the movie's diverse elements.

• • • • •

Ultimately, Altman's film was filled with delicious ironies and double-edged jokes. Even during the credit sequence, the announcer promised that the movie would proceed "without commercial interruption." *Nashville*, however, takes place in a world largely defined by commercial interruption — a world where political advertisements resound in the streets, where salesmanship casually intrudes upon social gatherings, where people conduct business even in a traffic jam. Fittingly, the movie opens with an ad, a poster for a third-party political candidate named Hal Phillip Walker. Throughout the film, his red, white and blue Replacement Party van appears and reappears, blaring vaguely populist sentiments from its loudspeakers.

The movie employs a deceptively loose structure, following the comings and goings of some 24 characters during a five-day period. *Nashville* begins with the birth of a record; it ends with the death of a recording artist. At the outset, Opal, a BBC reporter (Geraldine Chaplin), arrives to do a story on Grand Ole Opry star Haven Hamilton (Henry Gibson) as he records "200 Years," a ham-fisted ode to the U.S. Bicentennial. In another studio, Linnea Reese (Lily Tomlin), a white, upper-middle-class gospel star, cuts a record with a black choir. Across town, at the Nashville Airport — Berry Field in 1975 — fans arrive to welcome the reigning queen of country music, the fragile Barbara Jean (Ronee Blakley), who is recovering from a burn injury and a near–nervous breakdown. A folk trio, Tom (Keith Carradine), Bill (Allan Nichols) and Mary (Cristina Raines), breezes through town, while a rising country singer, Connie (Karen Black), seizes the opportunity of Barbara Jean's ailment to take her place on the Opry.

Crossing their paths are a variety of peripheral characters who never quite connect with the principals: a drifter (Jeff Goldblum) who performs magic tricks, a soldier (Scott Glenn) quietly obsessed with Barbara Jean, an elderly man (Keenan Wynn) monitoring his wife's illness in the same hospital where Barbara Jean recuperates. Over the course of the five days, while Walker's political advance man, the cynical apparatchik Triplett (Michael Murphy), attempts to round up entertainment for a rally, relationships dissolve, affairs commence, careers decline and fights erupt. The movie's many plot lines converge at an enormous rally outside the Parthenon, where an assassin's bullet robs the world of one country-music star — and another quickly rises to replace her.

In Altman's cracked post-Watergate vision of America, Nashville replaces Washington as the new symbolic center of the country. The president of the United States had hidden himself from the people, and even Hal Phillip Walker never actually appears onscreen. In the absence of political leaders, people searching for guidance look to the kings and queens of country music, whose messages provide comfort and reassurance. ("We must be doing something right to last 200 years," Haven Hamilton sings.)

In many ways, the America depicted in the movie seems more like a monarchy than a democracy. In her first appearance, Barbara Jean, greeted like royalty at the airport, is presented with a bouquet of roses; in the movie's shattering conclusion, she is deposed like royalty — by death — and her successor takes her place. In *Nashville* Altman predicted that, as media attention became a measure of status, the fastest route to celebrity would be to kill a celebrity. It's strangely appropriate that in the following year's similarly themed *Taxi Driver*, a poster for *Nashville* appears.

Nashville was the culmination of Altman's years of tinkering with densely layered sound and unconventional narratives. In the five years since his breakthrough commercial hit, *MASH*, in 1970, the director had experimented with an innovative technique for telling stories on film. He allowed plot, ambience and characterization to develop through overlapping conversations and an alert, yet consistently fluid, narrative style. New directors such as Steven Spielberg and Martin Scorsese employed highly kinetic techniques — comic-book angles, shock editing — to convey sensation, but Altman stood back from his tableaux like a man appreciating a work in a gallery, letting his camera zero in on any detail that he found worthy of attention.

Altman's reliance on improvisation and flexibility, coupled with the solid foundation of Tewkesbury's script, gives *Nashville* an overwhelming richness of detail. "He was able to bring out the creativity in everyone on the set," remembers Nashville illustrator Bill Myers, who frequently visited the set. It was Myers who created the painting shown behind the opening credits. "[Altman] was fascinating to watch," Myers says. "He inspired the actors to bring their own experiences into the movie." When the time came to shoot Barbara Jean's onstage breakdown, Myers recalls, Altman intended for Ronee Blakley to play the scene almost catatonically. Instead, Blakley suggested a rambling, disconnected monologue about home and family, one of the most pathetic and chilling moments in the finished film.

The director instructed his soundmen to mic every person in a scene, so that minute fragments of conversation would be captured on tape. "Everybody was walking around with these packs under their clothes," Myers recalls. When the conversations were layered together, the result was a tapestry of sound, an astonishingly lifelike effect unlike anything else heard before in American movies. Altman encouraged viewers to choose, listen and pay attention at will. For that reason *Nashville* rewards multiple viewings as few other movies do. The shock of watching *Nashville* today is one of liberation — the freedom of encountering a work of art that doesn't anticipate, manipulate or engineer its viewers' every response.

● ● ● ● ●

From a cinematic standpoint, it's easy to see why *Nashville* caused such a furor when it premiered in the summer of 1975. What's harder to see, after the sledgehammer excesses of subsequent media satires, ranging from *Network* to *Natural Born Killers*, is why the movie offended so many people, particularly Nashvillians. Compared to the genial condescension of a star vehicle like *Steel Magnolias* or the outright prejudice of a tub-thumper like *Mississippi Burning*, Nashville's portrait of the South seems downright generous.

Many details about the movie's depiction of Nashville still hold true 20 years later. Altman and Tewkesbury viewed Nashville in 1975 as a mecca for people with no roots of their own. Disenfranchised fans embraced country music, the music of working people, as the last tie to a heartland America where traditional values seemed to be disappearing. (The slogan of Walker's campaign is "New Roots for the Nation.") Locals who complained that *Nashville* was an outsider's view of the city missed the point that Nashville is a city of outsiders, from transplanted executives to country-music hopefuls with guitars slung over their backs. The movie captures the city's peculiar biggest-small-town-in-America ambience, a town where, even in a crowd of 1,000 people, you're sure to recognize at least one face.

The sad truth of the movie's characters, though, is that they're as isolated from each other as they are from their country. A repeated motif in the movie is the struggle of people trying, and failing, to reach one another through music. A budding country singer (Barbara Harris) gets a chance to sing at a raceway but is drowned out by the roar of the cars. Haven's son (Dave Peel, one of the only real singers in the cast) sings a little tune to Opal, which she blithely ignores. When the elderly man's wife dies, a soldier clumsily attempts to reach out to him by gushing about Barbara Jean. Country music in the movie is portrayed as both painkiller and panacea — the movie's constant refrain, "You might say that I ain't free / But it don't worry me," becomes a sort of group mantra in the moments after the assassination.

None of the movie's political observations particularly galled the premiere audience at the Martin 100 Oaks. What infuriated them most was the music itself. With the aid of music director Richard Baskin, Altman encouraged his actors to write their own songs. Thematically, the decision was an unquestionable success. The songs the cast contributed comment directly and indirectly on the action, from Henry Gibson's "Keep A-Goin'" (which ultimately reveals a much more noble side of Haven's personality than we expect) to Keith Carradine's plaintive "I'm Easy," sung at the Exit/In. (In a brilliantly conceived and executed scene, he sings to an audience of adoring former conquests, each of whom believes he's singing to her.)

Within the movie, the songs worked perfectly, providing running commentary and parody. On the movie's soundtrack album, however, they came across as limp, badly sung, one-dimensional cartoons — and that's exactly how the Nashville audience of musicians and industry figures heard them. To them, bypassing the city's wealth of gifted singers, songwriters and musicians in favor of a group of L.A. dilettantes — and then presenting the actors' off-key warbling as an accurate reflection of Nashville music — seemed an insufferable slap in the face. "How easy it would've been to get Harlan Howard to write those songs," Charlie Monk observes. "It was just another attempt to do a parody of something we were very serious about, and the general public thought it was sincere."

So did high-minded reviewers, who added injury to insult by using the movie's fake country to indict the real thing. Anyone who thought Nashvillians were being too thin-skinned had only to read the musings of conservative columnist George F. Will, who lambasted the filmmakers for lampooning middle America. Nashville, Will said, "is to America what country music is to music — not a close approximation."

"Nashville and its Grand Ole Opry have so little to do with the rest of the nation," complained Rex Reed, "that it seems like a poor metaphor for the disintegration of American society."

By 1975, Nashville's music industry was already in the midst of its own identity crisis, an ongoing debate about its own roots and authenticity. In 1975, the Country Music Association awarded its highest honor, the Entertainer of the Year Award, to non-Nashvillian (and, many argued, non-country) artist John Denver. The award incensed country purists, who rated aw-shucks buffoonery such as "Thank God I'm a Country Boy" only a notch above the songs recorded for *Nashville*. Performers such as Denver, Olivia Newton-John and Anne Murray topped both the pop and country charts, while stone-country reliables such as Hank Snow and Webb Pierce found it increasingly difficult to get airplay. In Nashville, musicians and record labels alike began to wonder what really constituted country music.

That same uncertainty extended to the rest of the city. The dominant image of Nashville in the country's mind, as Charlie Monk puts it, was "people jumping up out of a cornfield." Civic leaders who wanted to attract new industry to Tennessee in the mid-1970s found themselves confronted by the public perception of Nashville as *Hee Haw* and hillbillies. At the Chamber of Commerce, Eddie Jones remembers, "there was some concern that a country-bumpkin image would run off East Coast types." Meanwhile, Jones says, the Chamber "wanted to establish Nashville as a metropolitan area with a reliable labor supply, a good work force and a good interstate system." To civic boosters, *Nashville* merely shackled the city once more with the image it so desperately needed to shake.

• • • • •

Still, even the movie's detractors predicted *Nashville* would be a tremendous commercial success. They were wrong. Nashville grossed a modest $10 million, which paled alongside the year's commercial blockbuster, *Jaws*, the unprecedented success of which altered forever the scale and expectations of major-studio filmmaking. At the Academy Awards ceremony the next year, Nashville received six nominations, including Best Picture, Best Director, and two nods for Best Supporting Actress, one to Lily Tomlin and the other to Ronee Blakley. It lost every award but one — the award for Song of the Year, which went to Keith Carradine's "I'm Easy."

Joan Tewkesbury went on to a major career as a writer and director, as did Altman's assistant director, Alan Rudolph, who made such films as *Choose Me* and *Mrs. Parker and the Vicious Circle*. Jeff Goldblum went on to star in *Jurassic Park*, the highest-grossing movie of all time. Scott Glenn, Lily Tomlin, Keith Carradine, Geraldine Chaplin and costars Ned Beatty and Shelley Duvall have all enjoyed subsequent success and critical acclaim.

After *Nashville*, Robert Altman's career entered a long stretch of artistic and commercial frustration, a decade-long struggle with studios, projects that never got off the ground, and uneven material that was often unworthy of his talents. Starting with 1990's *Vincent & Theo*, Altman mounted an artistic, critical and commercial comeback capped by *The Player*, a delirious portrait of Hollywood skullduggery that had the assurance and technical mastery of his best work.

In a final juicy irony reported in Patrick McGilligan's critical study *Robert Altman: Jumping Off the Cliff*, Altman became in 1983 a member of a privileged club: He was the co-writer of a No. 1 country hit, the John Anderson song "Black Sheep." (Altman's co-writer, Danny Darst, was to achieve his own screen immortality by portraying one of the two cops butchered by Hannibal Lecter in *The Silence of the Lambs*.)

How has the movie itself held up as a metaphor for America? In the 20 years since *Nashville* was released, America has witnessed an unparalleled explosion in the popularity of country music, the ascendancy of not one but two Southern presidents, the courting of country-music stars by political parties, the assassination of a popular musician, and the rise of a third-party candidate who launched a grassroots campaign with an elusive populist platform. In the meantime, Rex Reed became the cohost of an obscure public-television movie-review show that had been abandoned by at least one previous pair of reviewers.

Coincidence? Maybe the audience at *Nashville's* premiere at the Martin had a reason to feel uneasy. Life, especially in the age of movies, has a habit of imitating art. (*Nashville Scene*, Nov. 9, 1995)

● ● ● ● ● ● ● ● ● ●

Fade to Black
Can the Watkins Belcourt Be Saved?

What was the best moment you missed at the Watkins Belcourt in the past three months? Hard to say. Maybe it was an uncharacteristically large audience of 50 people roaring at the Marx Brothers' classic mirror routine in *Duck Soup*. Maybe it was a somewhat smaller crowd of 11 people sitting in rapt silence at the climax of Preston Sturges' *Sullivan's Travels*. Or maybe, just maybe, you caught the glorious close-up of Giuletta Masina's face, radiant with renewed hope, that ends Fellini's transcendent *Nights of Cabiria*. That was at a Saturday afternoon screening that sold five tickets. I went alone, and bought two of them.

But if you didn't go to the Watkins Belcourt in the past three months, you've probably missed your chance. On Jan. 28, one week from today, Nashville's only art-movie theater will close its doors for good.

For Nashville to lose its sole arthouse is sad enough. Over the past few years, the Belcourt has brought movies to town that would never have come here otherwise, giving local audiences a chance to see the same films that regularly play larger cities. Many of these were movies too controversial or obscure for the local megaplexes. They were also true independents, released by scrappy small distributors who had to elbow their way into the marketplace.

But the Belcourt's imminent loss is troubling for more reasons than just movies. For the better part of the century, the theater has been the anchor of Hillsboro Village. Built in 1925, it was the former home of both the Grand Ole Opry and the Children's Theatre of Nashville. As the only neighborhood theater remaining in Nashville, its loss would remove a vital chunk of the Village's character at a key transitional period in its development.

There's more, and worse. If the Belcourt ends up demolished — a likely possibility — it will join the beautiful old Tennessee Theatre, the Inglewood, the Belle Meade, and all the other historic movie palaces that we allowed to fall or be closed. Each theater was irreplaceable, a measure of our civic history and aspirations. More importantly, it was Nashville's alone — not a chain, not a mass-produced structure, but a singular entity that set us apart from every other city on the make. Lose the Belcourt, and we lose one more irretrievable piece of our identity.

Other cities — some larger, some much smaller than Nashville — have managed to save their historic theaters, often through nonprofit organizations and civic fund-raising campaigns. Such efforts have required an outpouring of volunteer support. They have even proved successful, both as businesses and as civic attractions. Yet the Belcourt has already been saved once, and public support proved so weak that the theater is again in dire straits. No one argues the Belcourt is worth saving. Going to the trouble to save it is another matter.

● ● ● ● ●

By all rights, the city's one locally owned theater should be succeeding. Just five years ago, the Belcourt was literally falling apart, but it drew regular crowds of loyal patrons. Ironically, the theater's now in better shape than it has been in the past decade, and its seats are largely empty. If the theater had been showing awful movies — such as its disastrous run of *Species II* one week when the product well ran dry — its losses might be understandable.

But it wasn't. What made the Belcourt exciting, like the Darkhorse Theater in its early-'90s glory days, was the possibility of seeing something different — something different and good. First-run American indies such as *Buffalo '66* and *Unmade Beds* alternated with an incredible series of reissues ranging from the re-edited version of Orson Welles' *Touch of Evil* to Martin Scorsese's career-making early film *Mean Streets*. Audiences could see some of Hollywood's greatest films the way they were meant to be shown, on the big screen: *Casablanca, The Lady Eve, The Adventures of Robin Hood, The Searchers, The Wild Bunch, Blade Runner.*

This last point is not minor. We're so used to seeing movies mangled on television — censored, chopped to fit the small screen, speeded up or slowed down to accommodate commercial breaks — that we sometimes assume that's how the movies were made. The same goes for rented videos, which adhere to the stunted pan-and-scan format. In the year that marked the 100th anniversary of the cinema's birth, the Belcourt's revival programming made these films alive and whole again for a new audience. We're not talking egghead esoterica here: we're talking James Bond movies, John Wayne movies.

Which makes it that much harder to figure out why people stopped coming. As late as 1991, the Belcourt was a run-down Carmike Cinemas theater showing first-run mainstream movies. Inside the city, with only two screens, it did a fraction of the business Carmike's outlying mall 'plexes did. Faced with sagging attendance, Carmike started stocking the Belcourt with the left-of-center indie titles that used to play Fountain Square. Within a year, the Belcourt was doing brisk business with films such as *Reservoir Dogs* and *Howards End.*

In the fall of 1996, the theater was bought from under Carmike by a group of investors led by developer Charles Hawkins. In a remarkable philanthropic gesture, Hawkins and other investors who served on the board of the downtown Watkins Institute agreed to give Watkins a 25-percent stake in any profits from the theater's ownership. In that spirit, the theater was renamed the Watkins Belcourt, and it quickly reopened that October. It started trying to show the same arthouse hits that had kept the theater afloat under Carmike.

The new Belcourt had problems, sure. For starters, it reopened without making overhauls in sound and projection that Carmike had put off for years, causing grumbles immediately. Without Carmike's clout, the theater also found itself suddenly forced to share movies with its competitors. Thus its market share for films such as *The Wings of the Dove* was slashed — especially when Regal opened its enormous Hollywood 27 complex at 100 Oaks last January. In desperation, the Belcourt tried to show "commendable mainstream" titles such as *Out of Sight* and *Good Will Hunting* — an ill-fated experiment that led to empty houses throughout the first two quarters of 1997.

By last summer, however, the Belcourt had fixed its programming by converting to a two-screen calendar house. One screen showed current releases; the other showed classics and recent reissues. The theater started bringing in movies that customers requested, such as Takeshi Kitano's *Fireworks (Hana-Bi)* and *Nights of Cabiria.* It also installed a new sound system and did frequent maintenance on its near-decrepit projectors. In fact, the Belcourt's new management did more to address customer concerns in six months than Carmike had in the previous six years.

• • • • •

At several points during the year, the Belcourt seemed to have turned the corner with its ambitious programming, which was being booked by Watkins Film School cofounder David Hinton and New York–based booking agent Jeffrey Jacobs. An unexpected success was Abbas Kiarostami's *Taste of Cherry,* a superb Iranian film that drew patrons from as far away as Alabama. There was the triumph of the revitalized Nashville Independent Film Festival, which after its move to the Belcourt increased its attendance by more than 90 percent. *Fireworks, Touch of Evil, Mean Streets,* and retrospectives of Hitchcock and David Lean all drew crowds. So did Halloween screenings of *Evil Dead 2, Suspiria* and *Dead-Alive,* the theater's best-promoted venture.

For every week of success, though, there were three of crushing disappointments: A week of John Cassavetes films will never be forgotten by the seven people who took a chance on them. Two weeks of Preston Sturges' comedies — some of the funniest films ever made in this country — played mostly to single-digit audiences.

I might as well share the moment that broke my heart: The Belcourt was showing an amazing double bill of Jean-Luc Godard's *Contempt* and François Truffaut's *Day for Night* — two movies available on TV and video only in the most washed-out, dispiriting condition. I was seeing a movie on the other screen, but I snuck for a moment into *Day for Night,* which I'd seen earlier. Onscreen was the scene in which Truffaut, playing a movie director, dreams that he is a child again, swiping stills of *Citizen Kane* from the lobby of a neighborhood movie theater. Truffaut the director deepened my love of movies; Truffaut the critic made me want to write. I wondered how many other people in the auditorium were sharing this impossibly perfect moment. The room held 400. I counted eight. I bought two more tickets, just to make it 10.

How to explain such dismal turnouts? The Belcourt's lack of focus behind the scenes didn't help. Despite the noblest of intentions, the number of owners and competing interests made it impossible for any one vision to take hold — hence the six months of indecision before last summer. As the chief backer, Charles Hawkins was forced to act as liaison between the theater and his understandably uneasy partners.

That Hawkins and his fellow investors, who include Tuned-In Broadcasting president Lester Turner and members of the Massey family, held on as long as they did is an act of commendable civic charity — especially as their monthly losses ran into the tens of thousands. (Hawkins, a warm, unfailingly polite gentleman who speaks of the theater with genuine feeling, even reportedly financed equipment upgrades out of his own pocket.) Yet the absence of a single unifying figure, a showman/greeter/huckster who was synonymous with the theater (like the Belle Meade's legendary E. J. Jordan), kept the Belcourt from developing much personality — or visibility.

If another group purchases the Belcourt, it could learn from these and other mistakes, including the theater's uncertain marketing. There are countless inexpensive marketing ploys the Belcourt never tried — theme nights, cross-promotions, co-sponsorships with foreign-language organizations. Until recently, the Belcourt never even reached out to the many large ethnic communities here starved for films from their homelands. Julia Ann Hawkins, who handled the theater's advertising, deserves credit for allowing outside promoters to show Hindi films, which draw as many as 150 people each Sunday and Wednesday. It's an excellent idea — one that should be copied, should the Belcourt somehow remain an operating theater.

Yet despite all its problems, the theater was never guided by less than the best of intentions. When you see the Belcourt's employees and investors, tell them thanks for trying, OK? That goes double for Charles Hawkins, who tried so hard to make it work. If the old Varallo's were still open, I'd say he deserves a king-size three-way.

● ● ● ● ●

Even if the Belcourt can be saved, though, why would new owners have any better luck getting Nashvillians off their asses? The theater's biggest enemy isn't Regal or Blockbuster; it's the city's stupefying complacency where any kind of arts programming is concerned. That isn't entirely the audience's fault. As a local critic groused recently, one Nashville theater company's biggest supporters are always flying to New York to see current dramas the company will never stage — because it says there's no audience for them.

Yet local audiences don't receive better because they haven't been demanding or supporting it. If dull familiarity is what Nashvillians want, they'll be amply rewarded — either by *Patch Adams* on three screens at every megaplex, or by the umpteenth production of *Smoke on the Mountain* at the local playhouse. If these represent the pinnacle of our intellectual curiosity, it's a sad joke that we're investing in a $15 million downtown arts center. What will we enshrine there? Paintings of kittens and sunsets?

Even so, it's unfair to blame the Belcourt's failure on the vast majority of local moviegoers, who know what they like and choose a movie or two a month accordingly. They pick the Hollywood 27 because it has every big current movie they want to see, and the lines and the flashing tote board create a sense of activity. Plus it's clean and has state-of-the-art seating and sound. No shame there.

The sad fact is, the group that has let the Belcourt down the most is its target audience. Last March, when the theater was voted the city's best in the *Nashville Scene* readers' poll, it was struggling to meet its utility bills. If only lip service paid the rent. When asked, many of the people now eulogizing the Belcourt admit they've been going more frequently to Regal's Green Hills Commons 16, which took up the Hollywood 27's slack with so-called mainstream arthouse titles like *Elizabeth* and *Waking Ned Devine*. One Belcourt employee recalls a couple telling him how sorry they were about the theater's closing. All he could notice was the sack of microwaved popcorn they had sneaked in — at a time when the theater needed every dollar of revenue it could get.

That's the danger of viewing each new addition to the local horizon — be it an arthouse, an arts center or a pro sports team — as a civic acquisition: Active participation tends to stop once the purchase has cleared. Yet such things must always be works in progress. I hate to sound like a PBS fund drive, but without ongoing support, these concerns shrivel and die. And when they do, they invariably leave conditions worse than before.

Case in point: Does anyone think Regal will show the Belcourt's brand of indie and foreign films and reissues? The signs aren't good, even though the Nashville Independent Film Festival just announced that for this year's festival in June, it will move to the Green Hills Commons 16. Along with an admittedly generous $10,000 corporate sponsorship, Regal has donated two basement screens and the use of its perpetually desolate downstairs area.

Since December, though, Regal has bumped back dates for a number of films from top-notch smaller distributors like New Yorker and Zeitgeist, including the terrific Japanese comedy-drama *The Eel* (last year's Palme d'Or winner at Cannes) and the controversial Indian erotic drama *Fire* (which has been delayed so long that it's now on video). Last week came notices that *The Eel* and *Fire* have been postponed indefinitely, without rescheduling. Regal's reason is a pip: The parent company of the Hollywood 27 and Green Hills 16 is "short on screens."

Big deal, you say; so we won't get *Modulations*. Right — and we won't get *Touch of Evil*, or *Taste of Cherry*, or *Cabiria*, or the Warner Bros. 75th Anniversary festival. The picture will be even bleaker when Vanderbilt's Sarratt Cinema scales back its bookings, as is rumored. Suddenly the choices will seem a lot narrower, as they were only a year ago. And without exposure to the full range of cinema, how can Nashville's own slumbering film industry turn out anything other than mediocrity? It's no coincidence that Steve Taylor, one of Nashville's most creative and inquisitive music video directors, just got on VH1 with a Sixpence None the Richer clip inspired by Truffaut's *Jules and Jim*.

I think I even saw Taylor in the audience a few years ago when the film played at Sarratt.

And if the Belcourt building itself disappears, we'd do well to wonder what will replace it. Consider the Tennessee Theatre, one of the last Art Deco movie palaces in the country. It was demolished 11 years ago, and for what? A high-rise Church Street apartment building so architecturally nondescript and forgettable it constitutes a beige hole in the skyline. Yet the new building's bland façade is right in keeping with the city's persistent attempts to replace the old with something shiny and uniform. The loss of each Tennessee Theatre, each Jacksonian, brings us one step closer to erasing our past and losing the qualities that make us unique as a place to visit, or to live. Come to Nashville, the Stepford City.

● ● ● ● ●

The Belcourt is hardly the only theater of its kind in jeopardy. Across the country, small independent arthouses are falling by the wayside: the famed Biograph and the Key in Washington, D.C.; the Guild in Albuquerque, N.M.; the Vogue in Louisville, which closed just recently. The reasons cited are numerous, from chain consolidation to the birth of a video generation that has no sentimental attachment to the neighborhood theater.

"Distributors generally do not care about the little theaters that keep them in business," says Martin McCaffery, director of the Capri Theater in Montgomery, Ala. As even arthouse chains convert to four- and six-screen 'plexes, McCaffery says the days of the single-screen neighborhood theater are disappearing fast. Small-town theaters such as the Lincoln in Fayetteville and the Franklin Cinema in Franklin are the exception, not the rule — which is too bad for diehard movie lovers. "People who didn't grow up with video," he observes, "aren't used to bad sound and picture."

Yet McCaffery's own theater is proof that historic indie arthouses can survive — in cities smaller than Nashville. Built in 1941, the Capri was being run by a large regional chain as a soft-core adult cinema until it was shut down in the early '80s. In 1983, a group of Montgomery residents banded together to save the theater, forming a nonprofit organization to run and restore it. Today, the renovated Capri shows art films such as *Pi* and *Happiness*, despite intermittent competition from Carmike's local multiplexes.

"Their interest [in the kind of movies we show] ebbs and flows," McCaffery says. "Some independent movie comes out and makes a lot of money, like *The Crying Game*, and suddenly they decide to do art. They might hurt us for a while, but they just don't know the movies. And we don't treat our customers like cattle."

The Capri is one of several historic theaters across the country that has managed to survive through concerted civic effort. Some have been converted into lavish dinner-and-a-movie attractions. Many are run by nonprofit organizations, which supplement their box-office take with grants, donations, fundraising events, and memberships. In Champaign-Urbana, Ill., community patrons bought the New Art Cinema and transformed it into a neighborhood arthouse. In Boston, the Coolidge Corner sells memberships that include discounts at area merchants.

In each case, the theater built a bond with its patrons by giving them a stake in its future — organizing volunteer workdays, creating outreach programs for kids and senior citizens, selling seats engraved with customers' names. A cynic could argue that cities like Montgomery and Champaign-Urbana would be more receptive because they don't have much else to do. But movies are only a small part of the overall experience these theaters provide.

From a business standpoint, a low number of screens is a drawback — one dud movie can kill business for an entire week, as the Belcourt learned all too well. Yet it's that very intimacy, that warmth and sense of community — those intangibles we lost when the mall theaters took over — that make these small cinemas as representative of a city's personality as a quirky coffeehouse or a favorite meat-and-three. And when one fails, that says a lot about a city too.

• • • • •

There is a faint hope for the Belcourt — faint because the current asking price for the facility is $1.85 million. A Nashville native named Julia Sutherland, who recently moved back here from New Mexico, was stirred to action when she learned of the theater's closing. "It's sad to have that kind of experience only when I'm out of town," she says. So she and six partners are attempting to form a nonprofit organization to continue the Belcourt as a theater. She has been joined by a diverse group that includes Vanderbilt and Harpeth Hall instructors, country musicians and local filmmakers.

Sutherland readily admits she's only starting to secure backing. But in her talks with other theaters around the country, such as the Capri and New York's Film Forum, she says she has received nothing but encouragement. "They want it to work," she says. Some groups have even offered to share information on starting a nonprofit theater.

Thus far, Sutherland's is the only plan I've heard about that involves keeping the Belcourt intact as an arthouse. It certainly beats the alternatives that have been rumored — an apartment complex, a restaurant, office space and a parking lot.

Off the top of my head, I can think of a dozen reasons why the Watkins Belcourt should be saved. Because it's a piece of our history. Because the cutting edge of an art form as democratic as film shouldn't be the exclusive property of bicoastal snobs. Because it makes Nashville a richer place. Because going to the movies is a relatively cheap thing that can bring you in contact with other people and make your life a little better for two hours — sometimes a lot better.

If the Belcourt is to survive, it'll take an effort that lasts way beyond any initial meeting or purchase. It'll mean a month-by-month commitment that extends into the next century and doesn't stop. It'll mean taking a chance on some movies you've never heard of. It'll mean Gene Wyatt, a supporter of offbeat films here for more than 30 years, will have to clear Gannett's dunderheaded wire reviews out of the *Tennessean*. And if the Belcourt doesn't survive a second rebirth, if it joins all those other ghosts in the civic boneyard, we should harbor no illusions about who put it there. (*Nashville Scene*, Jan. 21, 1999)

Intermission

Live-music reviews in the *Scene* appear under a single pseudonymous byline: "The Spin." By tradition, this is done regardless of author. Part of the fun for regular readers is trying to guess who wrote what, and part of the fun for contributors is bending to the ur-style of the column (including referring to oneself in the third person) enough to keep readers guessing. When Jim submitted his summation of Bruce Springsteen's sprawling 28-song set at Bridgestone Arena in 2014, music editor D. Patrick Rodgers decided to forego the usual contrivance for the first time in The Spin's history. The review was posted under Jim's byline because, as everyone on staff agreed, there was no mistaking who had written it.

A Springsteen show is a genre whose conventions are well known, well trod and somehow satisfying all the same for their familiarity — like the Western, a film reference Jim manages to slip in. (Note: Nashville Cream is the name of the *Scene*'s music blog, and the Long Players is a long-running ensemble, boasting some of Nashville's best musicians, that convenes to play their favorite albums in their entirety for appreciative crowds.)

There's not a wasted sentence in the whole sweat-soaked, fist-pumping thing. As a tribute, Nashville Public Radio produced a segment in which five friends — then-*Scene* editor Steve Cavendish, Rep. Jim Cooper, writer Noel Murray, former *Scene* editor Liz Garrigan and the Belcourt's Stephanie Silverman — read one passage in particular that had taken on a kind of talismanic effect for its affirmation of love in the face of life's long odds. You'll probably be able to guess which one.

• • • • • • • • • •

Bruce Springsteen and the E Street Band at Bridgestone Arena, 4/17/14

"A Springsteen show is like Paris," The Spin emailed someone in the hours before Bruce Springsteen and the E Street Band took the stage at Bridgestone Arena Thursday night. "See it and die satisfied." A whiff of mortality colors a Springsteen show today the way clouds of green smoke once affected his Municipal Auditorium shows back in the '70s. The music still sounds terrific, the band still fires on all cylinders like the great sky-pawing beast of a machine it is, but your mood is definitely altered a little. But in a good way, The Spin would argue, still high from a three-hour-plus set made all the more moving by the band's invocation not just of shared history, but of a common fate.

Even without the late Big Man and Danny Federici — who loom in the show not so much as absences but phantom presences, licks or flourishes you sometimes hear even though they're not there — the E Street Band lineup was unusual, missing key players and making unusual substitutions. The band, that fascinating organism of equal parts sports team, long-running family drama and traveling tent revival, bears additions that represent every stage of Springsteen's career, like rings in a tree trunk: guitarist Nils Lofgren from the *Born in the USA* switchover, violin player and vocalist Soozie Tyrell from the *Lucky Town* wilderness years, the Dixieland horn section from the *Seeger Sessions* project. The latest is former Rage Against the Machine guitarist Tom Morello — probably not the first name you'd pencil in for the redoubtable Little Steven Van Zandt while he's off shooting *Lillyhammer*.

It works, though, for the same reason the shows themselves are such a jubilant spectacle: They contain multitudes, and within their sprawl there's room for all. Forsaking what Nashville Cream's resident Bruceologist Adam Gold termed the "region-specific cover" openers of recent dates — Brisbane, no joke, got a killer "Stayin' Alive" — Springsteen, yeoman percussionist Ernest Bradley and the E Streeters set the show's tone with the urgent, defiant optimism of the cover that gives the new *High Hopes* album its title. Yet the response it got from the (gratifyingly) full house doubled in volume once "Professor" Roy Bittan sounded the familiar piano chords of "Badlands." The sound of 15,000 people singing those fist-pumping "whoa-oh-oh-ohs" in unison was the first in a night full of heart-swelling communal moments.

Not that the intense sense of community, and the demands that go with it, can't be something of a mixed blessing. Like Bob Dylan, Springsteen has spent the past four decades as the object of daunting adoration and expectations, two pressures that can be paralyzing for an artist with any ambition. Dylan's late-career response has been to some degree sabotage: He sings generation-defining songs like a cagey, addled wizard finding scraps of half-remembered spells in the sleeves of his robe, testing if they still have any power.

Well, Springsteen knows his spells by heart, and he knows they work: the obligatory may-I-have-this-dance routine in "Dancing in the Dark," the obligatory audience-sung verse to "Hungry Heart" — hell, the obligatory "Hungry Heart." If anything, they work too well — that's a lot of obligation. During the lengthiest working-the-room moments there were times Springsteen appeared reduced to a prop in an endless procession of audience selfies. At times, the stiff-legged, geezerly trudge he affected early on — as in an epic "Spirit in the Night," where he played his age for laughs by slumping mid-song (and mid-arena) into a conveniently materialized director's chair — didn't seem entirely an affect.

What kept the show from lapsing into a shtick marathon was Springsteen's unmatched ability to create a sense of intimacy and one-on-one engagement in the vastness of an enormodome. (Case in point: the "Dancing in the Dark" routine, which became sweetly amusing once the chosen dancer stopped the show to negotiate getting her mom onstage instead. The punchline was even funnier: Each demanded her own selfie.) No other artist — with the possible exception of Bono — has so boldly explored the arena-rock grand gesture as an artistic form in itself, down to the thrill of those bellowed "HAH-WAHN! TWO! THREE!" count-offs. Springsteen did this most affectingly on *The Rising*, using the stadium-pitched incantation as a rhetorical device to raise vanished loved ones, lost rescuers and the hopes of a stricken city.

He turned to that device repeatedly Thursday night, invoking the anthemic exhortations of "Land of Hope and Dreams," "Waiting for a Sunny Day" and *The Rising*'s goosebumps-raising title track to get audiences of young and old shouting as one. The cumulative emotional effect was like the gradual swell and crash of a wave. There was little obligatory about the set, which was filled with curveballs and unexpected selections. With the arena floor divided into two general-admission sections by a mid-arena runway, Springsteen used an unexpected stage dive to gather fan-made request posters to his chest as the crowd passed him along over its head. From those, he selected — and nailed — a cover he said the band had performed only once before, Elvis' "Burning Love."

Better (and more surprising still) was a cover of "Satisfaction" with a preteen girl selected from the crowd as his duet partner. (Throughout both numbers, E Street bassist and part-time Nashvillian Garry Tallent must've thought he was back in the Long Players.) A two-song nod to *Nebraska* climaxed with a blazing "Johnny 99" as the horn section led by star-in-the-making Jake Clemons teetered on the stage's lip, gunning the song's motor with a swaggering "Night Train" riff. By this point, it was clear the 64-year-old frontman was pacing himself like a canny athlete; to drive the point home, he later slithered down the mic stand in a frankly erotic backbend, parallel to the floor on the toe tips of his boots as the crowd uttered a gasp that can only be described as orgasmic. The Spin's companion looked on ruefully and said, "I couldn't do that when I was 20."

Many of the night's most chill-inducing moments came from less familiar, more socially conscious material: the Amadou Diallo protest anthem "41 Shots (American Skin)," the solemn Vietnam Memorial ballad "The Wall," which Springsteen introduced with a eulogy for fallen Jersey friends that hushed the crowd to a pinprick drop. "The Ghost of Tom Joad" is a song that has stubbornly failed to ignite for The Spin, either by Springsteen or by Morello's solo. We're not sure we could have taken Morello's jaw-clenched earnestness and rock-face guitar acrobatics on his own — in his nightwatchman's garb, he sometimes resembled a progressive action figure the *Nation* might give away with subscriptions. But the energy and camaraderie he inspired from Springsteen, standing shoulder to shoulder with cocked arm pumping like a piston, electrified them both; it made the song a live showstopper.

Even the hits offered some surprises. Gold had seen Springsteen 22 times without ever hearing "Born in the USA" live; the 23rd proved to be the charm (thanks for reading, Boss!), with Mighty Max Weinberg rising to the occasion with a 50-cal barrage of a drum solo. By the time the band polished off the climactic trifecta of "Born to Run," "Dancing in the Dark" and "Tenth Avenue Freeze-out" — a song that has morphed over the years from origin story to eulogy to "look how far we've come" — the sea of extended hands and straining fingers across the arena looked like a wheat field in a windstorm.

The fact that Springsteen is still capable of surprise after all these years, while delivering elements fans have come to rely upon the way Western lovers await shootouts at high noon, speaks to his mastery of the concert as an art form. Watching him pause interminably as disembodied hands rub his head, or acknowledge yet another kid seeking his attention in the audience, would be hard to take if affection didn't overcome resignation. In a sense, he's the Bill Clinton of rock stars — without you, he's nothing. And yet he's attentive enough to seize moments of spontaneity fronting a band the size of an FBI task force. There's something thrilling about a guy barking "E flat!" at roughly a dozen people and expecting order to result, like hearing a man at the helm of a locomotive holler, "Turn left!" As for the selection itself, whoever thought anybody could again make "Shout" something more than a frathouse reunion-band cliché?

Time throws you off a rooftop the day you're born, and the fall you have to the pavement is called a life. The Springsteens of the world are there to remind us the object is to never stop kicking and punching and straining for the sky, all the way to the inevitable finish. You can complain Bruce Springsteen mugs too much, indulges too many little kids and weepy middle-aged moms, does too many of the same things again and again. You know who else you can make that complaint about? The people who inspire the most love from you — the people who have demonstrated their resilience, and their willingness to be there for you even when it's not convenient, and who have lifted their chin to face the hard times we know will eventually have to come.

The Spin was thus happy not to be the only person who got choked up when a little-girl guest singer handed the featured attraction's tambourine back to him, to his clear surprise, only to have him offer it to her to keep. And we were happy not to be the only person brushing away tears at the night's overwhelming benediction, an acoustic "Thunder Road" full of ache, shared experience and tenderness. But that wasn't surprising. Nobody ever left a Springsteen show feeling alone. (*Nashville Scene*, April 18, 2014)

Lost in a reverie, 1987.
Photo by Collin Wade Monk.

Jim and Alicia get hitched, 1993.
Photo by Jeanne Forsythe.

Jim and Alicia at Oaklands High School reunion, 1992.
Photo by Jennifer L. McMillion.

With former *Nashville Scene* managing editor Jonathan Marx, circa 1995.
Photo by Lee Weidhaas.

FREE
NASHVILLE SCENE
NOVEMBER 3, 2005 • WWW.NASHVILLESCENE.COM
Ridley's
Believe It or Not!
A guided tour of Nashville's strangest sights, weirdest phenomena and oddest oddities...
Is the Sounds stadium deal really that exciting? p. 16
Local band Ghostfinger create a new kind of classic rock. p. 45

Cover of the Nov. 3, 2005, *Scene*.
Photo by Eric England.

Opposite page:

As Kate Smith, onstage with Mayor Phil Bredesen at the Best of Nashville party, 1996. Photo by Vicki Beckwith McMahan.

Reporting for duty at the former Eighth Avenue *Scene* offices, circa 2003. Photo by Martin Brady.

Texting Alicia from
his office, surrounded
by stuff, 2014. Photo
by Steve Haruch.

Sporting a Janus Films T-shirt at the Belcourt, 2015.
Photo by Jon Keller.

Clockwise from upper left: Jim, Alicia, Jamie, Biscuit and Kat at home in South Nashville. Photo by Galyn Glick Martin.

At Burgess Falls, Tennessee. Photo by Alicia Adkerson.

Innocence and Experience 7

One sensation that returns again and again in Jim's film writing is the thrill of a movie whose grand scale sucks him in — "feeling like an awestruck 10 year old," as he puts it in his review of *Once Upon a Time in the West*. Allowing that sensation to take over was one of Jim's enduring abilities. And while that feeling of childlike wonder drove many of Jim's moviegoing fascinations, it didn't limit them. He loved movies that complicated childhood, too, especially ones that took care not to simplify kids or condescend to them. This chapter is dedicated to reviews that consider childhood, innocence and coming of age in all its messiness and revelation.

Jim was also willing to forgive gross technical incompetence if a movie rang true, hence his celebration of the ineptly staged but compelling *Pump Up the Volume*. (A side note: Chagall Guevara, the Nashville band Jim identifies on the soundtrack, included Steve Taylor, who went on to direct the *Jules and Jim*–inspired video for Sixpence None the Richer's hit single "Kiss Me" and the film adaptation of *Blue Like Jazz*.) Jim also loved Wes Anderson's *Moonrise Kingdom*, not only for its unabashed romanticism (see: Demy, Jacques), but the deeper truths under its stylish, fussed-over surfaces and its games of dress-up. "It's only by trying on these wardrobes that the characters arrive at workable lives," Jim writes.

He was not afraid to be frank about how differently some movies hit you once you're a parent — no matter how uncool that might look to some readers. His *Toy Story 2* review considers the movie from the vantage points of its two very different demographic targets. He preferred a flawed movie that's honest to a slick one that risked nothing. And he was willing to forgive some sappiness or too-tidy closure where he could find a kernel of honest optimism. For instance, his

Opposite: Preparing for induction into the
MTSU College of Media and Entertainment
Hall of Fame, 2016. Photo by Nancy Floyd.

review of *Akeelah and the Bee*, about a young girl who gains confidence in training for spelling bees, both admires (mostly) and admonishes (gently). It also hits a little differently now that Jim's star turn as a dad has been cut short.

● ● ● ● ● ● ● ● ●

Toy Story 2
Dir. John Lasseter
1999, G, 85 min.

Toys in the Attic

For a 34 year old who's about to be grandfathered out of his coddled 18–34 demographic, watching the pop-culture agenda skew steadily younger is like living in Menudo Nation — a land where the members are routinely drummed out and replaced once they're old enough to shave. Whenever I encounter some inexplicably popular slasher-movie retread or pre-fab 'N Sync tune, I feel one step closer to whittling outside some retirement-home bunker labeled Sunnydale. Just because you're not old now doesn't mean you're not old enough to become culturally obsolete.

In an odd way, that explains why almost every adult I know responded so strongly to *Toy Story* — and why they responded to it so differently from kids. Kids and adults both were tickled by the zany pace, the shiny look and the ingenious gimmick of what toys do when their owners aren't looking. But adults seemed to identify with the toys a lot more than younger viewers did.

Kids are possessive of toys, sure. Adults, though, are sentimental about them, and that isn't remotely the same thing. In its most poignant scenes, *Toy Story* reminded grown-ups of all the toys they'd left behind — the detritus of last year's passing fad or obsession, like the rings in a tree trunk. It's no major leap from there to getting left behind yourself.

That's a pretty depressing way to describe one of the funniest movies in recent memory. But if the *Toy Story* sequel manages to construct even wilder gags, and to stretch even further the idea of the secret life of toys, it also leaves an even more bittersweet aftertaste. Like the first film, *Toy Story 2* is partially organized around the idea of obsolescence — only this time around, adults will feel its pang a lot more sharply. At its most heart-wrenching, this chipper cartoon is also a parent's stricken fantasy of being outgrown.

At some level, being a parent means anxiously treasuring each moment of a child's development, while realizing ruefully that each new step is charting his eventual departure from your life. In *Toy Story 2*, that fate is represented by "the shelf" — the dingy ledge reserved for discarded toys. In a single tear of his toy sleeve, the cowpoke Woody (voice of Tom Hanks) is suddenly sidelined from a week at cowboy camp with his freckle-faced owner Andy. Instead, he's left to gather dust with Wheezy, a squeaky penguin who don't squeak so good no more.

Woody saves Wheezy from a fate worse than the shelf (yard sale!) only to wind up in the clutches of a maniacal collector who sees toys as untouchable commodities, not playthings. It's in his sterile care, however, that Woody discovers that he has a history: He was once part of a matched set with a wonder horse, a cowgirl named Jessie, and a grizzled prospector sidekick. When the reunited set goes up for sale, Woody is faced with a toy's version of an existential crisis — either be enshrined behind glass for eternity in a museum display, or enjoy what few years he has left with Andy before the boy outgrows him.

As hilarious as the slapstick rescue efforts of Buzz Lightyear (Tim Allen), Mr. Potatohead (Don Rickles) and Woody's old pals are, it's the former scenes that give *Toy Story 2* its peculiar resonance. In the movie's most affecting moment, Jessie (voiced ideally by Joan Cusack) recalls getting left behind by an owner who simply grew up. The scene is shot from a toy's point of view, but the primal fear it expresses — of fading from a child's memory as he or she grows older — is only too parental.

This montage didn't affect the tykes in the audience much (not the ones kicking my chair, anyway). No surprise there: What does the passage of time mean to an 8-year-old? The adults around me, on the other hand, wept like a Scout troop at *Old Yeller*. Somehow, that made watching *Toy Story 2* an even more poignant experience. It brought the gulf between young and old into startling view, even as we sat enjoying the same thing.

Toy Story 2 draws a distinction between toys as pristine works of art and as rough-and-tumble playthings. The movie itself is the latter: It backs off from some of its more painful themes, and it stretches out its delirious airport climax a bit too long. But its mix of silliness, affection, and piercing nostalgia — and yes, artistry — keeps the separate halves of the audience engaged simultaneously. Kids experience their toys in the present tense, while adults eventually view them only in the past. As delightful as these movies are, they stand a good chance of being part of everyone's future. (*Nashville Scene*, Dec. 2, 1999)

• • • • • • • • • •

Son of Rambow
Dir. Garth Jennings
2007, PG-13, 96 min.

Blood Brothers

No adult has ever been able to codify what separates a good movie from a classic. In kid terms, though — those favored by *Son of Rambow*, a chipper tribute to the cinema as both supplier and repository of dreams — it's literally a matter of steps. A good movie merely sends you bounding home from the theater. A great movie demands some further physical response, some sluicing of pent-up excitement: You just gotta pick up that volleyball and conk your neighbor off his ladder. And a classic? Simple. A classic makes you want to make movies.

Long ago, in the distant 1980s when *Son of Rambow* is set, "classic" wasn't the word anyone would have used to describe *First Blood* — at least not anyone above the age of consent for chocolate milk. A moody, proficient revenge thriller that heralded a coming wave of post-Vietnam sulking, it nonetheless begat Sylvester Stallone's segue from mush-mouthed punching bag to mush-mouthed killing machine. As a thrill ride, it's a lot slower to crank up than the early '80s' other celluloid 'coaster, *Raiders of the Lost Ark* — which famously inspired three Mississippi 12-year-olds to spend six years risking life, limb and one kid's basement filming their own VHS shot-for-shot remake.

Watch *First Blood*, however, from the POV of a lonely, picked-on tween-age boy — i.e., the sensibility that pervades it — and it's a projector-beamed bolt from the blue. In that light, John Rambo looks like Mattel's own adolescent-angst action figure: ostracized, misunderstood by the world, preyed upon by authority figures (and best of all, unencumbered by girls). No wonder the misfit heroes of writer-director Garth Jennings' whimsical comedy — two enterprising British schoolkids who set out to make their own Stallone-derived fireball-a-palooza — feel less kinship to Indiana Jones, the keeper of covenants, than to Rambo, the army of one.

Introduced bootlegging *First Blood* at the neighborhood movie house, scruffy little hustler Lee (Will Poulter), an Artful Dodger with bat-wing eyebrows and con-man cheek, has only the company of movies and a bulky camcorder. (The movie regards its '80s artifacts the way an archaeologist might peruse a stone ax: a shoebox-sized wireless phone looks like something Patton might've used to order troop maneuvers.) All but abandoned by his parents, mistreated by his caddish older bro, the conniving Lee takes a page from Rambo and passes along the hurt to someone else: a dreamy, repressed tyke named Will Proudfoot (the elfin Bill Milner) whose religion makes the sign of the cross against demon cinema.

Will may quietly adorn his notebooks with cartoon explosions and flip-corner mayhem — flights of fancy that Jennings renders in endearingly herky-jerky line animation. But Lee has to cajole, bully and guilt-trip his naïve new chum into top-lining his top-secret home movie. What it takes, ultimately, to make a believer of Will is a glimpse of Hollywood's forbidden fruit on Lee's VCR. The movie's cleverest, most exuberant sequence follows Will dashing home as his head buzzes for the first time with celluloid excess. The excitement of new sensations fuses with the dream language of movies: Lee's overhead fluorescent lights morph into Universal-horror thunderbolts, while a neighbor's noisy pooch becomes a literal dogfight pilot.

Jennings, part of the celebrated Hammer & Tongs production team, finds a tone here that's more winsome and less desperately wacky than his film version of *The Hitchhiker's Guide to the Galaxy*. As when kids act out the playground equivalent of fan fiction, the movie-within-a-movie mutates into quirkily revealing psychodrama. Escape into cinema proves contagious for the rest of the school — especially once a glamorously bored French exchange student (Jules Sitruk) staves off ennui long enough to kick some ninth-grade ninja asses. The project is powerful enough to overturn the school's hierarchy of cool. Soon mousy Will is pogoing to the crazy new sound of Depeche Mode with a roomful of Space Dust–chugging hipsters — while Lee looks on miserably, hopelessly upstaged.

Their falling-out seems trumped up to provide last-minute conflict, as does the heavy-handed subplot involving the oppressive brethren of Will's church — boilerplate complications that keep the movie away from Will and Lee's set for (too) long stretches. But at its most likable, *Son of Rambow* evokes the rush of discovery that turns budding cinephiles into lifers — that delight in finding a film that seems to express or coalesce some inchoate yearning, including a yen to share.

Why is it that kids playing dress-up in blockbuster tropes rarely gets old? Perhaps more to the point, why does the idea of rough-hewn DIY cinema seem so appealing now? *Son of Rambow*'s comrades and/or antecedents include not just the *Raiders* adaptation (itself being considered for filming) but also *Rushmore*'s Max Fischer Players, Jonathan Caouette's *Blue Velvet* high-school musical in *Tarnation* and the homemade video-store knock-offs in Michel Gondry's *Be Kind Rewind*. In differing ways, means and styles, each celebrates the sandpapery texture and tenacity of scrappy personal visions, whose flaws and grit are a welcome respite from generic mainstream gloss. More a modest pleasure than a rousing success, the gentle-natured *Son of Rambow* may not inspire anyone to make movies, or even to bean their neighbor with a volleyball. But it'll quicken your pace on the walk home. (*Nashville Scene*, May 22, 2008)

• • • • • • • • • •

Little Man Tate
Dir. Jodie Foster
1991, PG, 99 min.

Little Big Man

Jodie Foster's *Little Man Tate* has the sensibility — and the honesty — of a classic children's story, the kind in which intelligence is a mixed blessing, but a blessing nonetheless. It puts us inside the mind of a frustrated 7-year-old boy named Fred Tate, whose misfortune was to be born brilliant in a stupid world.

Like many other 7 year olds, Fred hates school, but for a different reason — it doesn't challenge him. He's completely stifled. While his classmates slog dutifully through elementary arithmetic, Fred composes operas, reads novels and dreams of standing in Van Gogh floral studies. His teachers love him; other kids hate him. He prefers to be alone with his books.

His mother, a waitress named Dede (Foster), worries about him while she struggles to support them. She thinks he needs a birthday party, or a summer vacation, but she's frightened. She's afraid it won't be enough. His intelligence intimidates even her — it's a part of him she doesn't understand.

It's also the part of him that attracts the notice of Jane Grierson (Dianne Wiest), a famed educator who operates a special institute for child prodigies. Dazzled by Fred's gift. Dr. Grierson proposes to take him on a three-week "odyssey of the mind," a trip that will give him the intellectual stimulation Dede can't provide. When the trip leads to a chance to begin college at the age of 7, Fred is torn between the worlds of the mind and the heart.

Movies about prodigies are irresistible. Everyone wants to know what it's like to be a genius, to see and understand things that no one else can. When filmmakers can't fulfill that promise, the disappointment is particularly sharp. As acclaimed a film as *Amadeus* was, its Mozart remained a hopelessly vague figure. It never gave a single insight into the processes of someone who composed symphonies as a child, let alone the way in which he must have perceived the world. A convention of Salieris couldn't have made a more ploddingly respectable, unimaginative film.

That makes the achievement of first-time director Foster all the more remarkable. Her *Little Man Tate* does what Amadeus didn't dare to try: It shows us the world through the eyes of a genius — the eyes of Fred Tate.

When Fred first walks through the Grierson institute, past a display of illuminated geometric figures, Foster keeps him and the figures in the same shot. She wants us to see what he's looking at and how he responds. The young actor Adam Hann-Byrd, who plays Fred, never disappoints us. His reactions are marvels of subtle, unaffected acting. His eyes may widen almost imperceptibly, but his mind is a universe exploding with possibilities. His intense seriousness has shades of puzzlement, sadness and understanding.

Foster shows us the speed of Fred's thought processes through a variety of ingenious visual devices. As Fred visualizes a complex math problem, numbers materialize before him and swim into place. When he watches a pool game, the trajectories of the balls streak past in light-blue lines, like the phantom trails of electrons. Foster even conveys Fred's spiritual nature in a poetic flourish. Riding horseback through Dr. Grierson's ranch, he envisions a treetop as a canopy of shimmering bells. The moment is brief, but it's piercing. You may never see a silver maple the same way again.

Little Man Tate has a strong script by Scott Frank, who wrote another of the year's best screenplays, the wonderful thriller *Dead Again*, although the two films share nothing but solid construction, quirky, well-defined characters and literate dialogue. Foster's astute, empathetic direction, however, gives the film its imaginative power. Her sense of color and composition enhances the movie's theme of balances. When the miserable Dede talks to Fred on the phone, the different shades of blue surrounding her could be thought balloons. To show Fred's apprehension in the large-scaled world, Foster emphasizes the space around him, dwarfing him in the frame or shooting him from high above. You don't expect this kind of visual attention and control in a first film.

Then again, Foster's performances in movies have been consistent only in their unpretentious virtuosity — her Clarice Starling in *The Silence of the Lambs* is a lifetime of experience away from her furious victim in *The Accused*, one of the all-time great film performances. Her Dede is just as memorable. Foster is an unusually natural actress. Her roles must demand a lot of preparation, but onscreen she just exists in character. You could swear you've seen Dede before, and you halfway expect to see her when the movie's over — she has that kind of presence. She's wrongheaded and nurturing in equal amounts, but you can see that Fred is the fulfillment of her imaginative side too.

Dede represents the side of Fred that craves love and normalcy, which places a tremendous burden on Dr. Grierson's character. She's the voice of unyielding intellect, a strain on any actress. In the role, however, Dianne Wiest has never seemed more appealing. Her warmth makes the character less schematic, redeeming even in the rather cheap scene in which she burns her first meatloaf while cooking for Fred. At the end, dressed in a pointy party hat, she's radiant and silly, the most blissed-out of good witches. Foster is the first director to capitalize on her incandescent smile.

When Dede and Dr. Grierson dance together in the film's lovely conclusion, *Little Man Tate* celebrates a sweet reconciliation of the heart and the mind, one that has its own dreamy logic. The one jarring note in this splendid film comes from watching children languish in classes that sap them of their gifts. In Tennessee, where jughead legislators enjoy free football tickets and Disneyland junkets while the education system starves, it's almost too painful to watch. To Tennessee audiences, it may be the only scene in *Little Man Tate* that doesn't look like something from an alien culture. (*Nashville Scene*, Oct. 17, 1991)

● ● ● ● ● ● ● ● ● ●

Akeelah and the Bee
Dir. Doug Atchison
2006, PG, 112 min.

Letter Perfect

Every year, when ESPN broadcasts the Scripps National Spelling Bee, a tiny flutter of hope rises in anyone who cherishes the life of the mind. *Spelling is a sport?* Sweet Jesus! For the duration of the competition, the brainy kid who gets his glasses stomped by knuckle-draggers on the playground is something more than a wedgie magnet. He's part of a brotherhood of athletes, a Michael Jordan who dunks with digraphs. It doesn't last — not at a time when mass-culture contempt for book learnin' and the eggheads who persist in it has never been higher, when the tangible value of an education is set mostly by *Jeopardy!* But for the length of the spelling bee, the fantasy exists of a meritocracy for any kid who's willing to learn.

It exists too in *Akeelah and the Bee*, a sweet-natured, immensely likable family film that recasts the bee's human drama — captured memorably in the 2002 documentary *Spellbound* — in the familiar terms of an after-school special. "Fantasy" may be the right word for a movie in which study alone overcomes all the savage inequalities of poverty, in which all bad people have some inner gold, in which circumstance ultimately favors the good at heart. Watching it, a parent feels a little like Terrence Howard's pimp in *Hustle & Flow*, who says that when his daughter asks him one day if she can be president, he's going to look her right in the eye and lie.

But these are fantasies worth believing in, and because of a remarkable young actress named Keke Palmer, we believe in the movie. Palmer plays Akeelah Anderson, a bright 11 year old languishing in an underfunded, underequipped South Central Los Angeles public school. To call attention to the needy kids and dire resources, the principal (Curtis Armstrong) hits upon the unlikely PR strategy of drafting a student to compete in the city's spelling bee, with an eye toward advancing to the regionals.

Writer-director Doug Atchison effectively sketches all the obstacles standing in Akeelah's way: a home where her widowed mom (Angela Bassett) fights to make ends meet, an at-risk neighborhood where her older brother (Julito McCullum) hangs with a shady local thug. Worst is the stigma of being smart. Almost against her will — she's bullied and branded a "brainiac" by dim-bulb classmates — Akeelah nonetheless performs well enough to catch the eye of a visiting UCLA prof, Joshua Larrabee (Laurence Fishburne, who also produced), who volunteers to serve as a sort of orthographic Mr. Miyagi. Making book study cinematically exciting is no easy feat, and Atchison doesn't exactly finesse the problem — not unless your idea of kinetic excitement is a montage of reading Latin dictionaries cut to "Rubber Band Man." (Like Larrabee, the movie largely pretends rap doesn't exist; in this maiden voyage of Starbucks Entertainment, the contemporary sound of ghetto aspiration and suburban envy is scarce as a two-dollar latte.)

But the movie doesn't need the hype. Its urgency comes from Palmer, who makes the prospect of learning seem transformative. Last seen as Tyler Perry's wayward charge in *Madea's Family Reunion*, Palmer doesn't have the fresh-scrubbed emotion-on-demand affectation that many child actors give off. Akeelah just looks tired and wary, and Palmer doesn't exaggerate her unhappiness — sitting at a PC Scrabble board, she's any kid lost in play, even under her late father's gaze.

Nor does she overplay Akeelah's growing self-confidence. As she makes it to round after round, her face brightens only gradually, as if one hard-closed inner window after another were finally starting to let in some light. But she's able to convey something almost ineffable: the difference that knowledge makes in a person's sense of worth. It's Palmer who makes the buildup to the national showdown compelling — not the trumped-up rivalry with an arrogant Chinese prodigy (Sean Michael), not the big secret that Larrabee's hiding in the wings. These elements all demonstrate the difference between conventions — the obligatory elements that you want to see in a piece of storytelling, because they provide satisfaction — and the clichés.

Instead, it's the movie's corny, stubborn good-heartedness that provides its most warming moments: the friendship between Akeelah and a supportive upper-class contestant (J. R. Villareal), the odd little connection between the girl and a local gangsta who was once a little kid with a trophy.

Knowledge, like dance, is one of those things that has value in contemporary movies only when it's used in competition. In the nifty finale, Atchison pulls a neat reversal that shifts tension to what's really at stake: decency, honor and a sense of accomplishment, not claiming a place on a plaque. If you can keep from biting your nails when Akeelah gets "argillaceous," or from tearing up at the resolution, you're made of sterner stuff than I. Someday my little girl will pop in this DVD, watch it with wide eyes, and ask if that's the way life really is. And I'm going to look her right in the eye, and lie. (*Nashville Scene,* April 27, 2006)

• • • • • • • • • •

Pump Up the Volume
Dir. Allan Moyle
1990, R, 102 min.

Talk Hard

By any objective standard of filmmaking, *Pump Up the Volume* isn't a good movie. The adult characters are cardboard cutouts, and their every line of dialogue sounds like a public-service announcement. The plot is pure cliché. The technical goofs are embarrassing: Teachers wear the same clothes day after day, while the record on a turntable might switch mysteriously in mid-song.

Here's why none of this matters.

Sometimes a movie that isn't very good captures the mood and spark of a moment better than a good one. *Pump Up the Volume* has a lot of problems, but it's more provocative and incendiary than many more artful movies. Its crude energy, punch and conviction get you worked up. The writer-director, Allan Moyle, bungles all kinds of small details (and some big ones as well), and his film is a sloppy piece of work. But it's sloppy because Moyle has his eye on the big picture. Like its teenage hero, Hard Harry (Christian Slater), *Pump Up the Volume* is more concerned with its message than its medium.

Hard Harry's medium is a short-wave radio set, which he uses to bombard his high-school audience with simulated masturbation, music and pointedly obscene jeremiads against the bonehead administration at Hubert Humphrey High. Hard Harry wants to shake up his listeners: He wants them to care about thinking for themselves. He also wants to reach someone: At school, he's too shy to talk.

When Hard Harry's broadcasts become a huge success, inspiring students to question the blind authoritarianism of the administration, the schoolmasters decide to shut Harry down. But the movement he starts is not so easily stopped.

Pump Up the Volume plays like a straight *Rock 'n' Roll High School*, and when the adult villains speak you may be reminded more of *Reefer Madness*. (The movie's lack of sympathy for adults panders to its young audience; the film never deals with adults as former teens.) But *Pump Up the Volume* is the only movie out now that portrays teens as literate, inquisitive, creative and smart. The young characters here read, play music, write avant-garde poetry and get politically involved. They don't all listen to the same music: Harry plays everything from Leonard Cohen to Richard Hell and a titanic Henry Rollins/ Bad Brains gang-up on the MC5's "Kick Out the Jams." The teens in *Pump Up the Volume* develop into a supportive community that tolerates difference by thinking for themselves, and that's a revolutionary message these days.

Pump Up the Volume is also the only movie to address head-on the censorship and intolerance snaking across the country. Harry isn't some nut spouting filth for its own sake: The movie makes it clear Harry's ideas are what's dangerous. His cheerful, imaginative, defiant obscenity is the excuse for shutting him down, not the reason. In Nashville, where the young owners of the underage Club Roar have been hounded unmercifully by officious pencil-pushers because of the way they think and the music they like, where we can see X-rated trash daily but not a serious, R-rated movie about the life of Christ, that message is revolutionary too.

The main reason *Pump Up the Volume* succeeds, however, is not the worthy message or the outstanding soundtrack (which features local heroes Chagall Guevara): It's the leads. When Christian Slater pulled a gun on two *Hitlerjungen* jocks in *Heathers*, he instantly became a symbol of freedom from dumb teen regimentation. Here, he's electrifying: He makes Harry's spellbinding rants into something positively iconic. The movie's other huge asset is an actress named Samantha Mathis, who plays a high-school poet: She projects a startling, erotic individuality. The two characters could easily become cult heroes, scratched on notebooks across the country.

The banding of the punks and yuppies alike around Harry isn't very believable: His music and message often wouldn't seem to appeal to either. But *Pump*

Up the Volume, in dynamic, vibrant terms, tells its audience things no other movie ever has. In the world of *Pump Up the Volume*, two kids decide they don't want to have sex after all, after a beautiful, halting moment of desire; a straight kid tells a gay kid that his tormentors are the ones that are sick, not him; and kids of all different backgrounds respect each other's individuality and revolt against censorship and oppression.

It may be a fantasy. But brothers, it's my kind of fantasy. *Pump Up the Volume*, flaws and all, is essential. (*Nashville Scene*, Aug. 30, 1990)

• • • • • • • • • •

Boyz N the Hood
Dir. John Singleton
1991, R, 112 min.

Street Smarts

In "Thank You for Talkin' to Me Africa," one of the spookiest and most hostile records ever made, Sly Stone slowly confronts the devil in a creepy, seemingly contradictory statement — "I begin to stop." The new film *Boyz N the Hood* begins with a stop, an ominous shot of a "STOP" sign at an empty intersection. It's the prelude to the saddest and most powerful vision of American childhood in years.

Taking its cue from a song by Eazy-E of the rap group N.W.A., itself violently divided by disputes, *Boys N the Hood* does something rare in contemporary movies: It shows how a kid's upbringing determines the man he becomes; it shows how a web of childhood loyalties can either bind or destroy. It begins when its protagonists are children; it ends when they have no childhood left.

The "hood" is the neighborhood in South Central L.A. where 10-year-old Tre Styles is sent to live with his father, Furious (Larry Fishburne). It's also the home of his two best friends, the athletic Ricky and his half-brother, Doughboy, who struggles in his shadow. Violence in the community is less a threat than an underlying fact of life. An afternoon may consist either of a game of catch or a look at the dead body crumpled in a field down the street. The three boys are fascinated and repelled by the gangland life around them, but Furious urges Tre to escape its senseless cruelty.

The test comes, however, when the boys reach the brink of adulthood. At 17, Tre (Cuba Gooding Jr.) and Ricky (Morris Chestnut) begin to look for ways out of the hood, while Doughboy (Ice Cube) deals drugs and swills beer all day. (The movie's condemnation of alcohol as a class weapon, along with drugs, is unusually gutsy — not to mention astute.) As the two straight kids struggle to leave the neighborhood, though, the tangle of alliances and violence draws them back.

In its unblinking, matter-of-fact portrayal of killing, *Boyz N the Hood* resembles Martin Scorsese's *Goodfellas*, another film about the allure a gangster's life holds for a destitute kid and the corrupting power of the American dream. But the best scenes in *Boyz N the Hood* have levels of surreal, understated irony all their own. The kids try to get a football back from a gang of neighbor hoods; the prospect of losing their ball completely obscures the dead boy that lies a few feet away. The scene works in several different ways. The theft itself is symbolic of the heartless crime ripping the community, but the boys' lack of concern shows that, in this world of commonplace death, a human life is as much of an object as a football — only it's worth less.

Another disturbing scene shows the teenage Tre terrorized by a cop — a black cop — who spouts racial slurs. The hatred and self-loathing the policeman must have endured is frightening; the way he vents it is more frightening still. A lot of credit for the scene goes to Cuba Gooding Jr., the remarkable young actor who plays Tre. With a gun at his chin, Tre refuses to show the cop any emotion until a single tear sneaks out the corner of his eye. Gooding angrily brushes his eye. His tears have betrayed him.

If all of *Boyz N the Hood* were as scrupulously tough-minded as those scenes, it would be the great film it's being touted to be. But Singleton's script and direction are uneven and at times downright uninspired. The movie's credibility isn't helped by Singleton's borrowings from other movies. Accepting something as a slice of life is hard when you've seen it already in *Stand by Me*. (Any director who would steal not one but three scenes from *Stand by Me* is a petty thief indeed.)

Other moments, however, are didactic and badly staged in and of themselves. A scene in which Furious lays out an economic theory for some onlookers is as inept as a Channel 4 public-service announcement. The actors wander up menacingly, deliver some stock responses and wait for their next cue.

Singleton's writing, so precise and penetrating in individual scenes and dialogue, suffers from a certain TV-movie flatness — less telling and more showing would have helped. Near the close, he exploits a moment of violence to rouse the audience, obliterating his own anti-violence message. That the victim is made to seem deserving doesn't make the moment any less hypocritical.

Balance against this, however, the towering strength and dignity of Larry Fishburne's Furious, moving performances by Gooding and Morris Chestnut, the pulsating, jittery nighttime captured by Charles Mills' cinematography and the piercing insights offered by much of the film, and the flaws seem much less important. Rap star Ice Cube even makes a funny, credible debut as Doughboy. (An amusing in-joke: The thief Doughboy beats up in the film wears the T-shirt of Ice Cube's enemy and former bandmate, Eazy-E.)

Boyz N the Hood is going to be underrated by some because of its low-budget limitations, which aren't very distracting. It's going to be overrated by others despite the occasionally poor staging. Whatever the consensus, it's a powerful, disturbing, often assured and ultimately hopeful film that deserves to be seen by as wide an audience as possible. Here's hoping someone pays attention to that stop sign. (*Nashville Scene*, July 18, 1991)

● ● ● ● ● ● ● ● ● ●

Moonrise Kingdom
Dir. Wes Anderson
2012, PG-13, 94 min.

Moonrise Becomes You

Wes Anderson's first feature, the 1996 caper comedy *Bottle Rocket*, is the movie that introduced one of the great comic archetypes: Owen Wilson's Dignan, a fidgety idea man who pours his inspiration into low-yield robberies that he micro-manages as if he were tunneling into Fort Knox. But it also introduced the worldview Anderson would refine and elaborate over his next six films — the folly of thinking you can control your life if you just map it out obsessively enough.

The heroes of Anderson's subsequent movies — *Rushmore*'s adolescent go-getter Max Fischer, *The Life Aquatic*'s scuffling Cousteau stand-in Steve Zissou, the fantastic Mr. Fox — are whizzes at elaborate planning. Over the years, Anderson has developed a visual style to match their fussiness: tidily composed frames that look like shoebox dioramas, every detail fitted into place with a *New Yorker* cartoonist's eye for sight-gag arrangement. The compulsive order becomes the joke: There's no way anything so maniacally organized can hold, like an Eiffel Tower of toothpicks awaiting just one big sneeze. If a spirit animal haunts this realm, it's not suave Mr. Fox but hapless Wile E. Coyote.

And if knocking down these characters' matchstick houses were all Anderson cared about doing, his movies would be exercises in twee sadism. But the elements that disrupt his heroes' best-laid plans — other people, the stray bottle rockets whose path nobody can predict — tend to produce something better by demanding to be acknowledged. And so it is with Anderson's seventh movie, *Moonrise Kingdom* — which in some ways is exactly what you expect if you've been following his career, and yet still the loveliest surprise you're likely to get at the movies this summer.

Scripted with unflagging comic invention by the director and Roman Coppola, *Moonrise Kingdom* is the outright romance Anderson's movies seemed to be leading up to, child protagonists and all. It begins with the discovery that a 12-year-old Khaki Scout, Sam, has gone AWOL and vanished from under the nose of his doggedly earnest scoutmaster (Edward Norton, born to wear an Eagle Scout's garb). On the other side of their coastal community is Suzy, the girl Sam plans to run away with once she escapes the angular house of her morose lawyer parents (Bill Murray and Frances McDormand). Since the orphaned Sam is an Anderson hero, this entails lots of maps, a stash of artfully arranged provisions and exact proto-GPS instructions about where to meet.

In a movie where precision of tone counts for everything, the casting of Sam and Suzy carries an extra burden. Somehow the filmmakers found two newcomers, Jared Gilman and Kara Hayward, who slip into their roles without a false or contrived move. The scene where Sam and Suzy come face-to-face, across a grassy cliché of a movie meadow, typifies the empathetic balancing act Anderson pulls off, a recognition that however affected the kids may act, the passions they feel are no less sharp, or real. It's a moment that could've been played for an easy joke — a goof on the ancient lovers-running-in-slow-motion wheeze. Instead, Sam clamps down on a pipe and affects a look as world-weary as Jude Law returning to Cold Mountain. It still gets a laugh — there's not a shot of him sagely puffing on that silly pipe that doesn't — but in a way that lets the character be seen as he sees himself, with the gentlest of deadpan ribbing.

As they set up a beachside idyll — their underwear-clad dance and awkward wooing to a Françoise Hardy chanson, like so much of the movie, is at once hilarious and curiously haunting — their flight disrupts the clockwork rituals of the surrounding adults: the lonesome patrols of the town sheriff (Bruce Willis, all hangdog decency), who's concealing his own furtive stab at romance; the watchful rounds of the scoutmaster, who dispatches a platoon of kid troops to track down the young lovers. No less than the runaways, these kids see themselves as participants in a movie adventure. The incongruity of their mouthing war-movie palaver ("If we find him, I'm not going to be the one who forgot to bring a weapon," one pint-size Private Ryan grouses) is all the funnier, and more unsettling, for how seriously they take it.

A second viewing of *Moonrise Kingdom* is essential, if only because the movie keeps the sight gags and marginalia coming so fast you can barely register every joke in the frame. (The breathless pace of *Jules and Jim*'s early scenes seems a key reference point.) Set in a storybook mid-1960s that suggests the Nouvelle Vague, the British Invasion and Saturday-morning TV of the period stirred together in a dreamy kid's noggin, *Moonrise Kingdom* is stylized even by Anderson's standards. In the early scenes, the camera scoots and sidles from one tableau to the next, as if sets were rotating past a fixed gaze. At the same time, Anderson's longtime cinematographer Robert Yeoman shoots in Super 16, and the result has a muted, autumnal palette like a home movie on the verge of dissolving into a sepia fog. The effect it triggers is immediately wistful, recognizable if you've ever picked up a faded old book you loved as a kid.

"Salinger-esque" is the label that's sometimes plastered on Anderson's movies: Taken as a pejorative, it's calling the director a preppy dilettante preoccupied with upper-crust ennui. But while his *Moonrise Kingdom* is a realm of precocious adolescents dimly perceiving the dissatisfaction and disappointment of the adult world, there's no judgmental posturing about "phonies." Everybody in *Moonrise Kingdom* wears a costume of some kind, whether it's a grown-up's work uniform or a kid's church-play outfit. Yet it's only by trying on these wardrobes that the characters arrive at workable lives. Anderson's generosity toward his characters slips just once, in the scenes with Tilda Swinton as an officious social worker. She's one of the only figures Anderson can't work up any empathy for, and it's a measure of her failure to come alive as a character that she has no name beyond her function, "Social Services."

But that's the merest of quibbles about a movie that still leaves me grinning every time some remembered detail comes back — the clever use of Benjamin Britten's "The Young Person's Guide to the Orchestra" (and its inspired bookending over the closing credits using Alexandre Desplat's twinkling enchanted-forest score), or the brilliant throwaway gag of Sam's *Shawshank Redemption* escape from his scout tent. As a big finish, Anderson resolves his many complications with a series of epic flourishes. The tidiness that governs Anderson's frame represents our fondest hopes, always imperiled; the restoration of order, in plot as well as composition, creates a euphoric effect, like the blizzard of best-of-all-possible-worlds reconciliations that ends *Rushmore*. It's the giddy, transparent contrivance of a Shakespearean comedy — the benediction of a creator who wants to send his characters home as happy as his audience. If that was Wes Anderson's intent with *Moonrise Kingdom*, score one for solid planning. (*Nashville Scene*, June 28, 2012)

Mister Lonely
Dir. Harmony Korine
2008, NR, 112 min.

Lonely Are the Brave

A man in a Michael Jackson outfit — red shirt, black jeans, white face mask — rides hunched over the tiny frame of a clown bike. Jutting out to his side, attached by a wire, is a stuffed monkey puppet with angel wings. The background is a nondescript go-cart track lined with brightly colored tires; the sky above is billowing blue haze. Time slows to a crawl as the bike circles toward the camera. All is silent, but for Bobby Vinton's bathetic croon over a featherbed of strings: "Lone-*leee* . . . I'm Mister Lone-*leeee* . . ."

A recap, for those keeping score of outré elements: Michael Jackson costume. Clown bike. Monkey puppet. The Polish Prince.

The scene should ooze flip and curdled — a forest of twee guaranteed to leave the viewer muttering about those goddamn facetious hipsters. But it doesn't. The song's majestic self-pity is undercut by the goofiness of the details, leaving only the spell of the music's dreamy abundance. The exquisite slow motion ("*I'm just a soldier* . . .") suspends the bike and its rider (". . . *a lo-hoh-nely sollllldier* . . .") in a languid extended instant, speeding (". . . *away from home* . . .") yet almost still (". . . *through no wish of my own*"). At the end of its wire, the monkey angel leaps and strains at its tether, its stubby wings feeling for the sky. The image exudes a kind of deadpan surrealist humor, sure — but also poignance, a wistfully recalled innocence, a fluky free spirit.

As a stand-alone, this three-minute shot constitutes a gorgeous short film. As the opening sequence of *Mister Lonely* — the third feature by Harmony Korine, once the reigning Man You Love to Hate of American indie cinema — it advances the plot not a frame, tells us next to nothing about the character, and (from a narrative standpoint) has no impact whatsoever on the film that follows. By the standards of a screenwriting seminar, that makes it expendable — a glorified DVD extra. And yet, as a self-contained unit, the scene offers mood, charm, the bittersweet loveliness of that floating slow motion, the striking image of man and monkey racing together toward some transcendent offscreen finish line — and not least of all, the elements of surprise and originality.

Which is to say that *Mister Lonely* — a plangent fable of faith, childhood's end and the search for artistic identity that sometimes resembles a cross between the allegorical whimsy of *King of Hearts* and the fleabag vaudeville of *The Killing of a Chinese Bookie* — succeeds at few of the things movies routinely do, even as it pulls off other things most movies never even try. The man on the cycle is Michael, a Parisian street performer living a lonesome life as a Michael Jackson impersonator; he's played by the winning Diego Luna, who brings a wide-eyed sweetness to his manchild-naïf role (and does a mean moonwalk to boot). Spotted exhorting the wheelchair-bound patients in a nursing home ("Live forever! Don't die!"), he's summoned by a Marilyn Monroe look-alike (a luminous Samantha Morton) to a commune in the Scottish Highlands "only for people like us . . . where everyone is famous, and no one ages."

What he finds is a castle populated by celebrity impersonators from all catwalks of life: a fake Pope, played by James Fox; a fake Queen Elizabeth, played by Fox's *Performance* co-star Anita Pallenberg; a fake Sammy Davis Jr., Buckwheat and the Three Stooges; even a fake paragon of presidential virtue ("I'm Abe fuckin' Lincoln!"). Their counterpoint a world away, in a parallel plot that never intersects, is a group of indistinguishable unknowns whose talent is both bizarre and singular: a Latin American convent of flying nuns, whose father-pilot is none other than Werner Herzog. "How is it possible that a nun can fly?" Herzog asks, with an admirably straight-faced delivery. "Who are we to doubt such miracles?"

That question, in its deliberate naïveté, is as much a provocation as the assaultive shtick in Korine's first feature as writer-director, 1997's *Gummo*. As a filmmaker, Korine, who made an instant sensation 13 years ago as the teenage author of the *Kids* screenplay — and earned the undying enmity of the entertainment press with his subsequent Andy Kaufman–esque mindfuck antics — combines an installation artist's eye (and patience for duration) with a Catskills comic's affection for the threadbare fringes of showbiz. Co-written with his brother Avi, *Mister Lonely* is startlingly straightforward compared to his underrated 1999 Dogme feature *Julien Donkey-Boy*, which pushed its digital graininess to severe and often beautiful effect. Like his earlier films, though, it stands or falls on the self-contained scene before you at the moment.

And it falls, often. As a metaphor for artistic development, a celebrity impersonator who must ditch his costume and go his own way is a perilously maudlin conceit, especially if you read him as the director's stand-in. (Then again, he's balanced by the movie's other directorial figure, a Hitler-like Charlie Chaplin played by a pathetically brutish Denis Lavant.) Given his prankster rep, Korine's biggest challenge to an already skeptical audience is the movie's sleeve-hearted sincerity — never more flabbergasting than when a heartwarming Iris DeMent country ballad is warbled by a chorus of eggs.

But letting a movie keep its intimations of chaos — letting a scene meander in search of a tone, letting an image last beyond its expected end, repeating scenes or business as if they were incantations, allowing digressions for their own sake — sometimes yields moments of surprise and wonder that might otherwise hit the cutting-room floor. The movie's opening shot, for example, or *Gummo*'s magical little scene of kids smooching in a rainswept above-ground pool — this unmoored imagery has a lingering plaintiveness not even its maker may be able to explain. Movies tell the same stories over and over, but I know of only one that evokes mourned innocence in just a three-minute shot of a clown bike. Harmony Korine may be finding his gift as the ringmaster of these barbed, indelible images. But as the nuns' haunting finale shows, embracing your talent is no guarantee of a happy ending. (*Nashville Scene*, May 15, 2008)

That Obscure Object 8

n American movie theaters, the onscreen depiction of sex "remains such a taboo that most viewers sit stock still," Jim writes, "afraid of betraying any show of emotion that might be read by a neighbor." This stands in stark contrast to the cathartic violence we have come to accept and sometimes cheer. Sex is only one aspect of desire — and arguably, violence is another — and it gets tangled up with all sorts of competing forces. This chapter explores desire — thwarted, hidden, weaponized, released.

In his customary way, Jim criticizes timidity in American films by praising the frankness he finds elsewhere. He chides the "smirky evasions" of major-studio films, but only to lift up the Norwegian import *Turn Me On, Dammit!* for its directness and, importantly, its centering of female agency around sex. Similarly, in reviewing the Chilean romance *Gloria*, Jim finds that in describing what makes it so refreshing, "it's almost easier to describe what it doesn't do." Namely, it doesn't use a middle-aged woman's body, or her sexuality, as a punchline.

From the playful to the pained, these films delve into human passion and its consequences, intended and otherwise, from an array of perspectives. From the mute, repressed Ada of *The Piano* to the bemused pin-up model Bettie Page, these characters find they are moved, often against their better judgment, by their desires, and they simply cannot be still.

● ● ● ● ● ● ● ● ● ●

Turn Me On, Dammit!
Dir. Jannicke Systad Jacobsen
2011, NR, 76 min.

Sex and the Single Girl

I love that for the past month, the hot cinematic topic in Tuscaloosa, Ala., has not been a superhero movie, a 3-D blockbuster or even a major-studio release, but a teenage sex comedy from Norway that hardly anybody in the heartland has even heard of. Thank whoever decided to yank a screening of *Turn Me On, Dammit!* from the Bama Theatre after complaints from local clergy, then restore it after equally intense public outcry.

But it's easy to see why pastors got hot under their collars, and other folks too. If all you're used to seeing are the smirky evasions of major-studio movies — yeah, that includes you, *Magic Mike*, penis pump and all — the short, bittersweet *Turn Me On, Dammit!* is a shockingly forthright blast of thwarted hormones, right from the opening sequence of 18-year-old lead Helene Bergsholm frantically trying to get off to a phone-sex worker's chipper spiel.

In fact, you can pretty much count the reasons Jannicke Systad Jacobsen's first fiction feature would never get made as-is in America: Teenage girls do all the talking about sex, and their concerns are foremost; they're not punished for their curiosity or manipulated by plotting into some melodramatic crisis; they don't all look like supermodels in training. (Sorry, pervs — nudity is in short, if strategic, supply.) But longtime documentarian Jacobsen evokes the desperate longing and confusion of adolescent sexuality so vividly — and so amusingly — guys are just as likely to sympathize.

The inciting incident is smartly scaled, too awkward to be threatening yet too invasive to be shrugged off: During a break in a party, gangly Artur (Matias Myren) pokes Bergstrom's Alma with his boner then won't own up to it, setting off a chain reaction that not only leaves her a school outcast but strands her with the nickname "Dick-Alma." This does nothing to help Alma calm her raging hormones, which seek outlets in fantasy interludes involving Artur, her best friend's vengeful sister, even her scruffy convenience-store boss.

Yet at every point where an American movie would deliver Alma a smackdown — you'll brace for the worst when the girl hitchhikes a ride with a trucker to Oslo — director Jacobsen resists the urge for afterschool-special moralizing. At the same time, the movie isn't blithe: Alma's choices carry danger that keeps us on edge even when things turn out well.

But Alma is a great character, tough, resourceful and funny, and first-time actor Bergsholm projects an active, restless mind as well as a libido. She carries the movie with a winning combination of resilience, unaffected sexiness and gawky comic timing. If older teens get to see the unrated *Turn Me On, Dammit!*, whether here at the Belcourt or in Tuscaloosa, they'll learn the most helpful thing to keep in mind during years of teenage frustration: They pass. (*Nashville Scene*, July 19, 2012)

● ● ● ● ● ● ● ● ●

Afterglow
Dir. Alan Rudolph
1997, R, 119 min.

Screen Kiss

When you look at an abstract painting and you see a human figure recast in an alarmingly unfamiliar way, do you ever imagine how our world must look to the subject on the canvas? It couldn't look any more stylized than the world in Alan Rudolph's crazily romantic movies, which avoid realism the way a vampire dodges sunlight. In jazzy fantasias like *Choose Me* and *Love at Large*, Rudolph's characters float through unnamed cities in a haze of torch songs and chance encounters and penny-dreadful regrets; at night a neon moon bathes their glistening streets. His films are so totally immersed in artifice that they go beyond a movie nut's dreams. They're more like a pulpy movie character's fantasy of what it's like to be human.

Afterglow, Rudolph's 15th movie, is a characteristic grab-bag of romantic obsessions, parallel stories, cinematic quirks, and plot twists that would seem ludicrous if the writer-director and his cast didn't give in to them so fully. In one story, a young stockbroker (Jonny Lee Miller, *Trainspotting*'s Sick Boy) sequesters his love-starved wife (Lara Flynn Boyle) in a customized apartment that's a Jacques Tati nightmare of modernity. Across town, a former actress, Phyllis (Julie Christie), compulsively watches her old B movies on TV — even as her husband, an amorous plumber played by Nick Nolte, tends to an ever-expanding clientele of lonely housewives.

That the plumber's name is Lucky Mann should be enough to tell you that Alan Rudolph has a streak of whimsy wider than Moon River. And it widens as *Afterglow* progresses: Lucky starts romancing the stockbroker's wife, and Phyl retaliates by taking up with a younger man — who turns out to be the stockbroker, natch. Just when you're losing patience with the musical-comedy plotting, however, the sad history of Lucky and Phyl's marriage comes to light, and their odd behavior suddenly takes on tragic significance. At that point, Rudolph's eccentric vision comes into focus, and his sleight-of-hand switching of farcical romance and enigmatic drama starts to work its magic.

As Phyl, Julie Christie is uncommonly broad; you can't tell where the character's overacting ends and hers begins, and her Best Actress nomination seems more like a reward for career longevity, the Oscars being something of a televised yearly tontine. But what a tender, multifaceted performance Nick Nolte gives as Lucky, the kind of irresistible rogue who melts women's resolve without even trying. Watch the scene in which Lucky unburdens his past, and you'll see Nolte segue from boyish charm to haggard sorrow in a single, subtly deepening scowl. Miller's cocky stockbroker is the least interesting of the four principals — even when his brogue surfaces at awkward moments ("moon-tain" for mountain) — but Lara Flynn Boyle is unexpectedly affecting in a role that requires near-instantaneous shifts of mood.

Afterglow was produced by Robert Altman, Rudolph's early mentor and career-long supporter, and there's more than a trace of Altman in the ready-for-anything tone, the fluid pacing and the wandering camera setups. (Except when Rudolph's camera wanders, it has an annoying tendency to zero in on the speaker, the way a shampoo commercial always finds the perfect head of hair in a crowd.) But Rudolph's movie-drunk romanticism is his own. The ending of *Afterglow* is about as corny as movies get, even without Tom Waits gargling "Somewhere" on the soundtrack. And yet you're moved by how desperately the filmmaker wishes the best for his characters. If everything they've lost can be restored in the last second of screen time, Alan Rudolph will do it, because that's something only the movies can do. In a dream world, it's the dreamers who make the rules. (*Nashville Scene*, March 12, 1998)

• • • • • • • • •

The Notorious Bettie Page
Dir. Mary Harron
2005, R, 91 min.

That Obscure Object of Desire

If you can tell a society by its smut, America in the 1950s couldn't have been just a Frigidaire of repressive hysteria. Hidden somewhere in the closets of Pleasantville and Peyton Place, after all, was a stack of fetish mags bearing the face and hourglass figure of Bettie Page, and all the mysteries they contain. Here was a brunette Amazon in a sea of soft and curvy blondes — an anti-Marilyn, dominant and demanding where Marilyn was compliant — who deflected the ravenous gaze of strokebook buyers with a look of defiant self-possession.

At the same time, the kinkier the scenario, be it girl-girl slap-and-tickle or a little night music for gag and rope harness, the more she looked like a giggly teen at a pajama party. By the 1980s, when Page reemerged as a pulp icon, her combination of severe bangs, growled come-hithers and strapping poses served as camp, nostalgia, an emblem of post-feminist subversion, and a fantasy figure for tops as well as bottoms. In her photos and one-reelers, she has the ingredient perhaps most crucial for obsession: an image capable of reflecting anything a viewer projects onto it.

That surface is where *The Notorious Bettie Page* dwells. Neither a mock-heroic cockeyed success story like *Ed Wood* nor a *Walk the Line*–style hagiography, Mary Harron's facile but hugely entertaining black-and-white biopic seems most interested in its subject — a studious Nashville girl who became the world's most celebrated fetish pinup — as an object. A zippy, startlingly sweet elegy for the relative innocence of postwar smut, it's also a tricky consideration of a viewer's transformative gaze — whether that viewer is a lonely bondage hound, a photographer looking to make a fast buck, or even a director aiming a camera at her unclothed star.

After an amusing waterfront-noir opening, a police sting staged as equal parts *Reefer Madness* and *Sweet Smell of Success*, the screenplay by Harron and her *American Psycho* collaborator Guinevere Turner begins in fairly conventional lives-of-the-famous terms. Framed by Sen. Estes Kefauver's porn inquests in 1955, to which Page was summoned but never testified, the movie briskly sketches her religious roots and unhappy adolescence in Nashville, a bad early marriage and a horrific encounter with some backwoods predators. To Harron's credit, these incidents don't come across as explanations or cheap psychology: There's no "A-ha!" moment that draws a line connecting Page's lousy experiences with men — or her religious background — to her career.

Instead, the movie's Bettie, played with sunny forthrightness by Gretchen Mol, passes from one eager shutterbug to another as a game if somewhat bemused subject, allowing the context to be set around her. The breeziest sections of the film involve her "notorious" bondage shoots with photographer Irving Klaw (Chris Bauer) and his mother-hen sister Paula (Lili Taylor), who provide taboo specialty material to discerning patrons. If Bettie and other impoverished girls can pay the rent by playing dress-up, paddling each other in pantomime before collapsing in a fit of laughter, who's getting hurt?

Nobody, the movie argues — not the customers, whose deviant tastes look quaint compared to the Caligulan excesses of the Internet, nor the women, who take the sting out of the violent fantasy scenarios by participating joyfully, just as leading ladies like Erica Gavin and Tura Satana would redeem Russ Meyer's most lurid misogynist constructs by seizing their power. Harron and cinematographer Mott Hupfel — whose work here is never less than gorgeous — break the monochromatic visual scheme for blazing color re-creations of 1950s men's-mag covers, as if the liberation they offered from the imposed moral standards of the time radiated like sunlight.

Ironically, in the role of a woman who survives in the public eye as a fascinating question mark, Gretchen Mol makes a bigger impression than she ever has onscreen before. Few things are as hard for an actress to pull off as unself-conscious nudity; if Mol ever let on that she were abashed by Harron's camera or simply showing off, the role would be a stunt. But she plays Page not as a sex bomb but as a wholesome downhome kid who saw no reason to believe she was doing something wrong by undressing or posing with a whip. In one of the movie's best scenes, Bettie strips nude for an acting student in a park, and something about the casual, unguarded way Mol slips out of her clothes and basks in the light removes any hint of prurience from the moment. She disarms the camera.

The story doesn't have a very happy ending. Page's modeling career in New York lasted only seven years; there are stories that her later years involved religious obsession, one violent incident and a subsequent stay in a mental institution. Harron stops the movie before it enters this phase: Her Bettie acknowledges her past, admits no shame, then keeps the rest to herself. The writer-director gives the audience no reason to think they've seen the real Bettie Page, just a lot of dazzling surfaces.

That seems fair, even if it renders *The Notorious Bettie Page* somewhat unsatisfying. An *L.A. Times* profile described the now 82-year-old Page as finally enjoying the fruits of her career. She signed autographs and spoke willingly, but there was one thing she would not allow the paper to have: her current photograph. Fifty years after the fact, the real Bettie Page has held on to the one thing collectors, biographers and even this diverting biopic have desired but never managed to capture — the person peeking out from behind the image. (*Nashville Scene*, May 11, 2006)

The Piano
Dir. Jane Campion
1993, R, 121 min.

Tickling the Ivories

In a year when relations between the sexes have been marked by total mis-
understanding — just look at Forklift Systems[1]— it's fitting that the most indelible screen romances of 1993 concern people who cannot talk to each other.
Whether the image is of two hands separating for the last time amidst a roar
of unspoken words in *The Remains of the Day*, or of Newland Archer in *The
Age of Innocence* turning his back forever on a life of open feeling, the message
remains the same: Men and women can no longer even communicate at the
level of basic speech — let alone reach a deeper, more sensual understanding.

At first, that list of severe, ascetic love stories would seem to include *The
Piano*, the breathtakingly accomplished new film by the New Zealand writer-
director Jane Campion. But the lush, startling romanticism of Campion's vision
couldn't be more different. Even though her characters cannot relate on any
verbal level, they are driven by the need to connect. Appropriately, the very
first image in her film is a barrier — a Victorian woman's fingers used as a
shield over her eyes — yet one that allows light to peer through.

On the soundtrack, we hear the voice of the woman, Ada, played by
Holly Hunter in one of the finest and most graceful performances in recent
films — but she informs us that it is not her speaking voice we hear but her
mind's voice: "I have not spoken since I was six years old. No one knows why,
not even me. My father says it is a dark talent and the day I take it into my
head to stop breathing will be my last." The inner voice of the mute woman
informs us that she has been married to a man she has never seen; she and her
young daughter Flora will leave their home in Scotland and join him in his
native New Zealand.

The only possession she cares about is an antique piano, from which she
coaxes music that expresses the depth of her feelings — but only in private
or with Flora. When she, Flora and the piano arrive in New Zealand, they are
met on a desolate beach by her husband, Stewart (Sam Neill), a group of Maori
tribesmen, and a local landowner named Baines (Harvey Keitel).

---

1   Harris v. Forklift Sys. (92-1168), 510 U.S. 17 (1993), *www.law.cornell.edu/supct/html/92-1168.
ZO.html.*

At that point, the characters enter a series of duplicitous secret bargains. After he hears Ada play the piano, Baines tells Stewart he will trade him 80 acres of land for the piano — a deal that thrills Stewart and infuriates Ada. Stewart insists she show Baines how to play, but the tattooed landowner isn't interested in learning. Instead, he offers Ada a shocking proposal: He will allow her to purchase her beloved piano back through a series of unusual sexual favors — one key at a time.

Theirs, like every relationship in the film, is hindered by an inability to communicate. Stewart doesn't understand Ada's sign language. Flora fibs incessantly, and none but Baines can speak the language of the Maori, the people closest to the land, though he can neither read, write, nor translate sign language. Only Flora and Ada can speak directly through signing. But when Baines hears Ada play the piano, he senses that they share a passion they cannot express. As their "lessons" become more physical, sex becomes the language they alone share — displacing Ada's reliance on Flora, who betrays her to Stewart out of a child's resentment and confusion. When Ada learns to communicate her developing feelings toward Baines through her body, she loses her dependence upon the piano, which represents the burden of her dormant emotions. In the stunning finale, the piano literally becomes a millstone around her feet.

The awakening of Ada and Baines gives *The Piano* an erotic charge more powerful than any movie in recent memory; not since *Last Tango in Paris* has a movie used sex as eloquently. Where the year's other period romances involve people who gradually dwindle under the weight of their inexpressible desires, Campion's characters blossom like carnivorous plants under the influence of flesh. The director stresses the power of touch, one of the many senses Ada has hoarded to herself since childhood. When Ada discovers the feeling of giving and receiving caresses, she's addicted; once her Eve has tasted the apple, she craves an entire orchard. In her sleep, she presses against Flora in a lustful daze; in a remarkable scene that will be discussed for years, she overwhelms the repressed whimpering Stewart with the intimacy he both wishes and fears. (It's a welcome shock to see a man for once lie back and think of England.)

Moreover, the sex scenes between Ada and Baines are bracingly adult, possessed of a tenderness and radiance absent from American movies. I always think of the ridiculous sex scene in *Indecent Proposal*, where the entwined Demi Moore and Woody Harrelson are edited into disconnected snippets of naughty parts; Campion instead stays at a distance that allows us to see the characters' entire bodies. How better to show Ada awakening to the sensation of being stretched out, naked and vulnerable, alongside someone equally naked and vulnerable, in a position of mutual trust? Campion is that rare commodity, a contemporary filmmaker who sees sex as a liberating influence rather than sensual enslavement. Her film is the story of a man and woman who use physical intimacy as a bridge to emotional understanding instead of an obstacle.

In the wrong hands, this material could have come across like a parody of D. H. Lawrence at his wheeziest, especially the parallels between Stewart and Baines and the subtext of sex as a return to nature. (If you want a quick jolt of horror, just imagine what Ken Russell would have done with this story.) But there's something raw and unaffected about Campion's approach that strips the story of any pretentions. The beautifully structured script may carry echoes of literary sources as diverse as Scheherazade and Emily Brontë, but the screenwriter-director has a rude, irrepressible wit and a voluptuous sensibility that give the film immediacy. Working with the superb cinematographer Stuart Dryburgh, Campion frames the story in the elemental imagery of Gothic romances — mud, water, rainstorms — while avoiding the bodice-busting excesses of historical fiction. Her images encompass death and rebirth, blood and flesh, demons and angels — Ada, the fallen angel, is framed by a black halo of a bonnet, while Flora wears a costume of snow-white angel's wings.

The movie's most stunning visual moments place the characters in the midst of natural settings that signify their relationships. Baines lives in a lush, verdant forest, while Stewart's house is surrounded by ankle-deep mud; in the movie's most horrifying image, the bloodied Ada sinks into the mud like a wounded animal, her hoop skirt puffing with air. (Here, as elsewhere, Michael Nyman's uncharacteristically melodic and understated score works wonders.) When Stewart, overcome with longing, tries to force himself on Ada, a thicket of tangled vines ensnares them like a spider's web. The movie abounds in ravishing images, in every sense of the word: the nude Baines wiping the piano with his shirt in reverie; a glimpse of flesh through a hole in Ada's stocking that transfixes Baines; Stewart witnessing his wife's joyous infidelity in rapt agony while a dog roughly licks his hand.

At the same time, each image, each scene carries us into rougher emotional waters than American movies ever dare. The complex relationships among the four main characters are consistently fascinating, particularly the one between Ada and Flora, who functions initially as her mother's mirror image but grows more willful — and vengeful — as Baines captures Ada's affection. Yet even at their most callous and cruel, the characters remain painfully human. Even after Stewart has exacted a gruesome, ironic revenge upon Ada in the movie's scarifying climax, Campion's pitiless compassion for her characters grants them each absolution.

Even if Jane Campion's obvious talent didn't mark her as an outstanding filmmaker, though, I'd say the film's casting alone would. The casting of the three leads is more than a masterstroke: It forces you to rethink these actors' abilities entirely. Harvey Keitel, who hasn't been given a remotely tender moment onscreen since *Mean Streets*, makes a strong, sensitive romantic hero, giving Baines the power and sensual nobility of a lion. Sam Neill, a handsome leading man a less perceptive director might have cast as Baines, expresses Stewart's thwarted desires so perfectly that he makes us care for the character even at his most violent and vindictive.

The most astounding revelation is the performance of Holly Hunter in a role that requires absolute silence for the entire length of *The Piano*. Hunter, a marvelous actress who has been given mostly pixilated comic characters to play, demonstrates a range here she has never been permitted before on film. She isn't afraid to emphasize a bird-like sharpness in her features for intense effect, because the grace and fluidity of her signing and playing reveal the sexuality to which Baines responds. And her gaze is bewitching. Near the film's end, Stewart makes a clumsy attempt to mount his unconscious wife; he looks up only to stare directly into her fully opened eyes. They signify horror, and compassion and, for the first time in their relationship, understanding. The camera settles right in front of her face, allowing the intensity of that stare to bore right through us. (*Nashville Scene*, Dec. 9, 1993)

● ● ● ● ● ● ● ● ● ●

Gloria
Dir. Sebastián Lelio
2013, R, 110 min.

Gloria in the Highest

To get at what's refreshing about *Gloria*, a funny, sexy and satisfying character study that's one of 2014's first arthouse sleepers, it's almost easier to describe what it doesn't do. It features a middle-aged woman as its protagonist, but it doesn't make her body and libido into punchlines. It has the basic premise of a sitcom — woman finds seemingly perfect lover, only to compete with the demands of his ex and grown kids — but doesn't treat the complications in dopey sitcom ways. That said, when a movie can set up a paintball-revenge scenario that results in anything other than forehead smacking, you're watching something special.

From the opening scene of its heroine, a divorced office worker and mother of grown children, mustering her nerve and scanning the slim pickings on a Santiago dance floor, we're not just watching a movie about someone we've known: We're watching a movie about someone we've *been*. She's played by veteran Chilean actor Paulina García, in the kind of performance routinely called fearless — "fearless," as Mike D'Angelo once pointed out, being critic-speak for "gets naked." But García deserves it, for inhabiting the role so fully without distancing.

On the dance floor, Gloria catches the eye of a divorced naval officer named Rodolfo (Sergio Hernández), whose occupation seems less a nod to the Pinochet years than to his exaggerated sense of duty — particularly to his adult daughters and ex-wife. Hot sex leads to warm companionship and what looks like a future. But to Gloria, who enjoys cooler relations with her own ex and grown children, the constant ringing of his cellphone starts to sound like a wake-up call: a sign he's only wedged another item onto his to-do list.

At a time when Lena Dunham can't make a move without touching off a referendum on her looks and likability, this crowd-pleasing Chilean comedy-drama — directed by Sebastián Lelio (*The Sacred Family*) from a sharp script he wrote with Gonzalo Maza — seems almost revolutionary in its matter-of-factness about its leads' aging bodies and immutable hang-ups. (Here's a glimpse of taboo male vanity you'll never see in a contemporary American movie: horny Gloria hungrily ripping off Rodolfo's girdle.) These are characters with experiences and complicated histories that can't be entirely explained away, and we can sympathize to an extent with everyone in Lelio's unusually intimate 'Scope frame — so much so that early audiences have taken sides whether Rodolfo really needs to "grow a pair," as Gloria seethes, or Gloria is too needy, neurotic and desperate to see his worth.

Both may be true. But so is the emotional immediacy of García's performance, whether she's eyeing a neighbor's hideous hairless cat with heavy-lidded disdain, undoing a blouse with cobra-stare confidence or trudging back to a hotel in a dejected shame-walk. As a send-off, director Lelio welcomes her back onto the dance floor, bruised but hopeful, for the jubilant pop pealing of Umberto Tozzi's original "Gloria" (the one Laura Branigan made famous in the U.S.). Your spirits can't help but lift hearing it. García makes us believe it was written for her. (*Nashville Scene*, Feb. 6, 2014)

● ● ● ● ● ● ● ● ● ●

Eyes Wide Shut
Dir. Stanley Kubrick
1999, R, 159 min.

Dr. Strangelove

There are great directors we can imagine dabbling successfully in hardcore porn. Hitchcock? Maybe, although the sickening mix of sadism, nudity and voyeurism in *Frenzy* doesn't exactly portend raincoat weather. Buñuel? We can only guess how he might've needled his audience's squeamishness about privacy and body functions, as in *The Phantom of Liberty*'s classic gag about diners excusing themselves from the bathroom to eat. But Stanley Kubrick? Apart from a coy lovers' game in *Barry Lyndon*, the most erotic scenes he'd shot in the past 35 years were in *2001: A Space Odyssey* and *Dr. Strangelove* — and as I recall, both involved docking aircraft.

That's not to say his films avoided sex and nudity, although you could be forgiven, after the chilling rapes of *A Clockwork Orange* and the peekaboo perversions of *The Shining*, for wishing they had. In these films grotesque sex was another manifestation of unchecked power and inhumanity, two of the director's great fascinations. But their coldness added to the raps Kubrick had taken ever since *2001*: that he had become a hermit and a heartless technician — a guy who could manipulate lenses, light and angles with mathematical precision, while brutalizing his actors with endless takes and his characters with merciless cruelty.

So when word came that *Eyes Wide Shut*, Kubrick's first movie in 12 years — and the one that would prove to be his last — was an erotic thriller of much-hyped explicitness, the notion made viewers a lot queasier than, say, the idea of Joel Schumacher doing snuff in *8mm*. On that count, we now know that no one should worry — to please the vigilant penis-snippers at the MPAA ratings board, the director digitally altered the movie's roughest scene to avoid an NC-17. (The hope persists that Kubrick, a brilliant marketer of his own movies, conceived the entire flap to score one posthumous PR coup.) The good news is that *Eyes Wide Shut* is a triumph not of explicitness but of intimacy, a gorgeous, human and fascinatingly flawed chamber piece in a career filled with symphonic works.

Not that you'd have known it from the unholy unions in films like *Lolita* and *The Killing*, but Kubrick has been remembered in recent tributes as a devoted family man and husband. After seeing *Eyes Wide Shut*, you can believe it: It's the fever dream of a man secure in home and hearth, for whom temptations are far away and vividly imagined. The movie is driven by something as simple as a husband's hitherto untested relationship with his wife — which turns out to be as dangerous, vast and ultimately unknowable as the universe of *2001*.

The movie opens with Tom Cruise and Nicole Kidman as Bill and Alice Harford, an affluent Manhattan doctor and his former-art-gallery-owner wife. They assume evening wear — costumes are important — for a gala at the home of one of Bill's patients, Ziegler (Sydney Pollack); within moments of arrival, they're whisked apart. Downing glasses of champagne, Alice winds up whirling around the dance floor with an insistently seductive Hungarian (Sky Dumont), who taunts her commitment to her husband. Her husband, meanwhile, faces temptation in the next room from two girls who want to show him "the end of the rainbow." By chance, an emergency involving Ziegler draws Bill away, leaving open whether he really planned to pursue the pot of gold.

That's what Alice wants to know. Stoned, she asks Bill that night at home whether he wanted to sleep with the girls. He glibly tells her he didn't because he's married; she takes this to mean he was honoring their contract, not acting out of love — the same reason he thinks she'd never be unfaithful. In a rage, she tells him that during a family vacation, a chance encounter once filled her with a passion that almost made her throw away her daughter, her husband and her future.

Kidman is astonishing in this long, wounding take, but it's here that the casting of Cruise really pays off. Cruise is a good actor, but at his worst he falls back on a cocky smirk filled with blithe entitlement. At the start of the scene, Bill pastes on this movie-star grin, and it annoys Alice as much as it does us: It sums up years of having her will and sexuality taken for granted as a possession. Like the wife in Joyce's "The Dead," who shatters her husband's illusions with a single confession of long-ago love, Alice undermines Bill's every certainty about his life and his wife in an instant. From then on, every time Cruise flashes his charisma in Bill's service, he gets slapped down.

In a trance of fear and desire — the words that kicked off Kubrick's feature-film career — Bill leaves their apartment and vanishes into a garish nightworld, a journey that leads from a jazz hangout called the Sonata Club to a secret orgy presided over by a hooded red figure. It's a test of his own fidelity and sexuality, and at every turn he gets to find out what it's like to be defined purely in terms of sex: by a grieving client (Marie Richardson), by street punks, even by a smitten bellhop (a wonderful cameo by Alan Cumming). In the course of the movie, he will attempt to wear a costume, to dabble in depravity and voyeurism, and his mask will always be his undoing.

Eyes Wide Shut evokes a dream state so fully that it leaves you feeling drugged and woozy: It's fascinating to note in retrospect how few steps Kubrick uses to lure us from mundane domesticity into perversity. Kubrick does this by inverting the privacy of the dream world, the landscape of fantasy and fear that manifests itself in your sleep. That world is the one Bill Harford walks through: It abides by the same leaps in logic and location. One sequence alone, in which Bill's steps are dogged by a man on an otherwise deserted city block, may be the most perfect representation of dream logic I've ever seen onscreen. The elements don't add up in the cold light of day without a load of backstory (who's the guy? what's he doing?), but Kubrick uses Bill's (and our) dread and curiosity as the glue that holds them together.

The movie doesn't proceed so much by plot as by motifs. Kubrick and his cameraman Larry Smith use color in ways that are almost musical. Splashes of lurid red and cold blue recur like the passages of Shostakovich and Ligeti on the soundtrack. Red throughout is the color of temptation; it marks every tantalizing threshold Bill wants to trespass — a hooker's door, the Sonata Club's awning, the plasma-like light inside — as signposts leading toward the climactic orgy. The Harfords' bedroom window is framed by a curtain as red and fleshy as Marilyn Monroe's lips; beyond it, the city at night gleams dark and blue.

The same blue light appears behind Alice when she starts to make her confession. This pale light, which illuminates the stage of the Sonata Club, is like an infection: As Bill faces each dark new truth, the light seeps from room to room until even their daughter's room is flooded — even their bedroom. Yet the red and blue are inextricable: They're in damn near every shot, even linked in the logo for the Rainbow Costumes shop where he picks up his outfit for the orgy. Which echoes the two girls' come-on to Bill at the party: Don't you want to know what's at the end of the rainbow?

He thinks he does, and so do we. Both times I've seen *Eyes Wide Shut*, the audiences throughout are dead silent: You'll recognize the uncomfortable quiet if you've ever seen an intense sex scene at a movie theater. Violence in film pushes our buttons and allows instant catharsis, but it's easy for viewers to whoop and holler at the release because acts of violence are acknowledged openly. Sex, however, remains such a taboo that most viewers sit stock still, afraid of betraying any show of emotion that might be read by a neighbor. Yet that's the reason everyone has come to see the movie — to see their fantasies projected. Like Bill, we want to experience some vicarious smut.

And so Kubrick sends Bill wandering through the orgy's parade of artfully arranged fornicators, each grinding away in plain view for our — oops! his — enjoyment. According to *Full Metal Jacket* collaborator Michael Herr in the current *Vanity Fair*, Kubrick had planned to film *Eyes Wide Shut* in 1980 as a comedy with Steve Martin. Herr pretty much scratches his head on this point, but it's in this scene that Kubrick's conception comes closest to black comedy, or the comedy of embarrassment and thwarted lust that flowered in his *Lolita*. Bill has come for titillation; what he gets instead looks like his every worst imagining of his wife's infidelity: positions 1 through 69, staged for an audience of gawkers. (I'm not sure the scene wouldn't have been better played more for laughs — the elaborate sex acts, which look like a cross between Victorian porn and Cirque du Soleil, are pretty silly, and the robed tribunal is downright hysterical, in every sense.) Bill's humiliation is complete when he arrives home to find Alice cackling in her sleep — at the notion she's cuckolding him before hundreds of onlookers.

The movie falters most near the end, when Kubrick and co-scripter Frederic Raphael attempt to impose too literal an explanation for the murky chain of events at the movie's center. There's an endless confrontation between Cruise and Pollack that resembles nothing so much as the psychiatrist's deadly dumping of exposition at the end of *Psycho*. Its sole redeeming factor is Pollack's dead-on portrayal of a wealthy, worldly Mephistopheles — an amiably corrupt publican who may represent why Kubrick turned his back on New York and L.A. (Harvey Keitel was originally given the role; the casting of Hollywood old-pro Pollack gives it a satirical kick that wouldn't have been there otherwise.) Here, Kubrick's rhythms become narcoleptic instead of somnambulant, and you long for a stray boom mike to disrupt his oppressively stunning compositions.

The closing scene, however, in which Bill and Alice must decide whether to start from ground zero — certain of nothing after nine years of marriage — catches Kubrick in a moment of unambiguous tenderness. How intriguing that a director noted for his coldness, his fascination with technology, and his supposed impersonality should end his career with a shot of a man and a woman in a toy store — surrounded by mechanical gadgets and gizmos, yet unable to focus on anything but each other. It's a farewell gift from a filmmaker who looked at the best and worst man had to offer, and never blinked. (*Nashville Scene*, July 22, 1999)

●●●●●●●●●●
Carol
Dir. Todd Haynes
2015, R, 118 min.

Carol of the Belles

The other night I decided to rewatch my two favorite movies this year — two movies that couldn't be more different, except for the love I feel for them. *Mad Max: Fury Road* is all maximalist gestures, painted in a palette of rust, dust, fireballs and speed — a motorpsycho hellscape out of Springsteen's "Born to Run," monster drums and electric guitar included. Yet beholding the mastery, kinetic panache and, yeah, beauty that George Miller marshals from that chaos is like watching a conductor coax Mahler from an orchestra of air-raid sirens.

Carol is quiet where *Fury Road* is loud, restrained where *Fury Road* is orgiastic, anchored in a recent past of suburban comfort where *Fury Road* cruises a dystopian futuristic desert. What the two movies share — besides a long road journey, and starting by following a male character who yields to a female protagonist — is uncommon command of the medium. Control isn't just the formal rigor that *Carol* exhibits from the very first scene: It's the stifling exactitude required of its two main characters, whose every public utterance and gesture must be delivered in code.

The movie establishes that as soon as a man walks into a 1950s hotel restaurant and glibly shouts to a young woman across the room. It will take roughly another hour and a half to learn why the woman and her dining companion react to his arrival with expressions a more attentive man might read as alarm. The women part, not in any way the man might notice; only we register the extra beat the elegant older woman leaves her hand on her tablemate's shoulder, and the slight nod of the head that acknowledges it.

From there *Carol* goes back in time, retracing the steps that led shopgirl Therese (Rooney Mara) and upper-crust wife and mother Carol Aird (Cate Blanchett) to lock eyes across a department-store display of perfect dolls and a toy-train utopia. It's as immaculate as the home Carol shares with her husband Harge (Kyle Chandler, a walking bruise of wounded masculine pride) and preteen daughter; yet Carol's every interaction with him seethes with desperation and longing for escape. The rest of the movie is what happens when Carol falls in love with Therese and tries to get away with her, only to learn it isn't enough just to stay secret in public.

The director, Todd Haynes, made the Julianne Moore melodrama *Far From*

Heaven, a fascinating experiment that played like a semiotician's painstaking re-creation of Douglas Sirk's brazen Technicolor weepies. It was an affecting movie, but every element of Sirk's style, from the saturated colors to the use of mirrors, still left a vapor trail of quotation-marked pastiche. Not *Carol*. Maybe his *Mildred Pierce* HBO miniseries served as practice, but Haynes' measurement of every hand gesture, every isolating frame within the frame, every glance or line charged with hidden meaning, has a precision that obliterates air quotes. *Far From Heaven's* interracial romance seemed itself something of a code as it pushed a subplot about Dennis Quaid's closeted husband off to the sides; *Carol*, adapted from an initially pseudonymous 1952 novel by the late Patricia Highsmith, is painfully direct about the stakes facing its lesbian heroines, who stand to lose children and homes if they drop their cover in a restaurant — or in their own bedroom.

The tension is keenly felt in Blanchett's exquisitely modulated performance. Pressed to maintain a public façade, Carol is different people as the occasion demands: a doting mom, a coolly poised wife at social functions, a huskily voiced seducer with Therese. The law and social strictures demand that these be exclusive, with Carol's friend and former lover Abby (Sarah Paulson, making explicit what was implicit in the true-blue Eve Arden gal-pal role) standing as proof of what comes to those who step outside. As the less experienced Therese, Mara has an open face that seems to be processing several contradictory things simultaneously — the opposite of Carol, who must be one thing at a time.

The lush atmosphere Haynes creates around them with his excellent cinematographer, Ed Lachman, isn't as sterile as the germophobic bubble world of his 1995 classic *Safe*, but it's very nearly as tense. The screenwriter, Phyllis Nagy, a filmmaker and friend of Highsmith's who shepherded the project for more than two decades and through myriad production setbacks, supplies a taut script that occasionally echoes *Brief Encounter*, even *Lolita*. It's smart enough to hand the hat-tipping statement to a minor character — the difference between what people say in movies and what they really feel — then to play it almost off-handedly. Sharper still (and masterfully delivered by Blanchett) is the gulf of heartbreak between Carol's two variations of her two-word refrain: "That's that."

Given the times and the situation, *Carol* seems headed for the requisite misery that marked (and marred) fiction about gay characters for decades. But gay readers loved Highsmith's novel back in the day because it ultimately had no patience for that well-of-loneliness jive, and neither does Haynes' film. *Carol* may begin in public with an interrogative, but it ends in public with a declarative all the more dramatic for not being voiced, conveyed with all the passion the minor chords in Carter Burwell's gloriously tormented score can muster. And that's another difference between my two favorite movies this year. *Mad Max: Fury Road* concludes with the promise of further exploits in its obsessively detailed wasteland — but it's *Carol* that ends with the advent of a whole new world. (*Nashville Scene*, Dec. 23, 2015)

A Boot the Size of Nebraska 9

One of Jim's many film-referencing T-shirts bore the immortal Roddy Piper quip from the 1988 sci-fi send-up *They Live*: "I have come here to chew bubblegum and kick ass . . . and I'm all out of bubblegum." Jim was very much a lover, not a fighter, so to see him saunter out of his office with a big grin on his face bearing this statement generated a kind of comic cognitive dissonance that was one of his hallmarks. There was never a sweeter, more unassuming guy who delighted so unabashedly in cartoon violence like the alien-busting shotgun rampage that follows the aforementioned bubblegum shortage. But more than anything, Jim loved the blast radius that only a movie gleefully caught up in its own delusions of grandeur can produce.

This chapter is dedicated to films in which even the most egregious flaws can be forgiven in the name of good plain *fun*. It begins with a review of *Playtime*, in which Jim revisits a recurring motif of his writing: likening the experience of a film to being a child playing with an erector set, rapt by the intricately interconnected bits that become a microcosm of life. It ends with the comedy *Hot Fuzz*, a movie that lovingly apes every cliché of police flicks — what Jim ingeniously refers to as "cop-socky" — to the point of sublime absurdity. Along the way, the sleaze-art inventions of *Pulp Fiction* ride shotgun with the social satire of *Serial Mom*, the depraved hijinks of *Jackass*, and the lush absurdity of *The Fifth Element*. (There's that toy skyline again.)

In his review of the Jackie Chan vehicle *Rumble in the Bronx*, Jim calls movies "both populist entertainment and conduits for unique, even unhinged, personal visions." Jim enjoyed both extremes. Playful choreography, wry satire, comedic athleticism, disgusting pranks, outlandish violence — all get equal consideration. Here, plot is a minor concern, if it's a concern at all — which is not to say that such things don't matter, just that they matter a lot less if a movie kicks enough ass to make you forget its shortcomings.

● ● ● ● ● ● ● ● ● ●

Playtime
Dir. Jacques Tati
1967, NR, 126 min.

City of Delights

If the movies are the best toy train set a kid ever had, as Orson Welles once said, *Playtime* may be the greatest toy railroad yard ever built. An impish, often wordless comedy of modernism run amok, Jacques Tati's 1967 film pulls off an almost impossible feat, maintaining magical lightness on an enormous scale. It reminds me of an erector set I had as a kid, one that came with snap-on plastic windows. I would peer through the exposed girders and dream of whole cities constructed of these see-through skyscrapers.

Tati actually built one. *Playtime* takes place in a gleaming, glass-case Paris *moderne* constructed to its maker's design, on a set so huge it functioned as a miniature city. As Kent Jones notes in the liner notes to Criterion's DVD edition, this "Tativille" had its own power plant and access roads and two glass-framed buildings, one with its own working escalator. At the time, Tati was a comic performer and filmmaker whose popularity rivaled Charlie Chaplin's. He essentially mortgaged his future on the movie — to get every giant window, endless hallway and congested street just so.

Typically, money smothers comedy faster than Ann Coulter kills an erection. Today, watching *Playtime* — which bankrupted Tati and curtailed his career — what's remarkable is how right the director was about the necessity of those details. Something about the exact positioning of a pane of glass, about a skyline's cartoon angles, about pointing all the cars in a parking lot one way, makes you laugh even when you can't figure out why.

The movie has no plot to speak of. The closest thing it has to a central character is Tati's version of the Little Tramp, his comic persona M. Hulot, a rumpled observer with hat, pipe and long coat who lopes past the world's absurdities in a stiff-legged gait, like a lock-kneed stork falling forward. And Hulot is not the focus here, as he was in Tati's international hit *M. Hulot's Holiday*. He's one among literally hundreds of characters, all bustling around a crystal palace of chrome, cubicles and sharp angles as anonymous as a suburban mall. The characters convene at a restaurant's ill-fated opening night. This tour de force of timed-release slapstick lasts for 50 eye-goggling minutes of bad service, collapsing fixtures and mounting chaos.

In place of a plot, there is only the city and the characters' interaction with it, staged in long takes that are choreographed as intricately as a toppling-domino *Mona Lisa*. Tati's sight gags place an absurdist frame around mundane civic activities and public space. Five men moving a plate-glass window become a chorus line of bow-legged dancers, thanks to the spectators humming below; an apartment building's glass façade turns into a bank of competing TV screens. But the absurdity was always there. No matter how hard people try to wall themselves off with some kind of chilly formal dignity, behind these shiny surfaces, their goofy, disruptive humanity finds a way to bust free.

That's why *Playtime* is among the movies' most charmed and elating portrayals of city life. Living in a city, we can't help but be reminded we're connected to a larger world that extends as far as we can see — something Tati evokes by treating the back, sides and edges of the frame as a playground where something always competes for our attention. Few comedies get funnier each time around; few movies so reward multiple viewings. *Playtime* was originally conceived as an interactive work to be projected so large that the audience would be engulfed in its mayhem. In its 35 mm form, it's still a transformative vision, one that casts public space in a joyous new light. In the marvelous conclusion, the city is revealed as a giant whirling carnival, hidden in plain sight, where a traffic roundabout becomes a merry-go-round and a tilting window turns a tourist bus into a rollercoaster. Then the movie sends us outside, onto our own midway. We find, to our delight, that the ride is just beginning. (*Nashville Scene*, Oct. 28, 2004)

● ● ● ● ● ● ● ● ●

Rumble in the Bronx
Dir. Stanley Tong
1995, R, 87 min.

Brute Farce

The formula for great action filmmaking doesn't involve loud explosions, a dozen smashing cars, and a survivalist-compound's worth of ammo. It involves nothing more complicated than an ordinary person trapped in a confined space with a limited number of options. Think back on the most entertaining American action movies of the past two decades — *The Warriors*, *The Terminator*, *Die Hard*, *Speed*. Their common thread is a series of scenes in which audience surrogates — people who aren't ex–Navy SEALs or steroid-stoked supermen — must puzzle their way out of hopeless situations, using only brainpower and whatever materials are at hand.

The precedent for this formula isn't other action movies; it's the work of silent comedians Buster Keaton, Charlie Chaplin and Harold Lloyd, men of impeccable physical ability who chose to portray 98-pound weaklings. They understood the appeal of an underdog who could overcome brute force through sheer pluck, and they devised challenges as enormous as their characters were puny. They dangled from clock faces, battled prizefighters and scampered across moving locomotives. That they did it for laughs often obscured some of the most brilliant, intricate action sequences ever staged.

As the years have gone by, action heroes have bulked up in size — usually in inverse proportion to the amount of fun you get out of a *Judge Dredd* or a *Street Fighter*. By comparison, the Asian superstar Jackie Chan could be snapped like a breadstick by a Stallone or a Van Damme — which is just what he wants us to think. With his mop-top hair, infectious grin and happy-go-lucky demeanor, Chan is the rare martial-arts hero who comes across as a buddy, instead of a badass like Bruce Lee or Sonny Chiba. That friendliness, combined with peerless comic timing and athletic skill, has made him a treasure in his native China. Like Chaplin, Keaton and Lloyd, Chan wears scrawniness as a badge of honor and humility in a world obsessed with power.

Blah, blah, blah. I could go on with all the movie-geek blather about how Chan as a martial artist combines Gene Kelly's athleticism with Astaire's effortless grace, or how Chan as a director shares Keaton's uncanny grasp of how far the camera should be placed from the performer. Both are true. But all you really want to know is whether Chan's new movie, *Rumble in the Bronx*, kicks ass. And I'm here to tell you that it does — with a boot the size of Nebraska.

You want plot? Go see *The Juror*. *Rumble in the Bronx*, the amazingly prolific Chan's 38th movie in two decades, has a plot that wouldn't fill two title cards in a silent movie, but it compensates with stunts and set pieces so miraculous they're practically the reason movies were invented. Chan stars as Keung, a good-natured Chinese innocent who travels to New York for the wedding of his uncle, a market owner in the city. To Keung's chagrin, the store is located not in ritzy Manhattan but in the rugged Bronx, here portrayed as a crime-ridden junk heap ruled by hookers and hustlers. No sooner has Keung pitched in at the store than he pisses off the scary neighborhood gang, a spike-haired, ripped-knees crew that looks like Adam and the Ants after they lost their record deal.

That sets up the first big fight scene, a showdown between Keung and some scurvy gang members in the market — and from that point on *Rumble in the Bronx* delivers one exhilarating whammy after another, the trademark of Chan's Asian films. From the age of 7, Jackie Chan was educated in the notoriously strict Peking Opera Company, which instructs students in the performing (and martial) arts with Draconian rigor; he emerged at the age of 17 in the burgeoning Chinese film industry of the 1970s, working as a stuntman, stunt coordinator and sometime actor. His background makes him the rare filmmaker with the ability to conceive, control, stage and perform his own stunts. At any time, one slip could kill him — as the injuries recorded in the outtakes prove.

But Chan was also blessed with a born entertainer's lightness of spirit, and it's this buoyancy that makes *Rumble in the Bronx* so refreshing. (Although the movie was directed by Chan's frequent collaborator Stanley Tong, the outtakes show whose vision guides the film.) Chan doesn't fight to crush his opponents, the way the colliding lunkheads in Joel Silver movies do. He fights to defend the innocent, thwart the guilty, and get out of a bad situation with his hide intact. (In one scene, he tells the gang he's just clobbered that next time he hopes they can all drink tea together instead.) With the element of sadism removed, we can appreciate the flying kicks and slamming punches as sheer kinetic overload — a Roadrunner cartoon drawn in flesh.

Chan approaches his fights not as death matches but as slapstick routines. He picks locations (a dock, a warehouse, a supermarket) just to exploit every possibility in the props at hand. And the simpler the situation, the more rabbits Chan whisks from his hat. On one side of an appliance warehouse is Keung, completely outnumbered. On the other side is an army of burly goons, advancing in all directions. The hero's only hope is to use the one object at hand — a refrigerator. (You can hear the gears clicking in Buster Keaton's head already.) What follows is a marvel of comic invention, a blizzard of motion in which Keung uses a Frigidaire as a weapon, a barrier, a fortress, and finally a holding cell, swinging and slamming its compartments with unflappable precision.

And the movie keeps topping itself. By the time Keung grapples for his life aboard a runaway Hovercraft in the harbor — piloted by drug lords with machine guns, in case you thought he was wimping out — you think Chan has reached the limits of his imagination. Then the Hovercraft reaches *land*.

As usual, the material surrounding the action scenes is weak, though not unforgivable. From the beginning, the details of street life seem hilariously off: Gangs race motorbikes over parked cars, dark-suited mobsters converse in *Dragnet*-speak and police wring their hands ineffectually. And then it hits us: The filmmakers (who filmed *Rumble in the Bronx* in Vancouver for Chan's loyal Asian audience) have gotten their impression of the lawless New York streets from the same place we have — bad American cop shows and detective flicks. When the movie's black characters literally pop up rolling their eyes and spouting jive, we're seeing the warped reflection of our own pop culture. The America we've broadcast to the world is being beamed back at us — and for a moment, we don't know whether to laugh or cringe.

But there's no meanness in Chan's vision. If he uses stereotypes, it's to bull-doze past them: He reacts with surprise to his uncle's African-American fiancée, only to assess her a moment later with a you're-OK smile. (In one deft gesture, he acknowledges and defuses racial tension, both onscreen and in the theater: The largely black audience I saw the movie with stopped mimicking the Asian characters shortly afterward.) And the cop-show clichés are simply the dramatic shorthand that sets up Chan's astonishing action sequences. They carry no more weight than the awkward small talk that precedes big numbers in a musical.

I hope *Rumble in the Bronx* creates an audience for Jackie Chan's earlier movies, particularly the 1986 *Police Story*, which still contains the most dazzling stunt work I've ever seen. (Wait until you see Chan leap from the fifth floor of an indoor mall onto a strand of Christmas lights.) Nevertheless, it restores your faith in movies as both populist entertainment and conduits for unique, even unhinged, personal visions. Just don't try manhandling your freezer doors at home, or launching yourself off your roof toward your neighbor's balcony. After you've seen Jackie Chan take a four-story fall as if he were strolling in midair, I guarantee you'll be tempted. (*Nashville Scene*, Feb. 29, 1996)

● ● ● ● ● ● ● ● ● ●

Serial Mom
Dir. John Waters
1994, R, 95 min.

Silence of the Moms

Most contemporary satirists are stranded by time on a road to oblivion lined with outdated targets. In John Waters' case, however, the slipstream of time has circled back and shot straight up his polyester pants leg. *Serial Mom* is the Baltimore filth maven's ninth movie in 25 years, and it's set squarely in the fabu-lous '50s lawn-sale suburbia that he has mined with increasingly uneven results since 1981's *Polyester*. But something significant — and extremely fortunate for Waters the satirist — has happened in the years since 1990's hit-and-miss juvie send-up *Cry-Baby*: The plastic America of the Eisenhower decade has been embraced once more as an antidote to contemporary evils. Waters' fractured '50s aesthetic, once verging on harmless eccentricity, now has real topical bite — and the bite draws blood.

With America entering a period of cataclysmic division and violence in the

1990s — the Them Decade — pundits and legislators across the country have demanded a return to the values of the 1950s: a stronger work ethic, more rigorous spiritual indoctrination and the preservation of the nuclear family über alles. New '50s men like E. D. Hirsch and failed drug czar William J. Bennett expound that the permissiveness of modern society, as expressed and perpetuated by the arts, lies at the root of horrific phenomena such as serial murder: Cap one, and you've partially solved the other. The one kink in that theory, however, is a fellow by the name of Charlie Starkweather, a James Dean wannabe who practically invented serial-killer chic by leaving a bloody trail across Eisenhower's heartland. The people who look back fondly upon the social regimentation of the 1950s have forgotten the responsive chord Charlie Starkweather struck in a generation staring down double barrels of ennui and repression.

Waters hasn't. Filmed in the dinner-mint pastels of an old Rock Hudson–Doris Day farce, *Serial Mom* suggests we never left the '50s. The world still looks like *The Donna Reed Show*, appearing normal still seems to be the primary family value, and violence is still infinitely more acceptable than sex. Nevertheless, the country has gone to hell. Once unshakable social codes (no white shoes after Labor Day) and rules of polite conduct (no popping and smacking of gum) are now transgressed at will. Somebody has to draw the line — and that person turns out to be Beverly Sutphin, a suburban housewife who wants the very best for her dentist husband (Sam Waterston), lovestruck daughter (Ricki Lake) and horror-fanatic son (Matthew Lillard). When a high-school guidance counselor dares to suggest her family is anything other than completely functional, Beverly is pushed to action — which means flattening out the twerp under the tires of her station wagon. From that moment on, Beverly finds a novel way to redress society's infractions: cold-blooded murder.

Waters has said in interviews that he wanted to make a movie in which an audience would root for a serial killer, which reflects a certain naïvete on his part. Virtually every movie these days about a serial killer, from Jason to Freddy, manipulates us into cheering on the killers. His point, however, is that life, not art, sends people on murderous rampages. Beverly's son may sit rapt before a Herschell Gordon Lewis splatterfest, but Beverly is the one who skewers her daughter's thoughtless date with such gusto that she rips out his liver. The pressure of enforcing a crumbling social order drives her to her killing frenzy, which drives home Waters' main satirical thrust: Serial killing isn't cured by a societal clampdown, it's caused by one — which makes capital punishment merely a ritualized form of serial murder. But that's all right.

As an apple-cheeked pastor explains, in a dizzying bit of Buñuelian heresy that's more shocking than any of the killings, Jesus must favor capital punishment — why else didn't He pipe up on the cross?

Lest anyone fear Waters has turned left-wing scold, though, his (literally) side-splitting script butchers sacred liberal cows with equal viciousness. In the movie's warped universe, failure to recycle constitutes grounds for execution, while anti-violence advocates are portrayed as earnest simps who reverently tote biographies of Gandhi. And if Waters' take on the mass-media enshrinement of monsters as celebrities seems oddly tame, it's only because satire is redundant in the wake of the Amy Fisher and Menendez feeding frenzies. In a culture where inexplicable monstrosities such as Ed Gein and Jeffrey Dahmer are immortalized on bubblegum trading cards, even the man who had Divine eat dog feces can't win an obscenity contest.

Waters can, however, coax hilarious deadpan performances from his game cast, particularly Kathleen Turner, whose demented homemaker Beverly — a sort of June Cleaver Gacy — seems wholesome even when she's eviscerating a neighbor for eating chicken. Turner has always been a top-notch comic actress, but the outrageous material unleashes a gleefully absurd radiance she's never shown before. When Beverly finds her son entertaining his friends with the infamous tongue-ripping scene from *Blood Feast* — a moment that would cause virtually any other parent to schedule electroshock therapy — she beams like Florence Henderson discovering how to deep-fry bread in Wesson oil. She's even funnier in a courtroom showdown with Waters regular Mink Stole, who portrays the key witness to Beverly's secret sociopathology. The ensuing exchange of epithets proves once more that no one knows how to make taboo words sound sillier than Waters.

Serial Mom represents an astonishing return to form for Waters, who displays a command of technique he's rarely shown as a filmmaker. At his best, as in Beverly's systematic humiliation of a snooty prank-call victim, he can make you laugh helplessly at mankind's sheer capacity for hostility, and there's something liberating about the unfettered rudeness of his wit. John Waters is a truly democratic filmmaker. He believes we are united as a people by our ability to cringe, and part of the fun of seeing *Serial Mom* with a big audience is hearing his satirical arrows strike different people at different times. As long as America has a sore spot, whether it's vegetarian piety, our penchant for mass murder or the general collapse of our loftiest ideals, we can rest assured John Waters will be there to rub salt in our wounds. (*Nashville Scene*, April 28, 1994)

• • • • • • • • • •

Jackass: The Movie
Dir. Jeff Tremaine
2002, R, 87 min.

A Confederacy of Dunces

A few weeks ago, on NPR, a *Vanity Fair* contributor complained that reality
TV had cheapened the concept of celebrity. If an Anna Nicole Smith or an
Osbourne clan could claim public-airwave real estate simply by opening a
voyeuristic window onto their fucked-up, fame-damaged lives, then the notion
of fame no longer had any value. The epithet she used, as I recall, was "tacky."
Why poor Anna Nicole is tackier or less worthy than whatever wife-killing
upper-crust scumbag Dominick Dunne profiles this month is a question we'll
leave aside for the moment. More interesting is the commentator's underlying
assumption: that celebrity should be for the privileged few — a gate to be
policed and protected, lest some lowbrow Visigoths trample their muddy Keds
on the perfume ads.

The MTV series *Jackass* is the worst nightmare of people who consider
fame some kind of meritocracy — a bunch of rough-trade hooligans winning
public attention by humiliating themselves and each other with imbecilic,
injurious pranks. *Jackass: The Movie* is more of the same, only grosser, grislier
and grubbier, without any attempt to pretty-up its surveillance-cam video
look. Reviewers cannot conceal their contempt, either for the movie or its
audience; a typical quip says it was "made by jackasses for jackasses." But
that two-pronged attack exposes the reviewer's own prejudice: Fame is worth
nothing when the thinnest of lines separates the haves from the have-nots.
How great can media access be when all it takes is firing a bottle rocket out
your ass?

That thought must terrify the celebretainment industry, much as the
unprecedented success of the camcorder-shot *Blair Witch Project* momentarily
shook up Hollywood. There is a vast and growing audience, fed by traded
MP3s and bootleg tapes, for whom star power and studio sheen mean next
to nothing. *Jackass: The Movie* has no pretense to story, to craft, to production value. It looks like (but isn't) something anyone with a camcorder could
do, provided he were sufficiently drunk or suicidal. Its appeal, though, is a
little more complicated. Watching *Jackass*, a viewer laughs like hell at dopey
pranks — say, trampolining into a ceiling fan — while getting a vicarious taste
of total embarrassment. That's the kind of stunt stars don't do.

The typical *Jackass* setup works like this: There are spectators and participants — or, more accurately, viewers and victims. The victim is the one performing the stunt: the armor-suited sap who rides a shopping cart into a convenience-store snack display, the guy who snarfs a snow cone of his own pee. The viewers, his friends and co-conspirators, usually lie in a heap of convulsed hysteria. There is no self-congratulation in their laughter. It is the kind of open, cathartic howling that can only be triggered by watching your buddy do the stupidest goddamn thing you've ever seen. I've heard it many times.

The difference isn't just that host Johnny Knoxville and his scurvy crew — Bam Margera, Steve-O, Jason "Wee Man" Acuña, et al. — have actually elected to take a bowling ball in the nuts for our amusement. It's that their idiotic japes are so shameless, so beyond the boundaries of self-respect and social behavior, that they have an anarchic adrenaline rush. One of the funniest is a variation on a joke from the cinema's great prankster revolutionary, Luis Buñuel: A Jackass casually strolls into a plumbing store and cops a squat on a display toilet. Buñuel, in *The Phantom of Liberty*, was ridiculing the arbitrariness of what passes for acceptable behavior, but not even he would show an actor performing the function on camera.

Jackass' DIY demolition derby is the latest ripple of punk's anyone-can-do-it ethos — or more precisely, of skateboard culture, which celebrates fraternal bonding through risk, skill, foolhardiness, a high pain threshold and a casual acceptance of injury. Early skate videos often ended with *Jackass*-style pranks and outtakes, a heady combination of slapstick, documentary and actual danger. That trickled down into the work of enthusiasts as diverse as Harmony Korine and *Jackass* producer/participant Spike Jonze, whose own movies (like *Being John Malkovich*) prowl a weirdo wonderland where reality, fantasy and celebrity form a head-spinning blur.

Skateboarding, like bootleg video or Internet claim-staking, is a world where anybody can achieve underground notoriety, which will be ignored by the mainstream at its own peril. Stardom is no longer some distant, unapproachable quality, something that Andy Warhol and John Waters knew while the rest of the media lagged behind. The tools of fame will be seized, used and ground down until they no longer work — as long as there is someone who will do absolutely anything to be noticed, and someone to notice. We have met the jackass, and he is us. (*Nashville Scene*, Nov. 7, 2002)

● ● ● ● ● ● ● ● ● ●

Pulp Fiction
Dir. Quentin Tarantino
1994, R, 154 min.

Kiss Kiss Bang Bang

From the first sun-blanched shot of a dingy coffeehouse to the grungy Dick Dale surf-rock on the soundtrack, everything about *Pulp Fiction* screams trash. The movie takes place in some deliberately crappy pop-culture grave-yard of a world, a washed-out landscape littered with Fruit Brute boxes and Mamie Van Doren look-alikes. Even the title promises nothing more than lurid events and cheap thrills, both of which the movie delivers in spades.

And yet if we think of art as some ideal marriage of form, content, style and medium, no matter how brutish or seemingly unworthy the subject matter, *Pulp Fiction* qualifies as resoundingly as the novels of Jim Thompson or the grotesque paintings of Robert Williams. With this delirious, uproarious and enormously entertaining film, the phenomenally gifted young filmmaker Quentin Tarantino has staked out a genre all his own: the anti-art movie, which combines all the sleazy, prosaic elements so-called art movies avoid and transforms them into something beautiful and provocative and perilous. Even though its title and content recall the days of penny dreadfuls, *Pulp Fiction* is anything but. Photographed by Andrzej Sekula in flat, Edward Hopper–esque tones, *Pulp Fiction* is so thrillingly alert to the possibilities of moviemaking that it frequently knocks the breath out of you. Sensations and images tumble around in your head for days afterward.

Superficially, the movie is structured like a crime fiction anthology, with three distinct stories of murder, betrayal and greed. At the movie's center are two skilled hit men, Vincent (John Travolta) and Jules (Samuel L. Jackson), who are assigned to retrieve a mysterious attaché case for their boss, the men-acing crime lord Marcellus (Ving Rhames). Each successive story relates either directly or tangentially to these characters. As the movie leaps forward and backward in time, the spotlight is seized by a number of peripheral characters, including an aging boxer (Bruce Willis) forced to take a dive for Marcellus, a fixer named the Wolf (Harvey Keitel) who cleans up murder scenes, and (most memorably) the crime lord's cokehead wife Mia (Uma Thurman), who tests both Vincent's loyalty and his nerve.

While the stories have individual chapter headings, just like in magazines, Tarantino combines and recombines them in fluid and exhilarating ways. He flips events to and fro in time so that a scene assumes new dimensions with each new spin, the way a cubist painter depicts a bowl from several different points of view at once. The effect is startlingly similar: We begin to understand how these characters occupy the same space in this deceptively chaotic world. The technique may date back to Stanley Kubrick's seminal crime movie *The Killing*, but Tarantino wants to show us more than the workings of a heist — he wants to create an entire pulp-fiction universe on film, one where everyone from Jules and Vincent to a surly waiter dressed as Buddy Holly (the wonderful Steve Buscemi) continues to exist whether he's onscreen or not. The tantalizing glimpses we receive of these people when they're alone — Mia's languid dance to Urge Overkill's "Girl, You'll Be a Woman Soon," Vincent quietly blowing Mia a kiss goodbye, the Wolf hosting some sort of elegant dress party at breakfast time — suggest an entire society functioning just outside the camera's reach. Not since Robert Altman's early films or Spike Lee's *Do the Right Thing* has an American filmmaker created such a richly populated and detailed world.

After his first film, the ferocious *Reservoir Dogs*, and his script for the woefully underrated *True Romance*, critics pegged Tarantino as some sort of smartass nihilist indulging an adolescent bent for violence. The truth is substantially different. Tarantino may love pulp fiction for its dark humor, existential dread and confrontational cool, but he's also drawn to its stern morality and complex codes of honor. In this milieu, where being tough and looking tough are both essential, much is made of the word "character." As the Wolf says, there's a difference between having character and being a character. The line is tossed off casually, but it's really Tarantino's thesis statement: His characters must all undergo tests that determine how strong they really are.

For that reason, the movie's hotly discussed violence must be equally strong. While some of the situations, including bits of horror slapstick involving a giant syringe and a gruesome accidental killing, explode into convulsively funny black comedy, the violence in *Pulp Fiction* is still scarier than we're used to seeing in American movies. Tarantino isn't interested in the pat-a-cake gunplay that transpires in most action flicks. When people draw guns here, they do so well aware that their own lives are likely to end. Therefore, everything in this world — people's reactions, their speech, their manners — is shaped by violence. Violence is free enterprise: Whenever somebody pulls a trigger, someone else prospers. It's also a way of life, and if you don't take it seriously you die.

Tarantino plainly loves these misfits and outsiders, and he can barely tear himself away from their conversations. Neither can we. Tarantino's specialty is a brand of lowlife fatmouthing that escalates into verbal warfare, an explosively funny mishmash of sitcom references, movie titles and flamboyantly excessive curses and threats. It isn't poetry; it's more like hot jazz — hearing Samuel L. Jackson say the word "motherfucker" is like listening to John Coltrane play "My Favorite Things." Pop culture and threats are the only links these characters have. When Vincent and Jules square off, their verbal battle enjoins everything from racecar driving to *Super Fly T.N.T.*

The time that Tarantino takes to establish these characters is reflected in the many superlative performances. As Mia, Uma Thurman displays a comic exuberance she's never shown before onscreen, her naughty eyes seem to be reviewing a ceaseless parade of sinful possibilities. Harvey Keitel, playing a suave version of his *Point of No Return* "cleaner," exudes an implacable Mr. Wizardly calm that gets some of the movie's biggest laughs. And John Travolta's Vincent is a brilliant creation, a slightly dopey mixture of inarticulate longing and cold-blooded skill, as if Warren Beatty's McCabe really *were* a master gunslinger.

But if any actor can be said to walk off with the movie, it's Samuel L. Jackson, whose Jules instantly joins the pantheon of the great movie tough guys: He wields a gun with terrifying authority, and his volcanic rages rival Cagney's for sheer eruptive force. His steely-eyed Jules, who starts out quoting Scripture as a remorseless killer for hire and ends up pledging to "walk the earth, like Cain on *Kung Fu*" for God, is the spiritual center of Tarantino's vicious world — the proof that no man is too evil for redemption. By the time Tarantino brings us to a final hair-raising test of Jules' new convictions, we're dazed by the journey we've taken over the course of two and a half hours, a journey from garish melodrama through inexplicable evil to a closing note of grace and salvation. It's as impressive as the transformation *Pulp Fiction* itself makes — the transformation of sleaze into art. (*Nashville Scene*, Oct. 20, 1994)

● ● ● ● ● ● ● ● ●

Wayne's World
Dir. Penelope Spheeris
1992, PG-13, 94 min.

Teen Prodigy

The rarest thing in contemporary comedies — other than wit — is a unified vision. In the early years of screen comedy, the great clowns created and populated their own little world, each attuned to its own comic logic. W. C. Fields inhabited a vengeful, fanciful universe, absurdly precise in its detail.

Buster Keaton lived in a world where the law of gravity had been repealed. His pratfalls had the quicksilver grace of James Brown crossed with Inspector Clouseau.

Few screen comedians these days can be bothered to create their own worlds. They're at the mercy of their demographic-generated material. Over the years, the worst of the lot have come from *Saturday Night Live*, which has produced a generation of unbearably smug, gutless screen comedians. Comic actors such as Dan Aykroyd and Chevy Chase, who were brilliant in five-minute sketches, ultimately showed neither the imagination nor the attention span to carry an entire movie.

So expectations for a whole movie of *Wayne's World* are no higher than they'd be for, say, a whole movie about Hans and Franz or that guy who annoys people by the Xerox machine. (I hope that doesn't give anyone ideas.)

That only makes *Wayne's World* an even more pleasant surprise. Filled with inventive gags and witty asides, *Wayne's World* unreels in a goofy parallel universe where Pacers are cool and rock stars while away their time backstage discussing the history of Milwaukee.

For anyone who's been in a cave for the past year, *Wayne's World* is the basement of the Campbell home in sylvan Aurora, Ill., where Wayne Campbell (Mike Myers) and Garth Algar (Dana Carvey) mastermind a no-budget community access cable show replete with catchy theme song (sample lyric: "Party Time! Excellent!") and flashy camerawork. (The zoom looms large in their legend.) When a sleazy TV executive — played by Rob Lowe, no stranger to public-access video — gets a load of the show and Wayne's dream girl (Tia Carrere), he launches a scheme to expose *Wayne's World* to a national audience.

Of course, Wayne and Garth might have to sacrifice some of their integrity. What's worse, they might have to stop hanging out at the all-night doughnut shop. Their dilemma serves as a springboard for a series of first-rate pop-culture jokes, as well as a showstopping recreation of the *Laverne & Shirley* opening credits.

Myers, who wrote the bright script with Bonnie Turner and Terry Turner, and Carvey seem to know Wayne and Garth from the inside out. All their details, from Garth's dumbstruck shyness around women to Wayne's sneaky laugh, are utterly authentic. They're a lot more convincing (and a lot funnier) than the similar Bill and Ted, who seem to have no individual personalities whatsoever.

Myers and Carvey are surrounded by a variety of amusing supporting characters. You're always aware of a world that exists even when Wayne and Garth aren't around. The movie has a generous, whimsical spirit: Even its satirical victims aren't humiliated excessively. And once in a while, there will be something bizarrely touching, like a scene set on a car parked near a landing strip.

People who didn't grow up in the heyday of FM radio and syndicated sitcoms will probably be bewildered by *Wayne's World*, which has an omnivorous love of the Me Generation junk culture. To anyone who's ever banged his head along with Queen's "Bohemian Rhapsody" — in high school, I actually looked up the word "Bismillah" in a dictionary — *Wayne's World*'s observation of middle-class teenage life will seem hilariously accurate. Wayne and Garth are the most comforting patron saints of frustrated adolescence since Elvis Costello and Kath Hansen.[1] Long may they hurl. (*Nashville Scene*, Feb. 20, 1992)

● ● ● ● ● ● ● ● ●

Orlando
Dir. Sally Potter
1993, PG-13, 94 min.

Womanly Wisdom

Like the Virginia Woolf novel that serves as its inspiration, Sally Potter's *Orlando* is a lark, a playful, invigorating jumble of images, ideas and artistic possibilities. It isn't as fluid as Woolf's novel, and in its weakest moments it seems more like a collection of blackout sketches than a movie — a *Saturday Night Live* fantasia dreamed up by a dozing grad student. But it's faithful to the book's impudent wit, and the filmmaking has a confident, offhand exuberance — this is clearly the work of people who relish their craft; their delight in the material is infectious. You leave the movie tickled, with scenes and images buzzing in your head. Not since the superb film version of *The Unbearable Lightness of Being* has a great novel been adapted so buoyantly, so imaginatively, to the screen.

Published in 1928, the year between the publication of Woolf's novel *To the Lighthouse* and her literary manifesto *A Room of One's Own*, *Orlando* mocks the solemnity of historical biography — and history itself, for that matter. Its young hero, Orlando, begins life as a 17th-century British nobleman doted on by Queen Elizabeth I in her dotage. He eventually becomes an aspiring poet, an ineffectual Turkish ambassador — and a woman. The novel ends at the

---

1   See Tracy Moore, "Hot Bands, Big Deals, a Buzzing Music Scene — Nashville's '80s Rock Scene Had It All," *Nashville Scene*, Aug. 10, 2006, *www.nashvillescene.com*.

precise moment the author finishes writing: "the twelfth stroke of midnight, Thursday, the eleventh of October, Nineteen Hundred and Twenty-eight." Orlando herself lives on, undiminished.

In other hands, such outrageous conceits could have descended into mere clowning or empty virtuosity. The book, however, like its ageless hero, never grows old. Woolf tempers her most whimsical fabrications with irony and piercing scorn for the rigidity of gender roles throughout British history; she treats the giants of English literature with a contempt that predates punk by decades. (Her portrait of Alexander Pope is a riotous bit of literary assassination.) And her asides — on everything from the alteration of the British national character to the limitations of spaniels in polite conversation — prove conclusively that digressions are the most overlooked pleasure of reading a novel.

If the literary spirit watching over Woolf's novel is Lawrence Sterne, the master of digression whose fake biography *Tristram Shandy* provides a dizzying demolition of fictional form, the spirit haunting Potter's film is Jean-Luc Godard, particularly in the use of words as visual elements and the constant reminders of film as artifice. Where Woolf's omniscient narrator addresses us directly through the book, our companion onscreen is Orlando him/herself, played by the delightful actress Tilda Swinton, who fixes us with a raised eyebrow from time to time before imparting her thoughts to us. While this device rarely works in film — our impulse when someone on the screen talks to us is usually to look over our shoulder — Orlando's asides to the audience are a clever way of translating Woolf's asides to the reader.

Potter also finds ingenious, amusing visual correlatives for Woolf's observations about the limited possibilities for women in British society. (Woolf wrote the book as a tribute to her confidante Vita Sackville-West, who as a woman was cheated by British law of an ancestral home bequeathed to her family by Queen Elizabeth I; the story also has similarities to Woolf's famous parable of Shakespeare's sister.) To show the confinements and restrictions of British society for women, Potter and her outstanding costume designer Sandy Powell imprison the female Orlando in a variety of absurdly oversized hoop skirts and dresses. When Orlando struggles through a room crowded with furniture while wrestling an enormous cream-colored dress, she appears to be locked in mortal combat with a meringue. Potter's image of freedom is even better: a glimpse of Orlando and her little daughter racing along in a motorcycle sidecar on a 20th-century thoroughfare, their flaming red hair streaming from beneath their helmets. Here, as elsewhere, the movie benefits from the talents of the splendid Russian cinematographer Alexei Rodionov, who gives this low-budget film a sumptuous sheen that makes Merchant Ivory look like Dollar General.

Tilda Swinton, a British actress best known here for Derek Jarman's *Edward II*, incarnates Orlando so fully that the movie is unimaginable without her. As a man, she moves with the gawkiness and casual arrogance of male youth; as a woman, she registers some barely perceptible softening of her features and gestures. Yet the two halves of her performance are linked by a knowing irony, a nimble wit that comes through in her expressions and her carriage. Swinton is most amusing in her scenes with Queen Elizabeth I, played in a remarkable bit of casting by Quentin Crisp; when they cuddle together, a woman playing a man and a man playing a woman, the bemused look Swinton shares with the audience is priceless. If anyone is capable of shattering forced gender roles and creating a perfect androgynous balance, my money's on Tilda Swinton.

The movie lapses into camp only in the disastrous final image of an epicene angel (singer Jimmy Somerville), a creepy, glistening, winged apparition apparently intended to represent a future devoid of gender limitations. It's more deserving of Orkin than *Orlando*. However, even this ghastly vision detracts little from the triumphant image of Orlando's little daughter at play in a golden field with a video camera. The scene is a call to people everywhere, especially women, to pick up cameras and begin telling their own stories, and it's Sally Potter's own sweet tribute to the impact Woolf's writing must have had on her life. Let's hope this intelligent, delightful and altogether satisfying movie inspires lots of people to make a film of one's own. (*Nashville Scene*, Aug. 19, 1993)

● ● ● ● ● ● ● ● ●

The Fifth Element
Dir. Luc Besson
1997, PG-13, 126 min.

Pleading the Fifth

Nothing dates a movie faster than its vision of the future. When you look at the hard futurist skylines and oppressive machinery of *Metropolis* now, after seven decades, you see the apprehensions of a world reeling from class revolt and rocked by advances in mass production. Fifteen years ago, *Blade Runner* literally projected fears of Asian domination onto the L.A. of the coming century — the movie's futuristic buildings blazed with seven-story ideograms and ads bearing Japanese faces. Someday our great-grandchildren will tune in 1993's

Demolition Man on their synapse-linked TV transmitters, and they'll gape at the specter of . . . rampant political correctness! (Far scarier is the movie's notion that decades from now we'll all be eating Taco Bell. To indigestion and beyond!)

So what will future generations glean from *The Fifth Element*, which takes place about 250 years from now? Well, they'll see plenty of those damned Golden Arches, a symbol more prevalent than the cross in late-20th-century movies. We don't see money in *The Fifth Element*, but we do see burgers changing hands; these meat medallions must be the New Currency! Maybe the Arches are futuristic dollar signs, or the mark of a sinister, all-consuming global concern — the muted postal horn from *The Crying of Lot 49*, with ketchup on request.

If our descendants viddy enough big-budget babies from the 1990s, they'll learn that both explanations are correct. They'll also figure out that the presence of the Arches brands *The Fifth Element* as a certain kind of expensive, explosive movie that flourished late in the century. The good news for us 1997 moviegoers, stuck arse-deep in a premillennial mudslide of disaster bashes, is that apart from that dreaded "M" and other concessions to form — an equation of weaponry with masculinity, the usual anorexic standard of feminine beauty — *The Fifth Element* delivers a lot of crazy, extravagant pleasures that have nothing to do with blowing stuff up.

The most obvious of these is the movie's eye-popping look. After a brief World War I–era prologue in Egypt, the action shifts to New York City in the year 2259. The early scenes are indoors; whenever a portal opens on the outside world, we practically crane our necks for a glimpse. (That's when I knew the movie would be fun.) But when Leeloo (Milla Jovovich), a striking yarn-doll of a woman in a fetching Jean-Paul Gaultier duct-tape ensemble, eludes a cadre of police by slipping onto the ledge of a mile-high skyscraper, the movie gives us our first good look at the future — and it's *cool*.

As with everything else in *The Fifth Element*, the details are swiped from other movies — the flying cars from *Blade Runner*, the high-rise hell of *Brazil* — but they're infused with a zippy, plasticene playfulness, as if Manhattan had been razed and rebuilt by Tonka. Bottomless vertical canyons yawn between buildings, and the space buzzes with thousands of bee-like autos. Leeloo peers for a moment into this buzzing void — and then launches herself off the building with a dive worthy of Olympia. This shot alone is worth the price of a ticket.

You'll notice I haven't said much about the plot. What's to say? Leeloo crashes through the roof of cabbie Bruce Willis, who's appealing and vulnerable in a way he never is in American action vehicles, and from there the movie careens madly from slapstick to musical numbers, from religious drama to

Raiders of the Lost Ark, all on several different planets. (The movie's anti-war message is somewhat undercut by the many gun battles and explosions.) That the director, Luc Besson, keeps the many plot threads as untangled as he does is miraculous. That he cares about this lunacy is beside the point.

The surprise is that a director at the helm of somebody's $100-million investment could permit himself so many flights of whimsy. As a routine action picture, by major-studio standards, *The Fifth Element* is something of a washout: The women aren't threatened with rape, the hero isn't tortured or beaten into lunch meat, and the villains are the motleyest bunch of under-achievers this side of a *Bill & Ted* movie. As a flood of breathtaking images and thrill-ride sensations, it's often overwhelming — it leaves you begging for more, not begging for mercy. You wanna see where those canyons lead? Besson sends the camera zooming straight down at vertiginous speed — at rush hour, no less. Even better is a long sequence aboard an interstellar resort ship that allows Besson to intercut an aria sung by a pastel-tentacled alien with some gymnastic Bruce Lee–style ass-kicking. Don't ask — just watch.

Besson is just as indulgent with his actors — especially Gary Oldman's mad-industrialist villain. Where most actors would've played this would-be dictator as a figure of menace, Oldman invents him as Elvis Hitler, a scrawny, bandy-legged klutz with Ross Perot's nasal honk. For some strange reason, the movie saddles Willis with a talk-show-host sidekick played by Chris Tucker; stranger still is that the part is conceived and played as a gonzo parody of Prince and Dennis Rodman. Far better is Milla Jovovich, whose feral punk-marionette act is by turns lethal and lovable. And memorable cameos turn up from *La Haine* director Mathieu Kassovitz as a spastic mugger and from Lee Evans, the gifted vaudeville comic of *Funny Bones*.

The Fifth Element is comically ineffectual whenever it apes the standard scripting of Hollywood thrillers. The scenes involving the U.S. president (Tiny Lister Jr.) are so inept they're surreal, and the exposition is so daft that the hero goes on his secret mission by winning a televised lottery. I found these failings charming. Luc Besson became a superstar director on the basis of his French thriller *La Femme Nikita*, a movie that many critics here and abroad despised for its imitation of cruddy American action flicks. The death of French cinema as we know it, the *New Yorker*'s Terrence Rafferty called the movie in a famous one-line review, and Besson's prints were all over the murder weapon. Now French moviemakers decry the homogenization of their national cinema, and Besson uses French money to make American studio product. What makes *The Fifth Element* such fun is that he can't quite sell out enough. Even with the stamp of approval of the McDonald's arches, this loopy, delirious thriller just can't turn itself into a rote piece of major-studio crap. Don't worry about the French cinema, which can't manufacture perfect knock-offs of our world-dominating assembly-line swill. Worry about *our* cinema, which can. (*Nashville Scene*, May 8, 1997)

● ● ● ● ● ● ● ● ● ●

Hot Fuzz
Dir. Edgar Wright
1997, R, 121 min.

Law and Disorder

In "The Simple Art of Murder," Raymond Chandler laments the dum-dum conventions of detective fiction, especially the cozy British model and its highball-sipping American cousins. The settings change, the murder weapons change, Chandler writes, "[but] fundamentally it is the same careful grouping of suspects, the same utterly incomprehensible trick of how somebody stabbed Mrs. Pottington Postlethwaite III with the solid platinum poignard just as she flatted on the top note of the Bell Song from *Lakmé* in the presence of fifteen ill-assorted guests."

Chandler gripes about the lack of psychological realism in the Agatha Christie whodunit, where murder is a parlor game with corpses instead of charade titles. But is the hard-boiled American cop movie, for all its perps and pistols, any less clichéd? Ask the TV 'tater who watches *Lethal Weapon 2* every other weekend on TBS: It's as by-the-book as that ubiquitous rookie who always gets paired up with the street-smart veteran. The tropes are trucked out more frequently than Miranda rights: The Bad Guy Who'll Have Your Badge for This; The Million-Bullet Shootout; The Fireball You Dive Away From in Slow-Motion; The Retiring Cop Who's Getting Too Old for This Shit.

"There are only four plotlines in all of cop movies," says Edgar Wright, who knows them more intimately than anyone not named Bruce Willis. As director and co-writer of *Hot Fuzz*, a delirious British homage to the rootin', tootin', assault-weapon-shootin' Hollywood cop movie — as well as its SWAT-teammates around the globe — Wright and co-writer/star Simon Pegg underwent what Wright calls "a total immersion in the genre." After diligently cataloging everything from the 1973 Robert Blake vehicle *Electra Glide in Blue* to the immortal Patrick Swayze–Keanu Reeves face-off *Point Break*, they devised a riotous mashup of cop-socky's greatest hits — without exempting the *Clue*-like legacy of Hercule Poirot.

Miles from the endearing slacker savior he played in Wright's *Shaun of the*

Dead, Pegg plays Sgt. Nicholas Angel, a gung-ho last-boy-scout type whose overachieving on the force gets him booted from the London constabulary. He winds up in Sandford, a picturesque village where the biggest emergency is a runaway swan and the doddering police chief (Jim Broadbent) runs a chummy precinct house with a swear jar.

But only Angel sees anything strange about the town's lack of crime but catastrophic accident rate. That's even before the corpses start piling up, including one spectacular gory death that rivals Kurosawa's *Sanjuro* for voluminous splatter. Aided by a blundering partner who owns every DVD ever made with a gun on the cover — Wright wisely reunites Pegg with *Shaun* scene-stealer Nick Frost — Angel soon learns that what looks like the Kinks' tweedy *Village Green Preservation Society* is closer to the fascist star chamber of *Magnum Force*.

Even with Frost doing his best Keanu surfer-dude grimace, the comedy is less *Airplane!*-style parody than a trickier, subtler mix of affectionate ribbing and fond re-creation. (You can see it on display also in "Don't," the amazing fake trailer Wright provided for *Grindhouse*: It condenses a century of old-dark-house clichés into a flipbook of comic terrors, made all the funnier by Wright's percussive editing sense.) Cop movies, after all, are reassuring for the same reasons as cozy mysteries: They restore order. The cop movie is the inversion of Robert Warshow's famous description of the gangster movie: It's the "yes" to society's "no" — the nightstick crack that reminds you who makes the rules.

But boyish Pegg and baby-faced Frost have an innocence that removes any hint of authoritarian bluster. By taking the bombast out of the cop-movie conventions, *Hot Fuzz* actually makes them exciting again. The blazing finale, in which Pegg and Frost turn into the Will Smith and Martin Lawrence of bucolic Britain, rocks as hard as any John Woo or Shane Black smackdown even as it kids the familiar slow-motion sideways leaps and villain impalements. It helps that they're surrounded by a top-notch cast of overseas thesps, from Edward Woodward (whose *The Wicker Man* is given a nod) and Kenneth Cranham as villagers to Paddy Considine as the Sandford PD's resident macho blockhead. (Watch also for cameos by Bill Nighy, Steve Coogan, director Peter Jackson as a very bad Santa, and an Oscar-winning actress who's covered up except for her twinkling eyes.)

Tell Wright that the result resembles *Murder on the Orient Express* crossed with *High Plains Drifter*, and he's a happy man. "That's it, right on," he says during a promotional jaunt with Pegg and Frost in Atlanta. While he says Britain has little cop-movie tradition to speak of — "In the U.K.," he explains, "it's faintly ridiculous to see an officer packing heat, and the genre iconography is all about packing heat" — he gladly immersed himself in anything from brutal Italian *poliziotteschi* to Jean-Pierre Melville's hitman reverie *Le Samouraï* looking to unlock the genre. His epiphany came, he says, "when I realized that [the Chuck Norris head-buster] *Code of Silence* and *L.A. Confidential* had essentially the same plotlines."

After ransacking the world's supply of cop clichés, Wright says there's one even he couldn't bring himself to include: the groaner where the hero angrily hands in his badge. But there are still plenty more where it came from — enough, perhaps, to stoke a sequel if *Hot Fuzz* catches on here the way it has in Britain. "Put enough chimps at typewriters," Edgar Wright says, "and eventually you'll get the screenplay for *Bad Boys II*." Roger that. (*Nashville Scene*, April 19, 2007)

Panning for Gold 10

arly in Jim's writing career, Nashville didn't always attract the variety and quality of films it does today. Sometimes, in the early '90s, Jim would instruct readers to stay home and rent something — on VHS tape, even — rather than squander their ducats at the megaplex. In lieu of a review, Jim might offer what we now call a "listicle," with quick-hit recommendations of classics, cult oddities and whatever struck his fancy. Once the Belcourt became a secure fixture — alongside programming at Vanderbilt's Sarratt Cinema, the Sinking Creek Film Festival (now known as the Nashville International Film Festival) and other venues — so too did a reliable influx of worthwhile films. This allowed Jim to more or less stay within his preferred mode: Don't waste space you could use to celebrate a good movie by tearing apart a bad one.

Anyone can say a movie is bad. More than ever, literally *anyone* can yell "sucks!" in a crowded Internet — and potentially gain a huge audience. The ability to engage in nuance and detail separates the tomato-hurler from the critic. For Jim, it was never enough to say a movie failed without giving a sense of what it could have been if it were better. This chapter collects some of Jim's best pans, starting with a few send-ups, including one written in the form of a short story that imagines a film executive in purgatory summoning Carl Theodor Dreyer to his office — a doff of the cap, of sorts, to Godard's notion that one should make a movie to criticize a movie.

The chapter moves gradually in a more serious direction, toward movies whose failings, in Jim's eyes, are as much ethical as technical. In the case of *Schindler's List*, there's also a reckoning with the movie's broad critical acclaim (including a shot at the "dailies," evidence of the soft rivalry between alt-weeklies and their more mainstream counterparts). Among the many lessons a young writer could glean from this review, an important one is how to take a stance contrary to popular opinion without merely being contrarian.

• • • • • • • • • •

Bad Boys II
Dir. Michael Bay
2003, R, 147 min.

Louder! Louder!

The target audience for a Jerry Bruckheimer action movie, especially one with director Michael Bay at the helm, is a guy who became a cop to get even with everybody who picked on him in high school. Property (other people's) is there to be smashed, blown up, run over and demolished with impunity. Bad guys are there to be crushed, vanquished, but kept alive long enough to acknowledge your superior manhood. Women are there to make things "personal," for those moments when a guy needs, say, a pretext for invading Cuba. Being the hero of a Bruckheimer/Bay joint means never having to say you're sorry.

"Unapologetic" may thus be the term that best describes *Bad Boys II*, a movie that starts by superimposing its makers' names over a machine that cranks out ecstasy tablets. Peddling synthetic highs has been the Bruckheimer business since the early '80s, when the producer and his genius-vulgarian partner, the late Don Simpson, applied a ruthless assembly-line dynamic to the manufacturing of mass entertainment. With *Flashdance* and especially *Top Gun*, they set in place a three-act heroic formula for building a better blockbuster. It leads unswervingly from challenge to crisis to triumph, with room in between for music videos and other commodities. The mix is still commercially potent: Last weekend Bruckheimer had the two top movies in the country.

In a sense, *Bad Boys II* is the culmination of the Bruckheimer house style, in the same way that a cheese-oozing instant coronary of a gordita is the ultimate Taco Bell product. If that's what you like, baby, you want it all. Movies-as-food may be the laziest simile in the lexicon, but it fits in Bruck-heimer's case. His movies are completely open about being consumables. They supply the loudest music, the fieriest explosions, the craziest, emptiest deaths and the biggest buck per frame, in bite-size bits that serve as thousands of self-contained advertisements. The skies will be tinted. The sun will blaze like Apollo's chariot, the better to silhouette some big-ass helicopter (or three). One exterior shot may out-gloss a year's subscription to *Vanity Fair* and cost more than the entire *Blair Witch Project*, and yet it won't appear onscreen for longer than a gnat's blink. Wretched excess, in the Bruckheimer canon, is underkill.

Rather than whine about this being the death of cinema — its thuggish bravado is pretty funny sometimes, though not for 147 freakin' minutes — I'd rather pop the hood and look a little closer at the machinery. *Bad Boys II*, like all of Bruckheimer (including the current *Pirates of the Caribbean*), is at once cunningly authoritarian and anti-authoritarian. The drug-cop heroes, suave Will Smith and shaky Martin Lawrence, are established up front as trouble-making rulebreakers. However, they are surrounded by plenty of weaker, geekier people to pick on — computer nerds, jerkwater Klansmen, even a kid's hapless date — and they get to boss around lots of agents and firepower. Their loyalty as a team must be tested, since teamwork, to Bruckheimer, is primary among virtues. So Smith sneaks around with Lawrence's sister (Gabrielle Union), who happens to be undercover DEA, while the jittery Lawrence applies for a transfer to escape his reckless partner.

You want car chases? This has two about as long as *The Matrix Reloaded*'s freeway jamboree. Boats explode. Cars explode. Cars crash into exploding cars, and explode. You want R-rated laughs? Watch Lawrence, disguised as an exterminator in a drug lord's lair, marvel at two copulating rats. You want ladies? At one point, Lawrence storms a mortuary and pulls the sheet off a busty female corpse, and the soundtrack actually lets out one of those wah-wah stingers, like when a hottie saunters by in a Mello Yello commercial. I repeat for emphasis: The movie actually ogles the boobs on a *cadaver*. The guys who made this movie would hump the liver of Bambi's dying mother onscreen if research said someone would buy a ticket.

Speaking of which, corpse desecration and mutilation are the movie's running gags, perhaps as some kind of litmus test of the audience's anti-PC fortitude. Stiffs become human speed bumps in a chase scene, and Smith reaches around for drugs in a squishy cavity. As a quiet interlude, a bad guy has his partner served up as sawed-off limbs in a barrel. Maybe director Bay is warming us up for his *Texas Chainsaw Massacre* remake this year. Then again, chopping is what Bay does best — or at least it's what he does. In the original *Bad Boys*, it's striking how few shots in his action scenes seem to follow one another logically: He cuts for percussion, not melody. Bay's attention-deficit direction gets more fluid with each movie, and at times, as in the insane commando finale of *Bad Boys II*, there's something almost exhilaratingly silly about his bullheaded barreling past common sense.

But this is the producer's movie, down to the Bruckheimer signature shot of macho men marching forward in slow motion. In principle, I love almost all the things *Bad Boys II* is trying to sell me — the cars, the stunts, the leads' explosive banter — but they're all but ruined by the volume of the tone-deaf pitch. Imagine this entire review written in all caps, with exclamation points the only punctuation marks. Now consider yourself lucky Jerry Bruckheimer is a producer, not a typesetter. (*Nashville Scene*, July 24, 2003)

● ● ● ● ● ● ● ● ● ●

Little Miss Sunshine
Dir. Jonathan Dayton and Valerie Faris
2006, R, 101 min.

Ain't No Sunshine

Like the shambling VW van its hapless characters steer from Albuquerque to Redondo Beach, *Little Miss Sunshine* is a rickety vehicle that travels mostly downhill. How this antic extended sitcom from first-time feature makers Jonathan Dayton and Valerie Faris left Sundance with an eight-figure deal and reams of enthralled press clippings is beyond comprehension, even factoring in its big-name ensemble and the predisposition of festival audiences to pat a film about lovable losers on the head.

A grating black comedy about the paralyzing fear of not being strong, successful or skinny enough, *Little Miss Sunshine* means to indict our national obsession with winners and the stigma of coming in second. The opening sequence introduces dad Richard (Greg Kinnear) delivering a motivational nine-step pep talk with mounting fervor. Big surprise: the very next shot reveals his audience as a few stragglers in a dingy classroom. At home, cantankerous Grandpa (Alan Arkin) settles in for his favorite leisure ac- tivity — snorting heroin — while mop-topped teenage Dwayne (Paul Dano) hits the weights in a sullen vow of silence under a giant Nietzsche poster. In the next room, 7-year-old Olive (Abigail Breslin) stares through glasses at a TV beauty pageant. The camera finally settles in a hospital ward, on the sodden misery of uncle Frank (Steve Carell) — a gay Proust scholar who cut his wrists after losing his lover to an academic rival. Over his scowling face, the words appear: "Little Miss Sunshine." This is called irony.

With Frank sequestered in Dwayne's room on suicide watch, the bickering household gathers for dinner — the movie pauses to chortle over a gauche Mayor McCheese cup on the table — just as a fluke announcement makes Olive a contender for the Little Miss Sunshine beauty contest. On the spot, gung-ho Richard convinces wife Sheryl (Toni Collette) to make the 700-mile drive in the family's decrepit van, and the others reluctantly sign on — for no better reason than that's what characters in shaky farces do. *Little Miss Sunshine* is the latest in a long line of Sundance clunkers, from *Happy, Texas* to

Me and You and Everyone We Know, that seems to have developed its impression of human behavior from incomplete space transmissions.

Why does Sheryl, who doesn't want to take the van because she can't drive stick, suddenly decide when they're already on the road that she needs to learn? So the gears can go out, turning the van into a rolling junkyard that requires group pushing. How does Richard manage to sweet-talk a biker into loaning him a ride? That scene, in a Preston Sturges movie, might've been a pip — an illustration of the power of can-do optimism, that pure-grade American snake oil, to hypnotize even the skeptical. The movie just breezes on by, as if it were the most natural thing in the world for a stranger to hand over his bike. By the time the family makes a hospital getaway with a loved one in the trunk, the characters have edged from foolish and flawed to humanly unrecognizable.

The pity is that there are strains of tenderness and generosity in the script and performances: an affectionate scene between Grandpa and Olive comes as sweet relief, mainly because Arkin's character momentarily becomes a person instead of a wheezy comic device. (Can anyone remember the last time the Foul-Mouthed Grandpa bit was funny?) And occasionally the directors capture an unexpected bit of beauty or freedom — like Carell's cakewalk bolt toward the rolling van's doors, or a lyrical shot from underneath a whorled overpass. More often, though, ugly details are hammered clumsily into place, like the rumple in a hospital waiting room's wallpaper — a lived-in touch in the background of a shot, until the composition changes awkwardly to place it center.

The movie's platitudinous payoff — winning isn't everything, beauty is in the eye of the beholder, etc. — would go down a lot easier if *Little Miss Sunshine* didn't roam from scene to scene searching for new characters to patronize. The script, by Michael Arndt, practically nukes its easy targets. A sequence with a brusque hospital "bereavement liaison" (Paula Newsome) comes off thuddingly sour, but the beauty-pageant finale is the nadir. To engineer a happy ending — the heroes mustn't look like losers — the movie has to make everyone else look worse. Thus the contestants are made up into grotesque little kewpie whores, while the adults include a helmet-haired harridan organizer, a leering emcee and an audience of snooty stage moms.

Even as a metaphor for What's Wrong With America — "Life is just one fucking beauty contest after another," offers one character helpfully — it goes past comic exaggeration into cruelty. And yet *Little Miss Sunshine* saves its one belly laugh for this scene, which not coincidentally is the movie's only left-field surprise: Olive's glaringly inappropriate (or is it inadvertently appropriate?)

talent-contest specialty, one of exactly two punches the movie doesn't tele-graph. (The other involves Carell's reading material, and it's not *Remembrance of Things Past*.) As for the rest of this desperately contrived farce — wouldja settle for Little Miss Congeniality? (*Nashville Scene*, Aug. 17, 2006)

● ● ● ● ● ● ● ● ● ●

Texasville
Dir. Peter Bogdanovich
1990, R, 123 min.

The Devil Takes His Due

A young film buff longs to become a director. Not just any director, but a popular moviemaker regarded as a film artist as well: a Howard Hawks, a John Ford.

Flash, bang, a puff of smoke: The devil appears. OK, here's the deal, says the devil. Your wish is granted, but only for a certain time. At the end of that time, I'll come back around.

After years of apprenticeship, the young film buff makes a well-received low-budget suspense film. As his follow-up, he chooses an acclaimed novel about teenagers growing up in a one-story Texas town in the early '50s.

The ensuing film establishes him as a superstar director, a master entertainer, with one stroke. For the next few years, his films are enormous successes; he is the subject of volumes of critical study.

And then the devil comes to collect his due.

Just what the devil got from Peter Bogdanovich is uncertain. What is cer-tain, however, is that ever since that string of fine early films, sitting through a Bogdanovich movie has been hell.

Has another director suffered such an immediate and shocking decline? (The jury's out on David Lynch.) Just after the hilarious *What's Up, Doc?* and the charming *Paper Moon*, Bogdanovich began the Operation Rolling Thunder phase of his career, a systematic and uninterrupted series of bombs so awful they made audiences question his initial promise. A director of lesser repu-tation, commercial or critical, would never have worked again after a howler on the level of *At Long Last Love*; his last film, *Illegally Yours*, was (justifiably) considered unreleaseable.

However, his new film, *Texasville*, is a much sadder fiasco. For Bogda-novich has returned to the site of his greatest triumph, 1971's *The Last Picture Show*, the film considered by many the finest of the decade, and the sad truth is it doesn't help.

When *The Last Picture Show* ended, old Sam the Lion died and the only theater in the town of Thalia closed, leaving high-school football buddies Duane (Jeff Bridges) and Sonny (Timothy Bottoms) with a sense of bewildering loss. Their obsession with the beautiful, shallow homecoming queen Jacy Farrow (Cybill Shepherd) led nowhere; Sonny's affair with the football coach's wife (Cloris Leachman) ended in heartbreak.

Texasville opens some 30 years later, on the week of Thalia's founding celebration. Duane is now an oilman one jump ahead of bankruptcy, with a shaky business and a marriage to match; Sonny is now the mayor, sinking steadily into mental illness. Both harbor wistful recollections of missed opportunities and glories that never were.

Duane and Sonny's reverie is shaken by a visitor from the past: Jacy, now a minor actress haunted by the death of her son. Jacy instantly befriends Duane's wife Karla (Annie Potts) and reawakens Duane's teenage infatuation. As the celebration approaches, Jacy becomes a catalyst for upheaval in his life, while Duane struggles with his unresolved feelings.

When Sonny returns to the football stands, the ironies are obvious: Like Sonny, Bogdanovich has gone back to the site of his early triumph, drawn by the hope that magic might strike again. But *The Last Picture Show* wasn't a work of magic: It was a work of craft, of skill and imagination, and *Texasville* isn't. Bogdanovich expects our memories of *The Last Picture Show* to do most of the work. He reintroduces each character with huge, mythic close-ups, as if they were legendary figures, and he expects the audiences to know them already. Unfortunately, *The Last Picture Show* has been shown rarely in the past 10 years — it isn't available on video — so anyone who hasn't seen it will be baffled by the allusions and unexplained relationships.

Much worse, however, is Bogdanovich's complete inability to get to the point of a scene, the most basic rule of filmmaking. In a scene in Martin Scorsese's *GoodFellas*, for example, gangsters force a restaurant owner to make them partners; once he agrees, they suck the life from the business, draining it of its resources and capital. There is one shot of the restaurant owner signing away his business that lasts only a couple of seconds, but it conveys a world of information: loss, anger, brutality, cruel irony.

Contrast this economy with Bogdanovich's endless scenes, which have the aimlessness of bad improvisation. As a screenwriter, Bogdanovich reduces Larry McMurtry's spiny anecdotes to creaky old-movie set pieces, but as a director he can't even get the intended effects from them. We've all seen the same movies Bogdanovich has; we know how these chestnuts are supposed to work. Therefore, such scenes as a curmudgeonly preacher getting egged at the celebration, or Duane and Jacy playing Adam and Eve in a pageant, are a double embarrassment: Not only aren't they worth doing, Bogdanovich can't even do them right.

And that doesn't even scratch the surface of *Texasville*'s egregious shortcomings. The character of Jacy is supposed to assume a ton of metaphorical weight. She's the free spirit sent to redeem the town, but when she arrives she's just pouty old Cybill Shepherd, still delivering her most reflective lines like an auctioneer. With Jacy a pretty, prosaic blank, the movie has a hole at its center; the promised epiphany never occurs. The other actors, with the exception of Annie Potts' savory Karla, are hamstrung by their mythic burden.

I still haven't mentioned the scenes that arbitrarily change in tone (as if they were shot on mood film), the awful dialogue or the washed-out photography . . . but why continue? There's no pleasure in watching Bogdanovich forget everything he ever learned about filmmaking. Peter Bogdanovich was the first director whose career I ever followed; when I was in second grade, he was a hero of mine. I loved those early movies, and I love them still.

For admirers of Bogdanovich, watching *Texasville* is like watching a former football hero take the field once more, clinging to an adolescent glory that is gone forever. Like everyone else, you want to avert your eyes, out of respect for the memory. But you watch, and you hope, and you don't crack a smile.

The only one smiling is the devil on the sidelines, waiting to claim whatever's left. (*Nashville Scene*, Nov. 1, 1990)

● ● ● ● ● ● ● ● ● ●

The Messenger: The Story of Joan of Arc
Dir. Luc Besson
1999, R, 148 min.

Message Received

Carl Theodor Dreyer, the late Danish director, has been summoned to the office of a production executive in purgatory. A new version of the story of Joan of Arc is being planned, and a courtesy call has been placed to the maker of *La Passion de Jeanne d'Arc*, the silent 1928 film regarded as one of the best movies ever made. A secretary ushers him inside, and the executive sits with a treatment of Dreyer's film on his desk.

"Carl, babe, loved that vampire thing you did," the executive says, giving the director's hand a quick wring and motioning him to a seat. "Listen, I've gone over that Joan of Arc picture you made, and it spoke to me. Seriously. Goosebumps. I can only guess what you'd do with sound and a Joan who's a little less butch. I've gone over your treatment, and I think we're on the same page here. Now, where'd I put those notes. . . ."

"Notes?" asks the director, nervously pushing his glasses back on his nose.

"Yeah, just a few. You know, you've got a great story here. A girl who hears voices, who fights like a man, who goes into battle and gets tossed on a bonfire — it's *Braveheart* meets *Carrie*. But your picture just starts with the trial. A bunch of ugly extras and that babe with the bad haircut. You're missing out on a load of backstory. I want to know what makes this Joan tick."

"Tick?" Dreyer replies, fighting back a growing panic. "She hears voices from God."

"Glad you brought that up," the executive says, producing a red pen. "Look, you've got this peasant girl who says God tells her to take France back from the British, and she's going to lead armies and whatnot. The talking-to-God thing works, don't get me wrong, but she also needs some kind of . . . payback. Suppose she's got some kind of sex trauma in her past? I see it now: She's a kid, and her sister's hiding her in a wardrobe from the British. All of a sudden, these big ugly rapist guys come in. While Joan's in the cabinet, one of 'em takes her sister, nails her to the door with a sword, and just starts banging her right there while the kid's inside. I can see the tagline now: 'Joan of Arc — This time it's personal.'"

"Dear God," says Dreyer, rubbing his eyes.

"About that," the executive says. "Without showing God, you did the best you could back then, with the spiritual close-ups, the upturned face, the yadda-di-yadda. But Carl, buddy — we've got ILM now! We'll do a CGI guy-in-the-sky, some time-lapse *Close Encounters* clouds, even this slow-motion dance I saw in a Sarah McLachlan video."

"But — but the presence of God is there in Jeanne's face!" Dreyer sputters.

"Jesus, Carl," says the executive, sounding hurt, "I'm starting to think you've never seen *The Ten Commandments*. But that's nothing. The battle scenes — nobody's ever shown what those fights were really like. Arms flying, blood spilling, all those catapults and cannonball contraptions — it'll be like that big fight in *The Phantom Menace* where all the robots got carved up. And believe you me, we've got guys who can do a decapitation that'll loosen your lunch."

Dreyer opens his mouth but cannot form words.

"Now the casting will be the key," the executive continues. "We need a Joan who can kick ass and wear short hair without looking like some Bulgarian women's pole vaulter. We got that chick with the duct-tape bra from *The Fifth Element*. Plus we've added a conscience who appears from time to time in the form of a stern cleric. I bet you're reading my mind on this one: Dustin Hoffman. As for the French king, only one actor could give the role of a treacherous 15th-century French monarch the kind of power and credibility it needs."

Dreyer looks up hopefully.

"John freakin' Malkovich," says the executive.

"Why are you doing this to me?" whimpers the director.

"Actually, Carl," says the executive, "I didn't want to break this to you, but it's already done. That French guy, Luc Besson — you know, *La Femme Nikita*? *The Fifth Element*? — wanted a crack at the story. He not only anticipated every suggestion we had to make, he added things we never dreamed of. I mean, who else would've thought of showing Joan's face getting roasted in the fire? And the scene where the guards rip off Joan's clothes? The guy's a French Joel Schumacher. He called his picture *The Messenger*. We'll have this baby on multiple screens in a thousand megaplexes come Friday."

"At last, I understand," says Dreyer, gathering his dignity and walking to the door. "I am in hell."

"Not yet," says the executive. "But if you'll take the escalator down to theaters 3 through 16, you can't miss it." (*Nashville Scene*, Nov 18, 1999)

● ● ● ● ● ● ● ● ● ●

Schindler's List
Dir. Steven Spielberg
1993, R, 195 min.

Chamber of Horrors

Based on a biographical novel by the Australian novelist Thomas Keneally, Steven Spielberg's *Schindler's List* tells the true story of a German industrialist and playboy named Oskar Schindler, a war profiteer who found a unique way to exploit the strictures placed upon Jews under the directives of the Third Reich. A manufacturer and distributor of military supplies, Schindler shrewdly surmised that with their rights dwindling and the Nazis seizing power, the Polish Jews would be a plentiful — and uncomplaining — source of cheap labor for factory production. He cultivated influential Nazi contacts through lavish parties and extravagant gifts, and met with Jewish community leaders in Krakow to discuss a plan: He would take their capital and use it to finance a factory staffed by Jewish workers.

A charming dilettante with a distaste for work, Schindler (played expansively by Liam Neeson) had little interest in running the factory and little interest in the people who would be working there. He therefore turned over the burden of managing the factory's accounts to a Jewish bookkeeper named Itzhak Stern (Ben Kingsley), who was charged with the responsibility of bribing Nazi officials regularly and ensuring the company's solvency. To secure government contracts, Schindler wined and dined the Third Reich officers who had herded the families of Stern and his other employees into a cramped, squalid ghetto. He seemed to be bothered little by the Nazis' growing ruthlessness toward his Jewish workers.

When the Nazis began herding the residents of the Jewish ghetto into concentration camps, however, Schindler started to realize the grave threat facing his workers (and his factory). Using the goodwill and the relationships he had established among Nazi officers, Schindler initiated a desperate series of maneuvers that would allow him to retain his employees and their families. As the Nazis set about the grim task of exterminating the Jews with unfathomable efficiency, Schindler devised a means of keeping his plant in operation — and keeping his more than 1,100 employees alive.

After seeing *Schindler's List*, which received the Best Picture award from the prestigious L.A. Film Critics Circle just last week as a prelude to Oscar contention, I wish I could tell you that I understood why Schindler changed from an exploiter of human misery to the savior of his employees. But *Schindler's List* is far more effective as a visual catalogue of the horrors of the Holocaust than as any kind of study of the nature or character of man — and frankly, that's just not enough anymore. The apocalyptic cruelties of the Holocaust have been documented so vividly — in the newsreel footage taken by Allied liberators at the concentration camp sites; in the documentaries of Marcel Ophuls and Claude Lanzmann; in the works of Elie Wiesel and Victor Frankl, to name a few — that any fictional treatment of these atrocities can only be a pale, redundant shadow at best. What is needed is an exploration of the particulars in human nature that allowed people to survive, to encourage, to endure, to participate in, and to forget barbarism that represented the ultimate corruption of the noblest attributes of man. That's what *Schindler's List* doesn't provide — and that's partially what makes it such a frustrating film.

Part of the problem is that by placing the emphasis on the enigmatic Schindler, the movie spends little time introducing us to the people on his list, which blunts not only the emotional impact of Schindler's achievement but also the full terror of the cruelties endured by the Jews. Spielberg shows us, in gut-wrenching detail, several people being shot point-blank in the head so that their blood drenches their loved ones; elderly Jews being stripped naked and forced to run a Nazi gauntlet until they drop from exhaustion; children being machine-gunned and used for target practice. What he doesn't show us is how the Jews managed to survive the ceaseless, agonizing threat of death during each conscious moment; or, more miraculously still, how they managed to preserve their faith in a God who watched impassively as they endured torments far more vivid and tangible than His works. We receive no insight whatsoever into the Jewish culture, so we don't know the full extent of what is being destroyed. Most exasperating of all, with the exception of Stern, a young concentration camp worker named Helen Hirsch (Embeth Davidtz), and a few incidental characters, the Jewish characters remain largely a faceless parade of victims; without any knowledge of them as individuals, their suffering is robbed of its specific horror. The violence is detailed so much more vividly than the characters that it throws off our perception: We're more aware of the fountains of blood than we are of the people losing them.

The Nazis, on the other hand, are the same stereotypical fiends we've come to expect, portrayed for the most part without the shred of humanity that would make them impossible to dismiss. Spielberg has apologized in recent interviews for the light portrayal of the Nazis in the *Indiana Jones* movies, but all he's done here is make their crimes more explicit. He hasn't illuminated the twisted logic of their reasoning or moral views. The movie's most prominent Nazi is the monstrous Amon Goeth (frighteningly played by Ralph Fiennes), commander of the Plaszow death camp, who starts out his morning with half-hearted calisthenics and rifle practice with prisoners as targets; Spielberg and screenwriter Steven Zaillian spend quite a bit of time establishing him as Schindler's mirror image (literally, at one point), as if to say this is what Schindler might have become. But the movie makes no more effort to understand him than Schindler — and thus the filmmakers duck the toughest question of all. Are some men born inherently evil, or are we all born with a latent capacity for evil? Within the answer to that question lies the lasting horror of the Holocaust — the fear that it will happen again.

Some of *Schindler's List* is so remarkable that I wish the rest matched its level. With the superb cinematographer Janusz Kaminski, Spielberg has shot the film in a grainy black-and-white pseudo-documentary fashion that is the complete opposite of his swooping, magically deft cinematic style; the technique achieves a truly horrifying effect during the recreation of the liquidation of the Krakow ghetto. A couple of brilliant, darkly comic sequences perfectly capture the despair of the situation, particularly a sequence involving a jammed weapon.

At more than three numbing, unrelenting hours, *Schindler's List* is a punishing experience. It represents a perverse triumph for Spielberg, who has submerged virtually every recognizable facet of his talent — the dailies call that "restraint" — only to receive acclaim for making the most personal film of his career. Indeed, the strangest thing about watching *Schindler's List* is that Spielberg seems ashamed of his genuine gifts for moving and entertaining an audience: He even leaves his name off the opening credits, presumably so we won't expect "a Steven Spielberg film." He appears to be so afraid of the honest sentiment in his other films that he muffles scenes that deserve dramatic heightening — when Schindler and Goeth play a game of blackjack that will determine the fate of a woman's life, Spielberg doesn't even show us the turn of the cards. When he does employ a bit of cinematic trickery, it's usually cribbed from another, more "serious" film: the flash-bulb-as-edit from *Raging Bull*, the crosscutting between a beating and a party from *Cabaret*, the dot of color in a black-and-white shot from *Wings of Desire*.

If the graphic violence and endless scenes of abuse convinces one of those boneheads who doesn't believe in the Holocaust that it really happened, then they're entirely worthwhile; it would be wonderful if the movie opened the eyes of some of the skinhead cretins wandering around who worship the Nazis. But I'm afraid that won't happen. There's an excruciating scene in which Goeth corners Helen Hirsch in a basement and runs his hands over the terrified woman's breasts; for all the movie's high-mindedness, it isn't terribly differ- ent from similar scenes in exploitative garbage like *The Night Porter* or *Ilsa, She-Wolf of the S.S.* It's still going to turn on swine who see the Nazis as the ultimate aggression fantasy — people who believe sexual politics are fascism, not democracy. If anyone can sit through Alain Resnais' searing 30-minute documentary *Nuit et Brouillard* and remain unconvinced, I doubt if Spielberg's three-hour drama is going to do the trick.

In the meantime, there's something annoying about the way Spielberg repudiates his past work in interviews now, as if his beautifully crafted pop entertainments were somehow embarrassing in light of the heavy-handed, well-intentioned *Schindler's List*. If art were determined by good intentions, then *Judgment at Nuremberg* would be the lasting work of film art and *Tri- umph of the Will* largely forgotten, instead of the other way around. And some of Spielberg's intentions seem questionable. In the mad rush by America's movie reviewers to canonize the director, has anyone given any thought to the scene in which a trainload of Schindler's female employees accidentally arrives at Auschwitz? The women are herded from the cars; the next day, they are stripped of their clothing and forced into the infamous showers where thousands of women and children were gassed to death. Spielberg's camera lingers for an eternity over the horrified faces and shriveled, shivering bodies. Suddenly, the lights go out; there is the sound of something pouring into the room, and the women begin to scream in terror. Surprise: It really is the shower — Schindler reached the commandant in time, and the women are being scrubbed before their journey. It takes a rare kind of filmmaker to use a gas-chamber switcheroo to work up an audience. Whenever I see the moist-eyed, pensive Spielberg on magazine covers or newspapers, all I can picture is the Jewish director standing high above the set and ordering the actresses to march into the gas chamber. These days, that's the kind of tasteful restraint that gets you an Oscar. (*Nashville Scene*, Dec. 6, 1993)

● ● ● ● ● ● ● ● ● ●

8MM
Dir. Joel Schumacher
1999, R, 123 min.

Hardcore Jollies

Poor Michael Powell. In 1960, the esteemed British director of *The Red Shoes* made a movie called *Peeping Tom*. It concerns a photographer, Mark (Carl Boehm), who films pretty girls through a movie camera with two special attachments: a knife that stabs the subject when the film rolls, and a mirror for her to watch. Mark then watches the films in his basement, searching for the perfect expression of fear. Today *Peeping Tom* looks remarkably prescient in its linking of sex, death and the viewer's own passive voyeurism. At the time, though, even as Alfred Hitchcock was reaping the rewards of the similar *Psycho*, Powell was vilified. He made only four more films before his death in 1990.

Had Powell been a sharp guy like Joel Schumacher, the director of *8MM*, he could've used sicker material and gotten a budget bigger than all his films put together — and, to swipe a line from John Prine, all he would've had to lose was his point of view. Well, he would've had to change a few things — starting with the similarity between his pervy movie buff and the popcorn-munchers who pay to see his exploits. Then, like Schumacher, Powell could've seen his grisly images flickering in mall cinemas all over America, instead of in the one or two cities where *Peeping Tom* is currently getting an extremely limited re-release.

To do that, however, Powell would've ended up making *Peeping Tom Lite* — which pretty much sums up *8MM*, a weak, murky shocker that fails to deliver on its own grimy threats. You know you're living in a great country when the mainstream film industry ponies up something like $60 million for a movie about snuff films, the mythical underground porn movies in which women are slaughtered during sex. But what's repellent about *8MM* isn't so much its subject as the way the movie packages and sells this hard candy to its audience.

In its basic premise and its unconvincing moralizing, *8MM* recalls the leering sexposés of smut's golden era, in which a crusading investigator inevitably played your tour guide through Sin City. Here he's detective Tom Welles, played by Nicolas Cage, who's hired to find out whether a dead millionaire's 8mm snuff film is real. Going underground as a buyer, Welles uncovers a black-market industry linked to slimy auteur Dino Velvet (Peter Stormare) and a masked snuff star known only as "the Machine."

Even in *8MM*'s own script, snuff movies are dismissed as urban legend. It's hard to get worked up about them these days — not when every calamity is camcorder material, not in the age of video nasties and *America's Deadliest Chases*. Our duplicity in watching this stuff, on the other hand, is a story worth investigating. Had *8MM* made Welles, our surrogate, more of an active participant in the snuff scene, the movie might've been a powerfully sick exploration of the casual atrocities we've come to accept as viewers. Instead, Cage recoils like Jerry Falwell at Wigstock, cueing us that we're all on his moral high ground. Fear not: you still get to see a little B&D, some doctored Filipino roughies and a stripper, and you can fool yourself into feeling morally superior at the same time.

Here, as in his overpraised *Seven*, screenwriter Andrew Kevin Walker mixes chamber-of-horrors jolts with dime-store philosophizing about human nature and Ultimate Evil. Yet what's on display here isn't the banality of evil so much as the evil of banality. Every wrong turn is exacerbated by Joel Schumacher, whose style is to art-direct a movie to death in every insignificant detail while fumbling the big picture. The porn underworld he presents is so fashionably hellish it's ludicrous: Every set looks like a Nine Inch Nails video.

Then again, would *8MM* really be any better if it were better made? The creepiest thing about this litany of ho-hum depravities is that we'd pay to see it, and that we'd still feel unaffected afterward. As an antidote, I recommend an Austrian film called *Funny Games*. Two clean-cut youths invite themselves into a vacation home, and for the next 90 minutes they beat, stab and torture the family inside. The kicker comes when they address you, the viewer, as their implicit accomplice, at one point helpfully rewinding for you. I resented every moment of *Funny Games*, but it asks the question *8MM* dodges: What will you accept in the name of entertainment, and why? (*Nashville Scene*, March 4, 1999)

Problem Pictures   11

I n the preceding chapter, Jim takes directors to task for glossing over difficult questions or ducking them altogether. Here, in a chapter dedicated to socially engaged films, he gives credit where it is due to works that delve into difficult subject matter — war, racism, violence, genocide — and along the way challenge easy assumptions.

In 2012, the *Scene* ran a cover story, which Jim edited, about a convention held in a Tennessee state park: a meeting of the so-called "alt-right." At the time, the gathering, however dark its intentions, seemed archaic and anachronistic. Now, it feels like an eerie harbinger of the more overt and bold displays of prejudice and racism that seem to appear with more regularity since the 2016 presidential election. So, too, do these reviews look different in the light of this moment. Whatever distance we may have felt from their subject matter has closed considerably.

Even so, the best films invite us to return to them, even as the urgency of their message waxes and wanes depending on the surrounding events of the era. Cinema can draw us in far enough that we are forced to imagine how circumstances could drive us to act immorally; it can ask us whether it would be enough to feel we were on the right side of history, and whether we still think we are. A richly realized film can make us believe that, even as war and revolution rage all around, the small or seemingly absurd acts, however self-delusional, are what can allow our humanity to survive.

● ● ● ● ● ● ● ● ● ●

Triumph of the Will
Dir. Leni Riefenstahl
1935, NR, 110 min.

Ill Will

The opening shot, among the most famous in all of cinema, is of clouds viewed from the cockpit of an airplane. As the plane circles the towering clouds, we feel almost as if we too are sailing around them, as if time is suspended. Then, suddenly, the view gives way to steep rooftops and spires. We are descending. As the plane arrives, what seems like thousands of people begin to cheer wildly, awaiting the figure inside. The ground crew approaches, the door opens, and out steps — Adolf Hitler.

Thus begins Leni Riefenstahl's 1935 documentary *Triumph of the Will*, perhaps the most notorious film ever made. A filmed account of the Party Rally at Nuremburg on Sept. 4–10, 1934, *Triumph of the Will* celebrates the power and determination of a Germany unified under Nazi leadership. With its breathtaking command of film technique and its overwhelming glorification of power, *Triumph of the Will* has developed a somewhat ludicrous reputation as a propaganda tool so irresistible that viewers can fall under its spell, like mice caught in the gaze of a cobra.

"I think we need to reassess the power of propaganda," says film historian David B. Hinton, who has studied Riefenstahl's work for two decades. "Propaganda can only work if the audience is receptive to the message. By attributing all the Nazis' power to the use of propaganda, we're letting the Germans off the hook."

Hinton's compelling study, *The Films of Leni Riefenstahl*, was received poorly when it was first published in 1978, perhaps because of his unfashionable championing of Riefenstahl's talent as opposed to her political opportunism. Now available once more through Scarecrow Press, Hinton's book strips away some of the myths surrounding the making of *Triumph of the Will*, and he rightly argues the director's status as one of the world's great filmmakers, regardless of the moral ambiguity (at best) or her position.

A Nashvillian who earned his doctorate at Vanderbilt, Hinton met Riefenstahl through Nazi architect Albert Speer, whom the author encountered while studying in Heidelberg. Introduced to Riefenstahl by Speer, who told him, "Tell her Al sent you," Hinton was granted access to her personal archives. Using Riefenstahl's documentation and correspondence, Hinton was able to correct some of the inaccuracies surrounding the film: that it was edited in chronological order (it wasn't); that it was financed by the Nazis (another myth — Riefenstahl demanded artistic control, and her own film company secured backing through the German film-distribution titan Ufa); and that the entire rally was staged for Riefenstahl's benefit (the many hardships in filming would have been solved by such planning).

For contemporary audiences, the hardest part of evaluating Riefenstahl's stance is determining just how complicitous the director was. Hinton believes that Riefenstahl is more an apolitical opportunist than a fascist ideologue, and it's important to note that *Triumph of the Will* was filmed long before Kristallnacht or even the Wannsee Conference, at which the Nazis mapped out their "final solution." The director also shielded non-Aryans from harm in her production company. (According to Hinton, Riefenstahl refused to help the Nazi effort after 1939, when she witnessed the massacre of Polish soldiers, who were forced at gunpoint to dig their own graves.) Yet we hear the ominous rumblings about "racial purity" and eliminating the bad element. Didn't Riefenstahl?

It is entirely possible that she did not. One can make fascist art without being a fascist; even though she never joined the party, Riefenstahl's romanticization of form, her objectification of beauty, certainly dovetailed with the Nazis' cold, chiseled, beautiful lines. Riefenstahl could simply have been overwhelmed by her proximity to such unrivaled, marshaled power — the ultimate realization of her aesthetic.

What are we to do in the face of such brilliant art and such human ugliness? Judge? Turn away? Condemn Riefenstahl's astonishing command of cinema along with her opportunism and her duplicity in the architecture of the apocalypse? Or do we separate her work from her subject — if indeed that is possible? These are the options we face when confronted by Riefenstahl's masterpiece, the triumph of the mind that celebrates the body — at the expense of the soul. (*Nashville Scene*, Oct. 22, 1992)

● ● ● ● ● ● ● ● ●

American History X
Dir. Tony Kaye
1998, R, 119 min.

White Man's Burden

The earnest neo-Nazi melodrama *American History X* has lots of problems, but Edward Norton isn't one of them. It may sound rash to call Norton the best screen actor of his generation after just a handful of roles in two years' time. Yet Norton has quickly demonstrated a range and intensity that shames most of his peers, coupled with an innate likability that convinces audiences to follow him down some pretty dark avenues. In *American History X*, he uses every ounce of his appeal to keep us from writing off a character we should rightly despise; his effort helps turn an often overwrought drama into an affecting, even powerful one.

Norton's Derek Vinyard isn't anywhere around when his younger brother, Danny (Edward Furlong, who excels at the troubled-adolescent roles Sal Mineo once played), faces suspension from high school for writing an admiring paper on *Mein Kampf*. But the principal (Avery Brooks), Derek's own former teacher, recognizes the older sibling's influence.

After the brothers' fireman dad was killed at random in a black neighborhood, Derek bulked up and became the ardent disciple of a radical-right hatemonger (Stacy Keach in a small but effective role). He started organizing the other disaffected, impoverished white kids in his Venice Beach neighborhood into a tight-knit clan of skinheads. And when Derek caught two black thieves trying to steal his car, he doled out a sentence. He gunned down one and "curbed" the other — made the thief lie face down and open-mouthed on a curb, so his teeth grated on the concrete. Then Derek stomped the back of his head.

Instead of punishing Danny, the principal proposes an alternative — a personally supervised history class called "American History X." The first assignment: Write about Derek and the influence he's had upon Danny's life. That sounds easy, since Derek is getting out of jail for the two killings that day. But after his eye-opening prison stay, the newly released Derek isn't the same person who relished beating blacks and destroying ethnic groceries.

For *American History X* to work, both as drama and as social commentary, the actor playing Derek must convince us of his anger and ruthlessness before prison. Yet he must also show us a human being underneath all that hate and bluster, or his eventual change of character won't wash. Edward Norton does both brilliantly. Viewers who remember him as the lovesick Jimmy Stewart–ish beanpole in *Everyone Says I Love You* will be shocked by his transformation here into a ticking bomb. But they shouldn't be. Norton doesn't disappear into a role; rather, he fills it with so much alertness, physical detail and urgency that he and the character fuse.

The flashback structure allows Norton to play Derek at varying stages. As Derek buys into white power, Norton tightens his gestures and posture, and the effect is like watching a snapshot develop into a hardened image. Nowhere is this clearer than in the contrast between the stooped, crying kid who lashes out at his father's killers and the muscular tough who stalks chin and chest first onto a neighborhood basketball court. Norton's performance is rich in these and much smaller details — the different way he handles a gun before and after prison, for example, or the regretful look he gives himself in a mirror, using a hand to hide his swastika-ed heart.

In its sincere, muckraking tone, *American History X* resembles one of Stanley Kramer's problem dramas from the 1950s and '60s — especially *Pressure Point*, in which psychiatrist Sidney Poitier tries to find out what motivates a rabid Nazi (Bobby Darin!). The screenwriter, David McKenna, makes a good, honest stab at addressing the roots of hate crime, something the recent *Apt Pupil* fumbled miserably. He details how the Vinyards learned bigotry at the kitchen table, and he demonstrates how fear, poverty and neglect spawn racism of all kinds. Here, as elsewhere, Norton's performance adds verisimilitude: It's startling to hear him espouse white supremacy as forcefully as he defended the First Amendment in *The People vs. Larry Flynt*.

Needless to say, this isn't material that needs to be hyped up for shock value. Unfortunately, that doesn't stop the director, Tony Kaye, who also photographed — a bad combination. *American History X* made headlines recently when Kaye engaged in a bitter fight with New Line Studios over the final cut. Kaye tried to remove his name from the film, and the Director's Guild refused; the director is now suing, claiming that Norton (who co-produced) recut the film himself to make his part bigger.

It's nearly impossible to determine who was responsible for what. But if Kaye gets credit for the handsome black-and-white camerawork that separates past from present, he also gets the blame for the many artsy flourishes that corrupt everything they touch. The hero takes one of those purifying slow-motion showers that benefits nobody but Culligan, and anytime we're meant to be suitably horrified, the film drops to half-speed and slathers on the opera music. (Anne Dudley's bombastic score constitutes an assault in itself.)

Worst of all is a garishly filmed skinhead riot in an ethnic grocery. As the looters pour milk over a terrified cashier's head (to make her white), the scene goes on for such a prettily photographed eternity that our anger shifts from the skins to the director. This sort of aestheticized brutality is no small matter: It exploits and falsifies the vicious acts it condemns. If Norton indeed OK'd the final cut, he deserves blame for not leaving this crap on the cutting-room floor.

Especially since the most telling moments in *American History X* are the least rabid. McKenna gives Derek several provocative speeches that blur the line where conservatism ends and fascism begins: When he talks about why

Rodney King deserved his beating, or why people need to clear the undesirables from their neighborhoods, lots of viewers will likely agree — to a point. It's how far along we're willing to go that makes the movie so compelling. We can sit and watch Nazi goons beat an Hispanic clerk and never feel the slightest pang of recognition. But when the same goons lower their voices and start talking about personal responsibility, and safe streets, and protecting jobs, the movie hits home with a vengeance.

At the very least, see *American History X* for Edward Norton's fine work. And give the movie points for never succumbing to the lazy nihilism that informs *Very Bad Things*, *Your Friends and Neighbors*, *Happiness* and the other Angry White Guy movies of recent months. The ending is harsh (and a bit too carefully foreshadowed), but it reinforces the movie's tough theme: Hatred is an investment that always pays back. (*Nashville Scene*, Nov. 26, 1998)

● ● ● ● ● ● ● ● ● ●

Army of Shadows
Dir. Jean-Pierre Melville
1969, NR, 145 min.

Cease and Resist

A breathless man — a French resistance leader in World War II — lunges into a barbershop. Facing torture by the Gestapo, the man has just cut an officer's throat and run blindly into the snowy night. The barber, all business, ushers him into a chair. The man looks up to see a boldly displayed poster of Marshal Petain, ruler of the Nazis' puppet Vichy government. The barber reaches for his razor. You can imagine the scene as Hitchcock might have staged it, tightening the screws with each scrape of skin. There is no playful release of tension in *Army of Shadows*, a 1969 thriller previously unreleased in the U.S. that ranks among the great cinematic rediscoveries of recent years. A gripping portrait of life during wartime, rendered with pangs of nostalgia by a former resistance fighter, it doesn't let up: the haggard man in the chair has nothing waiting outside but more Petain posters, more Gestapo.

The movie is the work of Jean-Pierre Melville, the flamboyant French director whose career has undergone a dramatic revival of interest. Best known for coolly fatalistic crime dramas like 1955's *Bob le Flambeur* and 1967's *Le Samouraï*, he adopted Herman Melville's surname as his handle during the Resistance and reinvented himself after the war as a Stetson-wearing cineaste with a jones for American muscle cars, gadgetry and genre movies.

An episode of the 1971 TV series *Cinéastes de notre temps* shows him strolling gut first, hands thrust inside his trench coat like a gangster. Yet his movies have an iciness and sophistication far beyond their reputation for fanboy cool. Essentially a series of increasingly tense vignettes, *Army of Shadows* was adapted by Melville from a 1943 novel by Joseph Kessel. The combination of Melville's distant perspective and Kessel's immediacy produces a striking effect — something like the feel of a flashback without the establishing framework.

Army of Shadows was made the same year as *The Sorrow and the Pity*, Marcel Ophuls' great documentary about the Nazi occupation of France, and it evokes the terror and paranoia that the subjects of Ophuls' film describe — the sense of never knowing who might turn you in. Stereotypical Aryans are nowhere to be seen: the heroes have the same Gallic features as their jailors, torturers and executioners.

That kinship gives the movie a special horror, especially as Melville shows the torturers' handiwork. "You do what you can in these lousy times," a Vichy guard jovially tells Philippe Gerbier (Lino Ventura), chatting up the captured resistance leader en route to an internment camp. On the outside, Gerbier connects with other members of his resistance unit, including the sad-eyed enforcer Felix (Paul Crauchet), who enlists the cocky scofflaw Jean-François (Jean-Pierre Cassel).

Essentially members of a cell, the members carry out their missions with grim single-mindedness, keeping their identities secret even from those closest to them. From our vantage point — and Melville's, in 1969 — we can see that the men's actions served the greater good. Melville allows them no such comfort. The characters never have a chance to ponder their nobility or the verdict of time: There is only the matter at hand. In a horrific early scene, the men capture a turncoat — a scared kid — and dispassionately discuss the logistics of killing him: whether a gun is too loud, which room has thickest walls, etc. The kid's murder is a foregone conclusion, and one history will vindicate; in the moment, they must bear the look of his widening eyes, and the sensation of wringing the life out of him.

When the fighters do stop to worry about whether they're doing the right thing — as with a fearless organizer (cat-eyed Simone Signoret, marvelous) who is undone by simple love — the humane course of action proves to be wrong, or worse for humanity. The casting of Ventura, a heavy-set, thick-waisted character actor with a perpetually weary expression, makes the weight of those awful decisions palpable.

The world of Melville's movie has had almost all the color leached out of it, and with it all of the moral certainty; the first glimpse of the Arc de Triomphe is off-center, as if the whole country had shifted out of whack. "Bad memories, I welcome you anyway," reads the aphorism that opens the movie; "you are my long-lost youth."

If Melville's memories of the time went into *Army of Shadows* — he cast actual leaders and scrupulously recreated resistance meeting points — so did his skill at constructing spare, nail-biting sequences of existential dread. The film builds to a devastating final coda that reveals the fates of Gerbier and his shadow soldiers — information that, like the verdict of history, is unknown to them, shown to us, and little comfort to either. (*Nashville Scene*, Aug. 17, 2006)

● ● ● ● ● ● ● ● ● ●

The Untold Story of Emmett Louis Till
Dir. Keith A. Beauchamp
2005, PG-13, 70 min.

Too Close to Home

As a document of the unfathomable depths of evil, Keith A. Beauchamp's *The Untold Story of Emmett Louis Till* belongs in the historical record alongside a movie like *Shoah*, Claude Lanzmann's monumental oral history of the Holocaust. But it affected me, a proud white Southerner, far more personally than films about the atrocities of Nazi Germany. An ocean separates me from the homeland of Hitler's willing executioners. An interstate connects me to Mississippi, where proud white Southerners seized a black 14-year-old boy, Emmett Till, and butchered him for the crime of wolf-whistling at a white storekeeper.

This isn't some outpouring of liberal guilt. If anything, the brutal murder of Emmett Till gave even bigots permission to feel superior to the animals who killed him. But Beauchamp's invaluable film permits no easy detachment, no glib moral superiority. The question it asks is the same one underlying every Holocaust documentary: What, if anything, would you or I have done?

The result of nine years of research and interviews, *The Untold Story of Emmett Louis Till* lays out the case with a sober lack of melodrama. A Chicago teen, Till had gone to Mississippi in 1955 to visit relatives. Cousins, now old men, remember him as a mischief-maker, the kind of wiseguy who would holler on a city street that his companions were looking for a fight. With chilling matter-of-factness, one recalls trying to warn him how to act in the South. In 1955 Mississippi, you didn't just answer a white man "Yeah," or look directly at a white woman.

Till's capital offense was that he whistled at a storekeeper as she walked to her car. For that, two men, her husband Roy Bryant and J. W. Milam, showed up at the home of his grandfather near Money, Miss. With the help of as many as 12 conspirators, they abducted Emmett Till. Three days later, his decomposing body was found in a bayou, bound with barbed wire to a 70-pound cotton-gin fan. He had been beaten so severely that one eyeball dangled on his cheek. The teeth his mother remembered as "the prettiest thing I ever saw" had been knocked out, all but two. His face was nearly cleaved from his skull. The details of Till's murder were evidently horrible enough to shame racists: The local sheriff pushed for a fast funeral.

Emmett Till might have disappeared in racism's cemetery among a thousand unmarked graves. When Beauchamp unearths footage of an attorney dismissing his death as "ordinary criminal activity in Mississippi," one wonders how many other bodies lie mute in the swamp. But his mother, Mamie Till-Mobley, refused to let him be buried without a fight. When a funeral director told her he was forbidden to open the pine box that held her son's remains, she asked for a hammer. She put his body on display in Chicago, where thousands filed past his open casket. A sham trial later acquitted defendants Bryant and Milam after an hour (which included a break for sodas). But the image burned into people's minds.

With documentaries, the issue often comes up: Why not just read or write a book on the topic? One of the movie's interview subjects, the Rev. Al Sharpton, has the answer when he talks about the photos of Till's unrecognizable face. "People can sort of deal with things they don't have to look at," he observes, and the enormous value of Beauchamp's film is in seeing the firsthand testimony he has gathered. We see the teenage companion, now a grown man, who heard Emmett Till whistle; he saw the storekeeper recoil when Till put a dime in the woman's hand. We see the woman, then a girl, who heard his distant screams in the night. Above all, there is the heartrending evenness of Mamie Till-Mobley's remembrances, recorded before her death in 2003, as she calmly describes sights no mother should ever have to see.

Beauchamp's organization of the interviews is simple and arguably artless. He tells the story chronologically, in chapters; the interviews often overlap and repeat small details. A more assured filmmaker might have trimmed the excess and whittled down the personal reminiscences. I prefer the cumulative power of his technique: The witnesses have room to explain what they saw, and their overlapping details have the impact of corroborating evidence. He buttresses their accounts with archival footage that renders any dramatizing unnecessary — not when the defendants smile with their own children for the camera, or when the Tallahatchee County sheriff complains everything was OK until "our niggers went up north and talked to the NAACP." Or when women peer into Emmett Till's casket and faint.

The Untold Story of Emmett Louis Till doesn't just refute the notion that "it can't happen here." It refutes the idea, raised from time to time, that it *didn't* happen here. The movie introduces a jarring note of self-congratulation in its closing scenes, but perhaps it's deserved: As a result of Keith Beauchamp's research, the Justice Department reopened Emmett Till's murder in 2004.

This competently assembled, quietly devastating film isn't history written in lightning, as Woodrow Wilson said of *The Birth of a Nation*. But it just may be history recorded in light. (*Nashville Scene*, Nov. 24, 2005)

● ● ● ● ● ● ● ● ● ●

Xiu Xiu: The Sent-Down Girl
Dir. Joan Chen
1998, R, 99 min.

Acting Director

Actors who step behind the camera all too often lack an eye — a precise sense of how to convey ideas and emotion visually. Joan Chen isn't one of them. *Xiu Xiu: The Sent-Down Girl*, Chen's deeply affecting first feature as director, co-writer and co-producer, is remarkable both for its lack of reliance on dialogue and for the ghostly power of its images. Which is just as well: The story Chen tells is too painful for words.

Set in the 1970s, in the waning days of Chairman Mao's Cultural Revolution, *Xiu Xiu* (roughly pronounced "sho-SHO") concerns one of the millions of young urban students packed off to the provinces for "re-education" in communist work camps. After a year in the fields, the adolescent heroine, Xiu Xiu (Lu Lu), thinks she will be rewarded with a trip back home. Instead, she is promised an assignment leading a girls' cavalry if she spends six months learning horse-herding at a desolate Tibetan outpost.

Her only companion — a brusque but gentle middle-aged herder, Lao Jin (Lopsang), whose emasculation at the hands of Chinese torturers left him a laughingstock — tries to ease her loneliness. But Xiu Xiu longs for her family. To Lao Jin's horror, that makes her easy prey for low-level bureaucrats at the nearest regional headquarters, who routinely take advantage of the thousands of girls in Xiu Xiu's position. Soon the remote camp is invaded daily by ravagers, who use the girl for the cost of an apple and empty promises of reassignment.

Chen is best known for roles in *The Last Emperor* and the *Twin Peaks* series, and her acting experience no doubt helped her elicit such complex, expressive performances from her leads. Lu Lu, who was 15 at the time Chen started filming, is particularly impressive. The gradual fading of her spirit and innocence, as registered in her humiliated glances, is devastating to behold.

But it's Chen's unexpected skill as director that keeps *Xiu Xiu* from wallowing in unleavened misery. With her excellent cinematographer, Lü Yue, she invests stock imagery like storm clouds, landscapes and rainbows with serene, pitiless beauty that's as timeless as a folk tale, and she uses the wide screen to emphasize Xiu Xiu's isolation from Lao Jin, even within his cramped tent. And she brings out Xiu Xiu's youthful glee, before the story's natural gravity pulls her down. *Xiu Xiu: The Sent-Down Girl* shows that Joan Chen isn't just another actor who fancies herself a director. If her work reminds you of any other movie, it's Bresson's *Mouchette* or Teshigahara's *Woman in the Dunes* — not Gibson's *The Man Without a Face* or Costner's *The Postman*. (*Nashville Scene*, Aug. 19, 1999)

●　●　●　●　●　●　●　●　●

Underground
Dir. Emir Kusturica
1995, NR, 167 min.

The Basement Japes

Emir Kusturica's *Underground* is, among other things, the first movie about the collapse of the former Yugoslavia that you could recommend wholeheartedly to a *Three Stooges* fan. It's also one of the great moviegoing experiences of recent years — a work of staggering sadness, vitality and comic invention that's as awe-inspiring a spectacle in its own unhinged way as *Titanic*. An inexhaustible salvo of slapstick routines, sleight of hand and political theater played out as deadly vaudeville, the movie's two-hour-and-47-minute running time whizzes by like a blizzard of bottle rockets. Yet at heart *Underground* is a monstrous, drunken wake for a country that killed itself. The casket's packed with booze, and the corpse puffs an exploding cigar, but no amount of desperate tomfoolery can diminish the loss.

Underground distills the last five decades of Yugoslavian history into a massive metaphorical construct that's part Marx Brothers, part lyrical tragedy and part metafictional hootenanny. The curtains open with a fairy-tale declaration: "Once upon a time there was a country." Then bang! Kusturica joins bang! pistol-waving loonies and a brass band in full oompah as they tear ass through the streets of Belgrade, as though it weren't 1941 and the Nazis weren't laying waste to Central Europe.

But it is, and they are. As best buddies Blacky (Lazar Ristovski) and Marko (Miki Manojlovic) indulge their gluttonous appetites for food and sex, a gentle zookeeper hears a whistling high overhead. He looks up to see Axis bombs shatter the cages and loose the imprisoned animals. A goose nips at a wounded tiger; the tiger downs the goose with a weary chomp. Meanwhile, in a hooker's apartment, Marko races the bombs to climax. Blacky, across town, doesn't mind the explosions as long as they don't interfere with breakfast.

With the city reduced to rubble, the scheming Marko convinces his rash, impressionable pal to help him hijack Nazi convoys filled with gold and arms. Blacky's all too willing to help, especially since his mistress, the faithless actress Natalija (Mirjana Jokovic), is courting favor with a Nazi officer. After brazenly kidnapping her in the middle of a stage play — a wildly farcical scene that dumps the characters into a fictional world, the first of many such instances — Blacky is captured and tortured, and Marko and Natalija come to his rescue in one of the most inept getaway capers ever filmed.

They stash the wounded Blacky with dozens of blinkered refugees in a cavernous underground munitions factory beneath Marko's house. There he joins a small civilization that includes his son, the zookeeper, a superintelligent chimp and the brass band, among others. But when the war ends and Marshal Tito comes into power, Marko fears the reemergence of his best friend, especially since he has seduced Natalija in the meantime. Therefore, Marko and Natalija will spend the next 15 years sustaining an elaborate hoax, a fiction designed to convince Blacky and the underground dwellers that World War II still rages on the streets — the better to live off Blacky's status as a martyr.

Forgive this clumsy synopsis, which conveys none of the constant surprise of the plotting (by Kusturica and playwright Dusan Kovacevic) or the pure dammit-to-hell exuberance of Kusturica's filmmaking. At play there's a kind of silent-comedy logic, which makes it perfectly acceptable for, say, an urban dweller to see his shoes swiped by an elephant. Vilko Filac's camera wanders through antic tableaux of Baltic revelers in takes that last minutes on end, and for variety the camera might swing on the muzzle of a tank gun, or whirl around on a lazy Susan crammed with tuba players. The whole thing is propelled by a frantic Goran Bregovic score that sounds like an army of ducks walking on bicycle horns. If the movie were any more boisterous, the reels would fly off the projector and carom off the walls.

But the noise, the raunchy humor and the visual bombardment never obscure the movie's gravity. When it won the Palme d'Or three years ago at Cannes, in a victory that sparked an international controversy, *Underground* was reviled abroad as Serbian propaganda, and the Sarajevo-born Kusturica was denounced as a traitor. (Perhaps that's because he includes newsreel footage of cheering Croatians welcoming the Nazi invaders during the war.) If indeed there are subtleties that show Kusturica favors one ethnicity over another, they're either lost in translation or lost on Western audiences.

What isn't lost is Kusturica's grieving for his fractured homeland, or his evenhanded indictment of his countrymen for their willingness either to exploit or to allow themselves to be exploited. The disintegration of postwar Yugoslavia, in the movie's terms, is a ridiculous fiction that required the collaboration of most of its citizens, whether they're the Markos who conspired to line their pockets by oppressing their comrades, or they're the Blackys who blindly accepted whatever leadership came to power. Nazi, Communist, whatever — the director greets each new shift in the power structure with the same ironic refrain of "Lili Marlene."

Kusturica doesn't even entirely trust the process of moviemaking, which strikes him as a little too close to Marko's brand of myth-making manipulation. Doctored newsreels coincide with the Rube Goldberg–like periscope that Marko uses to spy on the world underground. In the movie's most riotous scene, Blacky finally emerges from his hole only to blunder into a tacky biopic — his own.

As often in satire, *Underground*'s heroes are almost completely lacking in psychological complexity. Like carousers in a Fielding novel, the characters show happiness by breaking into a jig, and if someone feels racked by guilt, he's likely as not to express it by shooting himself in the leg a few times. And yet the movie grows almost imperceptibly more somber. By the film's final section, when father loses son and brother kills brother, the zaniness of the first two-thirds has given way to a long, sustained note of regret and to indelibly surreal images of devastation: a flaming wheelchair creeping in circles, a body suspended from the rope of an incessantly pealing church bell.

Underground closes with a coda of extraordinary sweetness and beauty, as Kusturica literally reassembles his country before casting it adrift forever on a sea of memory. We can only hope *Underground* draws more of an audience than the excellent *Welcome to Sarajevo* did a few weeks ago. If not, maybe local audiences can't stomach movies about the Bosnian conflict, however abstract and stylized, because they remind us that once upon a time there was a country where brother killed brother, and we lived there. (*Nashville Scene*, March 26, 1998)

● ● ● ● ● ● ● ● ● ●

To Live
Dir. Zhang Yimou
1994, NR, 133 min.

A Tale Well Told

Storytelling is a threatened art these days, and lazy moviemakers are perhaps the biggest threat. What began as experimentation with film technique has become an overdependence on cinematic shorthand. When Eisenstein began to experiment with film editing, he looked to *Finnegan's Wake*: If Joyce could combine three words in such a way that they created an entirely new meaning in sequence, why not do the same with images? Pictures of a gun, a rose and a woman shouting add up to something completely different when placed in a certain order: Our minds fill in the connective blanks. The problem is, in this visually besotted age, we have become so used to filling in those blanks that moviemakers have lost the art of constructing a narrative.

In *Legends of the Fall*, for example, Brad Pitt says goodbye to his lover on the Wyoming prairie, and in the very next shot he's commandeering a pirate ship somewhere on the high seas. A 19th-century novelist would have spent 100 pages explaining the information crucial to that narrative development. Now we're expected to assume the screenwriter's role along with the viewer's; in the process, the very things that hold our attention in a story — character development, anecdotes and incidental asides — are abandoned.

To Live, the new movie by the Chinese director Zhang Yimou, manages what these days amounts to a miraculous feat: It tells a story simply, beautifully and so completely that we're left with a sense of serene satisfaction. In the process, it restores the thematic richness and detail so lacking in most contemporary films — and so crucial to our enjoyment. *To Live* runs nearly two-and-a-half hours, and yet it is never less than spellbinding and visually stunning — a tribute to the filmmaker's craft as well as the storyteller's.

To Live opens in mainland China in the 1940s, in the years just before the revolt against Chiang Kai-Shek's nationalist army and the rise of Mao. The protagonist, Fugui, is an inveterate gambler and ne'er-do-well who subsists on his family's declining fortune. Against the protests of his wife, Jiazhen, who cares for his aged parents as well as his young daughter Fengxia, Fugui gambles into the hands of a conniving puppet master, a move that leaves him ultimately without shelter, family or honor. As political turmoil sends the country into upheaval, Fugui struggles to regain his family and fulfill one meager but daunting wish — "to live a quiet life."

The perils of telling a story against such a politically charged backdrop are numerous: The film could either have lapsed into strident melodrama, like the overrated *Farewell My Concubine*, or into anti-communist agitprop lacking in human dimensions. Director Zhang, however, the most important figure to emerge thus far from the so-called "young Chinese cinema," keeps his drama rooted in the intimate details of everyday life: keeping warm, finding work, sharing meals. The movie's subtle but damning portrait of communist inefficiency and brutality unfolds through incident, not speechifying or crude grandstanding. As in his previous films, most notably *Ju Dou* and the magnificent *Raise the Red Lantern*, Zhang includes elements of melodrama but addresses them in such a skillful, matter-of-fact way that they don't seem sensational: They seem merely another hazard of the flux of living.

In a fine piece of writing, character and plotting are inextricable. Once Fugui and Jiazhen have been introduced, they seem to seize control of their destiny, and the movie's as well. The movie spans three decades of warfare, violence and personal tragedy, but Zhang never violates his characters for the sake of plot mechanics or an ideological point. Even when a surprise twist occurs — and there are too many to count — the characters react with appropriate joy, outrage or vengeance. What makes *To Live* such a superb piece of storytelling is the accumulation of details that build interest: the feel of busy streets, the ever-shifting relationships between family, friends and neighbors, the seemingly insignificant choices that prove vital — or deadly — later on. When someone goes to war, we have seen the events that led him there, and we know how he will respond. The careful crafting of the central characters permits effortless shifts between comedy and tragedy, between humor and horror.

Fugui is a particularly rich creation, a flawed hero who, like Hardy's Mayor of Casterbridge, seems all the more human and compelling for his frailties. Ge You, the actor who portrays Fugui, won the Cannes Film Festival award for best actor. In his early scenes, as a cocksure gambler, Fugui's unlined face exudes arrogant self-loathing; when he loses his entire fortune — and his family — on a single unwise bet, the arrogance drains from his face, leaving a mask of pure anguish. The cry that issues from Fugui is acting that transcends all ethnic or cultural boundaries. His devastated howl cuts right to the soul, and yet we hear in it the music that will eventually save his life. Ge You has one of those faces that expresses the kind of humility shaped by years of misfortune.

Gong Li, Zhang's frequent collaborator as well as one of the world's most accomplished and beautiful actresses, provides the movie's conscience as

Jiazhen: Her painful decision to leave Fugui snaps him to life; and when he returns, her reproachful looks are tempered with affection. Theirs is the most moving, honest and adult romance in current movies. Jiazhen needles Fugui to keep him humble, while he draws upon her spiritual strength; both have resentments, passions and disappointments that never go away, no matter how dimmed by time. Yet the way their faces age together, not so much by makeup but by shared experience, embodies the movie's radiant promise of hope: By the movie's end, we have seen the survival of love despite crushingly painful blows.

Although it is easily one of the best movies of recent years, *To Live* was locked out of an Academy Award nomination for Best Foreign Film by stupid voting processes and outright censorship: The Chinese government refused to enter the film as its official Oscar contender, due to the movie's criticisms of the whims of Maoist doctrine. Avenge the filmmakers, then, by seeing the movie.

I've seen few movies in the past year that I enjoyed as consistently as *To Live*. I love the mysterious depth and beauty of cinematographer Lü Yue's images, particularly the emphasis on backlit screens and hazy alleyways. I love the use of food as a metaphor of family solidarity, and the many moments of bravery, and humor, and compassion. Most of all, I love the perfect, novelistic balance of Zhang Yimou's world, in which the meal that saves one man from starvation brings about another's death, and the act that destroys Fugui's life ultimately leads to his salvation. *To Live* has the impact of a great novel, or a story handed down over generations. The marvelous last shot leaves us with the suggestion that life goes on, for Fugui and Jiazhen and all the movie's flawed and fabulous creations, long after the image has left the screen. (*Nashville Scene*, March 23, 1995)

Forever Changes **12**

The one thing all movies share is that they must end. Some stay with us long after the final image leaves the screen. They revisit us for idiosyncratic, seemingly incongruous reasons. The same movie might resonate with us differently on subsequent viewings, and that is part of what makes film so powerful and intimate. And so this book ends with a chapter dedicated to films about death and memory. Included here are Jim's review of *The Last Picture Show* (Peter Bogdanovich's masterful elegy for a dying Texas town), *Mother and Son* (about a dying woman's final hours), and an obituary for director Robert Altman that considers the richness and influence of his half-century of filmmaking.

In a 2014 interview with the now-defunct film site *The Dissolve*, director Kore-eda Hirokazu says, "In my filmmaking, one of the things I am trying to do consciously is to show the things in our daily lives that seem banal and ordinary, but that are actually very, very special."[1] This was a quality in movies that attracted Jim Ridley, and one he takes care to admire. This is especially apparent in his review of Abbas Kiarostami's *Taste of Cherry*, whose glacial pace some critics found off-putting. Jim defends the film by arguing that its method, and not a lack thereof, matches its intent.

Movies ordinarily compress time artificially, but as Jim writes, "Kiarostami asks us to consider the weight of the moments in between — the moments that make up living." In that 2014 interview, Kore-eda also says that one thing he eventually learned as a director is that "the more personal you make it, the more resonant it'll be." This is also true of Jim's reviews. The anecdotes that find their way into his writing never shift the focus onto himself, but rather deepen the point he's making. Jim ends his summation of *Taste of Cherry*

---

1   Noel Murray, "Hirokazu Kore-eda on *Like Father, Like Son* and the Art of Making the Personal Universal," *The Dissolve*, Jan. 20, 2014, *thedissolve.com*.

with a personal anecdote — a turn that is at once unexpected and perfectly in tune with the emotion of the film.

This book ends as it begins, with Jacques Demy, in a sprawling appreciation of *The Umbrellas of Cherbourg* whose small autobiographical details are now, for me, inextricable from the experience of the movie itself. In this way, great film writing is like great film: It changes how we see the world.

● ● ● ● ● ● ● ● ● ●

After Life
Dir. Kore-eda Hirokazu
1998, NR, 118 min.

Remembrance of Things Past

In my dreams, heaven is a movie theater. Not a video shop with endless aisles, not a megaplex with an embarrassment of riches; just a simple one-screener with a different movie every couple of nights. Some nights I'd see bad movies that carry some kind of fond association — like *Dressed to Kill*, my notoriously inappropriate choice for a first date with the woman who eventually became my wife. Other nights there'd be movies that haunt me like a favorite tune, because they evoke so piercingly a specific joy — the way *Jules and Jim* captures the feeling of being young and so in love that the world whirls by in a watercolor blur.

It's not the variety of movies that gives this dream its power. It's the chance to shuffle through an unwinding reel of memories that sometimes involve movies only incidentally, as backdrops for dates, chance encounters, family outings. But what if you had to choose only one movie, and only one memory — would that be heaven at all? Those are the rules in *After Life*, an overwhelming Japanese film about the promise of life after death and the bittersweet trade-offs it entails.

A fantasy that uses the mundane to illuminate the celestial, and vice versa, *After Life* takes place in a purgatorial way station that looks like a high school converted into a traffic bureau. But it's not exactly limbo; it's a makeshift movie studio. Every Monday, about 20 new arrivals — the recently deceased — check in at the lobby office, and in six days' time, they'll be whisked off to heaven. In the meantime, though, they're given one last task: They have three days to select one memory, the happiest or most indelible moment of their lives. The rest of the week, they'll film a reenactment of that moment; that and the memory will be all they carry into eternity. All other memories, good and bad, will vanish.

It's the beauty of the saved memories, and the burden of those that are lost, that makes *After Life* so affecting. The film originated out of a documentary project by the director, Kore-eda Hirokazu, whose work characteristically addresses death and memory — one of his previous docs concerns a man whose brain damage causes his memories to fade after only an hour. According to *Film Comment*, Kore-eda began *After Life* by inviting people to share one moment they'd like to keep forever; he then incorporated some of these people into the film alongside professional actors.

His script follows a deceptively plodding path, charting the daily progress made by each person: a morose husband, a pilot, a grandmotherly woman who was happiest dancing as a child. I say deceptively, because it isn't until the movie's devastating resolution, a crisis of memory that affects two heavenly staffers for entirely different reasons, that you realize how beautifully the director has shaped the movie — he transforms the ongoing rituals of bureaucracy into a metaphor for death and renewal. The afterlife-as-bureaucracy angle has appeared before, in movies ranging from *Defending Your Life* to *Heaven Can Wait*. Here, though, the documentary solidity — the grounding of fantasy material in a prosaic setting — becomes a kind of serene poetry.

In some ways, Kore-eda's method resembles that of the Iranian director Abbas Kiarostami, who incorporates real events, nonprofessional actors, and even the process of making his films into his fictional frameworks, using the very limits of his medium as a vehicle for finding the truth. While tantalizing us with basic mysteries (why just one memory? who made the rules?), Kore-eda fleshes out his afterlife with tiny, truthful details, down to the comic imprecision of attempting to restage someone's life on film. And he manages to evoke transcendence without leaning on special effects. His scale is human, his wit humane.

The movies I love most are inextricable from memory; they fuse with past feelings, trigger complex emotions, summon unbidden responses even years later. Though one of its themes is the inadequacy of movies to fully capture human experience, *After Life* does what those movies do: It asks essential questions of your humanity. Days after seeing it, I'm still haunted by the query at its center: What memory would you take, and which memories could you live with losing? Someday, those heartrending questions may have to be answered. For now, I'm just happy I don't have to part company yet with the memory of seeing this wondrous film. (*Nashville Scene*, Nov. 25, 1999)

● ● ● ● ● ● ● ● ● ●

The Last Picture Show
Dir. Peter Bogdanovich
1971, R, 126 min.

We Lost It at the Movies

Few movies capture the ambivalence of small-town life as well as Peter Bogdanovich's 1971 heartbreaker *The Last Picture Show*, adapted from Larry McMurtry's evocative coming-of-age novel. It's sometimes seen as an anomaly in the artistic upheaval of 1970s Hollywood, a blip of nostalgia for classical moviemaking as doomed as the single-screen movie theater that provides its title; ironically enough, that's one reason it has aged so much better than many hipper, flashier films of the counterculture era. But it's more like something warped in from an alternate-universe 1949, saddened and wised-up, frank where movies of the time were coy, watched as if by its own stars from a wistful vantage point decades later.

The movie's a black-and-white elegy for a dust-blown Texas burgh's slow fade into oblivion, as its young folk move on and its storefronts close. It's a yearbook of pool parties, fumbling sexual encounters and bleating high-school football bands, regarded with the despondent awareness that for these kids, these lives, this town, this is as good as it gets. The movie doesn't mourn the end of innocence so much as the lack of anything better to replace it — except maybe the sorrowful understanding exchanged between Cloris Leachman's neglected housewife and Timothy Bottoms' unwittingly cruel youth in that heartrending finale.

Perhaps most keenly, the movie laments the passing of Hollywood's golden-age auteurs — directors like Bogdanovich's heroes Howard Hawks and John Ford, whose films play the modest Royal Theater that serves as the town's supplier of dreams and glamour. With his wife, the late Polly Platt, as yeoman production designer, Bogdanovich shot the movie with Hitchcock's frequent cinematographer Robert Surtees, and the spacious, monumental images, composed and cut with a master's precision, seem to impart something new in the style of something old: a chill of self-awareness about what is being lost. All these strains of regret meet in Western star Ben Johnson's iconic performance as the stern, upright father figure who runs the cinema and remains the local boys' one strong adult role model — until he too is gone.

Bogdanovich overdoes the dry wind and backlot-barren streets sometimes, but the starkness is leavened by McMurtry's rowdy humor, a vital soundtrack of Hank Williams and honky-tonk oldies, and a wonderful cast. There's Jeff Bridges, looking fresh-faced and unformed but there, so *there*, as Bottoms' roughneck football buddy; there's Cybill Shepherd in her first movie, breaking hearts onscreen and off as the rich tease who comes between them; there's Ellen Burstyn as her hardened mother, and Eileen Brennan as the tough-talking waitress and confidante, and Joe Heathcock, the distilled essence of character actor, playing that sawed-off squawkbox sheriff just nine years before he died in Nashville. To see them today in this black-and-white ghost world, even (or especially) for teenage viewers who know Bridges as the paunchy, dissolute Dude — or as *Tron: Legacy*'s frozen-in-time CGI avatar — is to sense that time has passed, time is passing, time will keep on passing by. To get the full impact, you have to see it in an honest-to-God movie theater, projected from celluloid. The way things are going, it may very well be the last picture show. (*Nashville Scene*, April 26, 2012)

● ● ● ● ● ● ● ● ●

Mother and Son
Dir. Aleksandr Sokurov
1997, NR, 73 min.

One More Hour

In a *Village Voice* interview recently, distributor Wendy Lidell devised a simple distinction between movies and films. "[T]o me, going to see a movie and a film are completely different experiences," she said. "Going to see a film is more like going to an art museum, where I'm going to be engaged and provoked but maybe not entertained."

That distinction is useful from a consumer's standpoint. If you've had a hard day at work, you might not want to tackle the cinematic equivalent of *Ulysses*. But Lidell's distinction between movies and films breaks down some if your idea of entertainment is *being* engaged and provoked. Perhaps there's a more meaningful difference — between movies that function as an escape from the world, and movies that serve as a vehicle for exploring it.

By most people's definition, Aleksandr Sokurov's 1997 feature *Mother and Son* (which Lidell's former company, International Film Circuit, distributes) is probably the polar opposite of entertainment: a plotless, almost wordless Russian drama about a son's last few moments with his dying mother. I'd be lying if I didn't say that the first time I watched it (on tape), I was exasperated by its painful slowness and its lack of narrative momentum. And yet, on a second viewing, it affected me so much I'm almost afraid to see it again. If you watch movies to be engaged and provoked — or simply to see the world in an unfamiliar and revelatory way — *Mother and Son* is nothing less than astonishing.

Sokurov explores the bond between mother and son, and the agony of impending loss, through a series of scenes that are nearly (but never quite) still-lifes. In a reversal of the parent-child relationship, the son (Aleksei Ananishnov) cradles his pale mother (Gudrun Geyer), combing her hair and carrying her outside for a last look. Clutching her to his chest, he trudges through a succession of stormy landscapes and birch groves.

These events are captured by an elaborate filming technique that distorts and refracts the image through mirrors and glass filters. At times the process gives an odd horizontal slant to the objects onscreen, as if the characters and the landscape were buckling under the gravity of grief. At other times, it creates pictorial effects of breathtaking stillness and solemnity. Sokurov has cited the 19th-century German Romantic landscape painter Caspar David Friedrich as an inspiration, and the influence is evident in his awe-inspiring gray mistscapes. Against these panoramas of undulating wheat and gnarled, elongated trees, mother and son are frequently reduced to a single inextricable speck.

The movie's less than 75 minutes long; even so, its running time feels like several hours instead of one. But the weight of time is central to Sokurov's depiction of loss. You're always aware of the slow passage of each moment and an accompanying pang of regret as one more moment passes — an apt way to evoke watching a loved one wither. Like the mother, the movie makes demands upon your patience; like the mother, the movie comes across as a living thing perched between death and transcendence. When the end comes for both, there is a howl of anguish for which nothing can prepare you; then darkness, silence.

In its insistence on forcing you to work through your own responses, both to Sokurov's rigorously controlled filmmaking and to the common plight of all parents and children confronting mortality, *Mother and Son* is certainly engaging and provocative. For those reasons, you can say it offers entertainment. What it doesn't offer is escape. (*Nashville Scene*, Feb. 4, 2000)

• • • • • • • • • •

Daughters of the Dust
Dir. Julie Dash
1991, PG, 112 min.

Dream Gullahs

Julie Dash's *Daughters of the Dust* is an epic that defies all contemporary ideas of what an epic should be. Its strongest characters are women, it takes place in an enclosed place in an enclosed period of time, and it has no grandiose action scenes. It doesn't proceed according to anything remotely resembling traditional narrative form.

And yet this independently produced film has a sweep that makes an effort like *Far and Away* seem arrested by tunnel vision. In its elliptical, mysterious way, *Daughters of the Dust* encompasses nothing less than the development of the 20th century, from the dissolution of the nuclear family to the assimilation of African culture into the American mosaic. It's a strange, mesmerizing film, one that works on an associative, imaginative level that few movies reach.

Against a background of the Georgia and South Carolina Sea Islands, *Daughters of the Dust* concerns the Gullah-speaking descendants of former slaves, a people who have lived in partial isolation from the mainland for well over a century. Dash's film takes place on a late summer day in 1902, a time when some elders still share first-hand memories of Africa — the very moment when the younger generation is preparing to move from the island to the fabled mainland North.

Various stories emerge — a husband agonizing over his pregnant wife's rape, the arrival of a scandalous relative, a photographer fascinated by a glimpse of his heritage. But Dash's film is more about the fabric of a community, and a way of life, than about any one narrative thread. Its approach is reminiscent of Robert Altman's *McCabe & Mrs. Miller*, in which the plot and the characters' relationships are discovered only from overheard conversations.

Dash approaches filmmaking in an imagistic, associative way. Instead of using a conventional narrative, she condenses her vision of Gullah life into poetic fragments. Usually, "poetic" filmmaking falls into the same lapse that makes for bad poetry: imprecision, pretension, self-indulgence. For the most part, Dash's imagery escapes these pitfalls. Her control of the medium and her own symbolism are astonishing for a debuting director. Her motifs — hands, craftwork, the juxtaposition of intrusive modern elements against untouched natural settings — show hope for the survival of tradition, even as they lament the inevitable disappearance of the culture that spawned them.

Dash's technique, which features speeded-up motion, slow motion and breathtaking naturalistic lighting, gives the movie a timeless feel, as if it were truly poised in balance between two centuries. Her pictorial effects are marvelous: A shot of two women perched in yellow dresses among a live oak's gnarled branches has a mystical beauty and wit reminiscent of Latin American fiction. When the surf suddenly turns to gold at a woman's feet, God himself seems to have ordered the lighting.

As much of a pleasure as its understatement is, *Daughters of the Dust* might be helped by a few more dramatic concessions. While the musical Gullah language is surprisingly easy to follow, the many relationships aren't; the movie has dozens of characters, many of whom are never addressed by name, and their family or community statuses are never made entirely clear. What's more, some of the performances are a little stilted, as if the actors couldn't decide whether contemporary gestures or a period stiffness were appropriate.

Daughters of the Dust, like this year's earlier *Mississippi Masala*, completely recreates and explores another America, and its few faults are trifling, given the scope of its accomplishment. As our cultures are increasingly consumed and homogenized by the global village, *Daughters of the Dust* defiantly embraces cultural distinctions and traditions. It's a beautiful, difficult movie — a film in which the difficulty, for once, is worth the effort. (*Nashville Scene*, July 9, 1992)

• • • • • • • • • •

The Long Goodbye
Robert Altman, 1925–2006

Last week, when word of Robert Altman's death had just begun to circulate, a co-worker sent the wire clipping along with a single comment: "His death took three hours, and his last words couldn't be heard because of the 40 characters speaking over them." It was a more appropriate tribute, in a way, than the outpourings of affection and admiration that followed. Love his films or hate them — and even the best ones provoked grudges of almost Balkan tenacity — Altman didn't make movies that people can consume and shrug off. They won't brook any condescension.

The features Altman made in a 50-year career, not counting a huge amount of varied and fascinating work for television, are a lot like the voices that crowd the soundtracks of his movies. Some are quizzical, like the muted 1979 science-fiction allegory *Quintet*, and others seem chilly and off-putting; still others — say, the overbearing fashion satire *Prêt-à-Porter* — have the kind of forced frivolity you'd cringe from in a crowded room. And yet something about even the least of them commands your attention. Each represents not just a story but a pathway of possibility — a dead end, sometimes, but worth exploring nonetheless. Put them together, the grand and the misshapen, all overlapping and crisscrossing, and out of that entropic maelstrom comes something the movies rarely evoke: a sense of life's richness.

That's not just true of the carnivalesque ensemble pieces that are synonymous with the director's name — buzzing biospheres such as *McCabe & Mrs. Miller*, *Nashville* and *Short Cuts* that teem with intersecting destinies. It holds true also for chamber dramas such as his spellbinding 1977 dream play *3 Women*, whose mysteries spiral endlessly outward. In his best movies, and even in ones with few admirers, Altman rewired moviegoers' receptors: He encouraged viewers to look, listen and seek without knowing exactly what they were going to find.

A viewer enters Altman's movies as the stranger who comes to town. The world has been functioning without us for some time, whether it's a Music Row recording session, a frontier village or the card-shark milieu of his 1974 gambling tragicomedy *California Split*: It is up to us to listen sharp and see what we can find out. Gone is the usual gum-wad of exposition that lays out everything we need to know. In *McCabe*, his 1971 opium dream of a Western, it takes some time before we realize that scruffy, mumbling braggart in the furry coat is the hero, even though he's played by Warren Beatty.

Some two-dozen characters pass the narrative focus of *Nashville* back and forth like a relay baton within the movie's breathless first half-hour. The camera movement that links these disparate movies is a kind of purposeful drift, as if the lens were a gently floating transmitter always seeking to lock in on a signal. Altman made viewers listen the same way. Except for Orson Welles, and arguably David Lynch, he did more than any other major American director to explore the possibilities of sound in moviemaking, and in storytelling.

In his commentary on the *Nashville* DVD, the director says he miked even extras within a scene who might not appear again in the film. It was a logistical nightmare for the sound recordist, but as with Altman's commercial breakthrough, *MASH*, the density of dialogue makes the movie seem funnier, faster paced, caught on the fly. It also creates a texture of roving spontaneity. We never know which of these characters might spirit the movie away.

The slam against Altman — besides that racket on the soundtrack — is that he was a cynic inviting us to chortle at a gallery of rubes and straw men. The movie that always comes up as Exhibit A is *Nashville*, his kaleidoscopic 1975 portrait of America as Music City on the cusp of the Bicentennial. Even today, it makes people want to settle Altman's hash: Some supermarket rag just tagged it on a list of overrated movies (there's a novel idea), and even obits last week for the director brought out usual suspects to vent their spleen all over again. Watching *Nashville* now, though, it's hard to see why the movie bitterly polarized people here 31 years ago — a reaction that had as much to do with Altman's not hiring the city's hit mill to provide the soundtrack as with any perceived slight.

The director allows his alleged "rubes" to surprise us again and again with new facets of feeling and depth, as when Barbara Baxley's hitherto comic character delivers a tearful, sincere reminiscence of the fallen Kennedys. Henry Gibson's Haven Hamilton may be a pompous elder statesman of country, but he's also quick to shout down a heckler's racist taunts (in a plausibly complex way) and to stand up bravely when an assassin's bullets riddle the Parthenon at the climax. Altman may have loved to come on like the maverick outsider who knew more about the inside than the insiders — a tone that gives his 1992 Hollywood expose *The Player* its edge of breezily nasty score-settling. But his best movies convey the bitter indignity of being on the fringe, and none does so more painfully than *Nashville*. The humiliation of Gwen Welles' talentless wannabe Sueleen at a smoker is the movie's emotional crux: she's the stand-in for all the country's broken hopefuls, chasing a dream that lets others use her. Her exit — bare naked, insignificant, watched forlornly to the very back of the frame — carries the director's outrage and sympathy, not his scorn.

Images of windows recur throughout his movies; the director's heart is with all those people whose faces are pressed against the glass — Sueleen, the pining McCabe, Elliott Gould and George Segal's desperate low-rollers in *California Split*. Even 30 years after his astonishing string of early-1970s masterworks, the way Altman made movies — as if they were events that took on lives of their own — continues to pose challenges to contemporary filmmakers, and to point a way out of commercial cinema's seeming blind alleys.

From *Babel* to *Bobby*, from Paul Thomas Anderson's band-of-outsiders epics to Richard Linklater's dazed-and-confused roundelays, Altman's influence is perhaps stronger than it has ever been. It's just the man himself who is gone — something his last film, this summer's *A Prairie Home Companion*, foretold as gently, sweetly and insistently as possible. In one particularly poignant exchange, someone asks the Altman surrogate, ringmaster Garrison Keillor, if he wants people to remember him after he dies. His reply is forthright: "I don't want them to be *told* to remember." Maybe that line is a bit obvious to cite in a remembrance. But when a man gets a chance to write his own epitaph, we can at least take down his dictation. (*Nashville Scene*, Nov. 30, 2006)

● ● ● ● ● ● ● ● ● ●

Taste of Cherry
Dir. Abbas Kiarostami
1997, NR, 95 min.

Life Is Sweet

The wonderful Iranian movie *Taste of Cherry*, directed by Abbas Kiarostami, is suspenseful in a humane, unforced way that's unlike anything else I've ever seen. For maximum effect, you should see it knowing as little about it as possible, which is why I'd recommend skipping this review until after you've seen it. Viewed without warning or explanation, it offers a quiet rebuke to the idea that cinema (and drama, and life) is nothing less — or more — than wall-to-wall incident and action.

For the first 20 minutes, we follow a middle-aged man, Mr. Badii, as he drives through the outskirts of Tehran. He's played by Homayoun Ershadi, a nonactor whose doleful face Kiarostami spotted in traffic. The director tells us nothing about him, not even where he's going; the credits don't even appear until 10 minutes into the movie. In his white Range Rover, Mr. Badii just pulls up alongside various strangers — some laborers, a kid at a telephone booth. Is he some kind of predator? Some kind of pervert? The director remains silent.

Mr. Badii picks up passengers, first a young Kurdish soldier, then a seminary student. They talk, but they're not shown together: The movie cuts from one face to the other, as if they weren't even in the same car. We're 20 minutes into the film before Mr. Badii finally explains his purpose. For reasons he won't mention, he plans to take an overdose of pills, crawl into an open grave and die. He just wants someone to return in the morning to fill in the dirt.

It's easy to make a case for living when the plain, uneventful moments are edited out of your life. But what if your life consists of nothing else? Either you treasure it for the chance that something good will happen, or you hold no such hopes and see no reason to continue. And so Kiarostami strips 95 minutes of screen time, of life, to its spare essence. Mr. Badii is joined by a Turkish taxidermist (Abdolhossein Bagheri) who can't imagine giving up forever the taste of a cherry. What follows is so simply presented, and so simply profound, it's like considering for the first time how it feels to breathe air.

The complaint I keep reading about in reviews of *Taste of Cherry* is that nothing happens. Things happen, all right, just not at the pace we expect from movies. A trip to the store, in standard movie terms, is accomplished in a matter of seconds: exterior shot of the supermarket, cut to the condiment aisle, cut to the checkout line. All the downtime — the leaving, the driving, the parking — has been removed, all action compressed. But a life in progress isn't a movie script; it's dots of occasion connected by mundane routines and moments that take shape only in retrospect. Kiarostami asks us to consider the weight of the moments in between — the moments that make up living.

Apart from *The White Balloon*, which he scripted for his former assistant Jafar Panahi, *Taste of Cherry* is the first film I've ever had the chance to see by Abbas Kiarostami, whose movies have rarely been shown in the U.S. Although Kiarostami has made numerous short films and features since 1970, he's best known for his "earthquake trilogy," which started with 1987's *Where Is the Friend's House?* — a film about a boy retrieving a notebook — and expanded to include the aftermath of a real-life earthquake in the filming area (1991's *And Life Goes On*) and even the filming of that previous film (1994's *Through the Olive Trees*).

This spiraling interplay of fact and fiction indicates something of his method. *Taste of Cherry* is visually simple but hardly uncinematic: The director uses a frame within a frame — the car window — as effectively as Peter Weir in *The Truman Show*. As viewers, we're always aware there's a world that extends not just beyond the frame of the camera but also beyond the time frame Kiarostami has chosen. *The White Balloon* ended with a piercing shot of a solitary boy uncertain where to go next — his story didn't end when the camera shut off. *Taste of Cherry* ends by refusing to stay within the bounds of fiction. A director who cares so deeply for even the most tedious aspects of living can hardly slam the door on his universe with the script's last page.

Five years ago, one of my closest friends killed himself. The night before he died, I thought about calling him, and I've wondered ever since what I would've said if I'd had the chance to change his mind. I imagine reciting the litany of precious small wonders in Lucinda Williams' "Sweet Old World": the breath from your own lips, the touch of fingertips. But at the simplest level of existence, you either want to live or you don't, and if you don't, the sweetest cherry in the world means nothing. *Taste of Cherry* reminded me of all the nights we drove around, drinking mint Snapples in silence, when I thought nothing was happening. (*Nashville Scene*, June 4, 1998)

• • • • • • • • • •

The Umbrellas of Cherbourg
Dir. Jacques Demy
1964, NR, 91 min.

A Finite Forever

Jacques Demy's *The Umbrellas of Cherbourg* won what is now the Palme d'Or at Cannes in 1964, launched a pop standard that has been covered by everyone from Frank Sinatra to Louis Armstrong, and made the 20-year-old Catherine Deneuve an international sensation. It has been revived theatrically at least twice since its initial release, each time playing to new audiences and wider acclaim. With a CV like that, you wouldn't think a movie would need defenders. And yet something about this film trips a wise-guy alarm in viewers who distrust musicals as a form, and who use "light entertainment" as a pejorative. The word that comes up repeatedly, in searches for the movie online, is *curio*.

The notion of Demy as the French New Wave's twee miniaturist has long trailed his work. It hounded him in the years that bracketed the meteoric flourishing of the Nouvelle Vague, when he was the guy who made a musical with Gene Kelly the same year that Jean-Luc Godard was dispatching revolutionaries to incinerate Emily Brontë, the classicism she embodied, and cinema itself. It clung to him in the waning years of his career, when self-styled sophisticates could look at a movie as politically seething and formally daring as his 1982 musical melodrama *Une chambre en ville* and write it off as, sigh, yet another tunefest from poor outmoded Demy.

By the mid-1970s, the received wisdom on Demy was that he was a dabbler in irrelevant genres whose time had passed. And none of his films sounded sillier in the abstract than *The Umbrellas of Cherbourg*, this oddity in which every line of dialogue is not only sung but sung in French. It didn't help that his movies grew harder to find in subsequent years, or that the superlatives of his style — brilliant color, exquisite framing, elegantly choreographed camerawork — were grotesquely ill served by the aesthetic abattoir of lop-and-chop VHS.

It wasn't until the mid-1990s that I saw *Umbrellas* for the first time, under near-perfect conditions — in a restored print at San Francisco's glorious Castro Theatre, with an audience so besotted that they anticipated the melodies. I expected a mawkish pastiche — the judgment rendered in 1964 by the *New York Times*' reliably fusty Bosley Crowther, who dismissed the film as "a cinematic confection so shiny and sleek and sugar-sweet — so studiously sentimental — it comes suspiciously close to a spoof."

What Demy delivers instead is the most affecting of movie musicals, and perhaps the fullest expression of a career-long fascination with the entwining of real life, chance and the bewitching artifice of cinematic illusion. More than any other film I know, *Umbrellas* affects people differently at different stages of life. When I first saw it, newly married but still remembering vividly the pang of adolescent crushes, it played as tragedy: the story of a young love snuffed out by war, fate, and economic hardship. Over the years, seen in the light of Demy's other films, it has come to seem more properly an exaltation of life's bittersweet balances and trade-offs — of unexpected triumphs made richer by the dashed hopes that offset them.

When Demy released his masterpiece in 1964, the big-budget Hollywood musical was a mammoth cakewalking on a cliff's edge. The musical as breezy, high-spirited entertainment had yielded to ponderous road-show events such as *My Fair Lady* and *The Sound of Music*; their success would beget extravagant decade-closing flops like *Star!* and *Doctor Dolittle*. On a genre noted for its lightness, prestige worked like carbon monoxide. The more these movies lusted for acclaim and recognition, the more stale, square and ludicrous musical conventions looked.

But in *Umbrellas*, Demy found an ingenious way to extend the form of the screen musical, restoring its effervescence in part by reducing its scale to something recognizably human. Rather than surge and lunge in elephantine production numbers, the entire movie would flow on an uninterrupted current of music. The singing and color would evoke the piercing immediacy of first love, even as the abstraction granted a very contemporary distancing effect.

Is there a genre that demands a greater leap of imagination from a viewer, a more sophisticated acceptance of blatant artifice, than the movie musical? Someone watching, say, Vincente Minnelli's *Meet Me in St. Louis* in essence enters into a compact with the filmmaker: I accept that characters will erupt into song and dance as naturally as conversation, and in return I will become their confidant, privy to their otherwise inexpressible longings. Accept those terms and a different emotional plane appears in the midst of Minnelli's boisterous, crowded household — a private space in which the characters open their throats, their hearts, directly to us. This is not the real world; this is a world with the veil of realism parted, allowing the passions beneath to peek through.

This is life as viewed through Demy's lens. But if *Umbrellas* uses the conventions of the Hollywood musical to express the immediate exhilaration of young love, it also subverts them to convey what's left when the illusions fade. Among other things — many things — the film is about how our lives measure up against the romantic ideals we see on the big screen. "People only die of love in movies," a character tartly observes — yet her pronouncement has an unmistakable note of regret.

Even before the title appears, Demy establishes a universe that fuses the commonplace and the cinematically heightened. The iris that closed on the black-and-white world of his 1961 debut *Lola* opens on the sepia-toned harbor of coastal Cherbourg, its workaday fleets of trawlers and naval ships. Without cutting — a seamless transition into the realm of stylization — Jean Rabier's camera tilts directly down on the waterfront's stone streets. A light rain begins; pastel umbrellas seen from overhead engage in delicate spatial choreography with the credits. On the soundtrack, we hear the first wistful iteration of Michel Legrand's "Je ne pourrai jamais vivre sans toi," the theme song that will follow the leads like the fading scent of prom gardenias.

In the first section, "The Departure," set in November 1957, handsome, brooding Guy (Nino Castelnuovo) waits to get off from his job at the garage so he can see his girl. It's not just any garage: as Demy's widow, Agnès Varda, points out in her loving tribute *Jacquot de Nantes* (released a year after his death in 1990), it's very much like the one Demy's mechanic father ran. And it's not just any girl: Deneuve is a vision of pristine loveliness. As Geneviève, the daughter of a single-mom shopkeeper, she's introduced here as the most desirable element in a store window filled with the titular *parapluies*. She and Guy cavort down thoroughfares hot with neon yellows and sultry blues, as if the intensity of their passion has caused the town to bloom.

Her mother (Anne Vernon) tries to tell her to consider her future, to think of Guy's callowness and the grim economic realities. (Another thing that changes over the years, as we watch the movie, is our grudging awareness that she speaks the truth.) She'd rather Geneviève cultivate a visiting jeweler (Marc Michel, in one of the earliest of Demy's intertextual movie references, portraying the same dejected-suitor character who pursued Anouk Aimée's dime-a-dance siren through *Lola*). Then comes word that Guy has been drafted for military service in the Algerian War. With only a night left together, Geneviève vows that she cannot live without him, and she offers up the same proof as the Shirelles in "Will You Love Me Tomorrow?"

At this point, the dizzying height of their infatuation, Demy cuts from the young lovers' tearful exchange to the two literally floating down the slickened street in an embrace, carried by the swelling current of their ever-ready theme song. I have yet to see the movie with an audience that didn't burst out laughing at the audacity of Demy's artifice, the boldest such moment in the movie. It may take a second viewing to realize that the director isn't just kidding their abandon but inviting us to remember the delirium of our own first loves.

They part in the time-honored fashion of movie lovers, with a railway-station farewell, but one that carries a whiff less of irony than of the drab everyday concerns that lie ahead. Then the next section — "The Absence" — begins, and the director starts to strip away the romance. Just as *maman* predicted, Guy's letters come less and less frequently. Worse, Geneviève is pregnant, the shop is failing and economic necessity demands that she find a provider. (The movie's frankness about money as an over-riding concern of marriage for women startles with each viewing; the topic helps Demy pass the Bechdel test with flying colors.) "I would have died for him," Geneviève confides, despondent and confused. "So why aren't I dead?"

There waiting, however, is Michel's suitor, Roland. In a remarkable sequence, he is brought to Geneviève in a showroom of bridal dresses, where she too stands on display. A dissolve transports her veiled face to the altar, making her transition from mannequin to trophy complete. And yet what's most striking is that Demy, the generous humanist, sees no reason to demonize Geneviève for her choice, nor to make Roland an ogre.

In the final section, "The Return," a scarred, disillusioned Guy comes home to a Cherbourg leached of color. The swooning, string-laden arrangement of Legrand's supple theme yields to louche marimbas and a down-at-heel cabaret ambience, as the wounded veteran limps past the haunts of a youth that now seems distant. He takes solace in booze and one of the cinema's least judgmental transactions with a prostitute, before an unexpected rescuer snaps him out of his misery: his dying aunt's caretaker, Madeleine (Ellen Farner), who represents a path to happiness that the movie hadn't even led us to consider.

The coda that follows, set four years later, in 1963, takes place at an Esso station at Christmastime. (In Jean-Luc Godard's 1967 *La Chinoise*, Esso's "Put a tiger in your tank" slogan would signify a cultural napalming by Western capitalism; for Demy, the gas station simply represents all the dully ordinary locales that prove to be the mysterious agents of our satisfaction.) Here, two young lovers who once vowed to wait for each other meet again a lifetime later, sadder and wiser. They now know the meaning of forever. The absence of the earlier color is stark. Their chance encounter is underscored by a hushed, mournful treatment of the Legrand theme — a dirge for a dream. As Geneviève drives away, Madeleine returns to the station with the couple's young son — and at this point, Legrand's score rises to an unprecedented crescendo. As in James Joyce's "The Dead," the snow that blankets the station falls on the death of a romantic idyll as well as the lives and loves that survive.

Is this the saddest happy ending in all of movies, or the happiest sad ending? The beauty, and profundity, of Demy's vision is that it's both. In *Umbrellas*' opening scenes, it seems that Demy is whittling the Hollywood musical's subject matter down to the particulars of daily life. But in this closing sequence, the converse is just as true: the movie urges us to see the color, hear the music in the currents of life and the rhythms of everyday speech. How different Demy's sympathetic stylization is from that of a fascinating experiment like Herbert Ross and Dennis Potter's lip-synched 1981 antimusical *Pennies from Heaven*, which considers its characters rubes for buying the tinny platitudes issuing from their mouths. Demy knows the limits of tuneful homilies, but he also understands why they lodge in our imaginations. They lodge in his too.

Demy would return to the musical throughout his career, starting with *The Young Girls of Rochefort* (1967), whose public-space-as-playground resourcefulness suggests Jacques Tati's *Playtime* as staged by Arthur Freed's MGM production unit. It's a beautiful film, but its airy expanses were eclipsed in the year of *Bonnie and Clyde* and *Weekend*. By the time of *Une chambre en ville*, a shocking recitative musical that makes explicit the violence that's always threatened or implied under Demy's pastel surfaces, the sailors of his earlier films had given way to union-busting storm troopers, and infatuation had curdled into murderous obsession. (Perhaps alone among directors, Demy might have made something more than kitsch from a movie-musical *Les misérables*.)

None of these films have ever approached the popularity of *Umbrellas*, whose influence turns up in the least expected of places. Even if they hadn't featured the undimmed presence of Deneuve, such dramatic musicals as Lars von Trier's *Dancer in the Dark* and François Ozon's *8 Women* would be unmistakable as tributaries of Demy's initial vision. Curiously enough, one of the strangest yet most astute homages to the movie is a 2002 episode of the animated science-fiction sitcom *Futurama*, in which the cryogenically thawed hero debates whether to clone a DNA sample from his dog, left a millennium earlier with the instruction not to move from his spot. He ultimately decides that the dog must have moved on and leaves the matter be — at which point the show cues a time-lapse montage of the dog waiting faithfully for his owner for years, until the moment he slumps to the sidewalk. The music playing over the montage is Connie Francis' recording of "I Will Wait for You" (the Americanized version of Legrand's song) — that anthem of a finite forever and an eternally preserved present that never loses its ache.

"One of the sad things about our times, I think, is that so many people find a romantic movie like that frivolous and negligible," Pauline Kael lamented about *The Umbrellas of Cherbourg* in a 2000 interview. "They don't see the beauty in it, but it's a lovely film — original and fine." And it's just as lovely today — its color just as vivid, its hopes just as fragile and delicately suspended. When I watch it now, it reminds me of the doorjamb in my grandmother's house with my height marked in pencil over the years, or the dresser with my own children's measurements notched along the edge. In it I see the person I was and the person I turned out to be, but the object itself will always be the same. It will wait, forever. (*The Essential Jacques Demy* (The Criterion Collection, 2014)

Acknowledgments

This book would not exist without Alicia Adkerson.

I'm also grateful to many people for their help and encouragement. Margaret Renkl of Chapter16.org said it simply needed to be. Steve Cavendish, Nancy Floyd, Elizabeth Jones, Patrick Rains and D. Patrick Rodgers of the *Nashville Scene* all pitched in. Special thanks is due to Casey Sanders, who tracked down decades-old bound volumes of *Scene* back issues and hauled them across Nashville so I could scan them. Nina Cardona read and provided generous responses to the original book proposal, as did Jennifer Fay, who also provided crucial feedback on the first draft of the manuscript. Kogonada, Noel Murray, Sam Smith and Allison Inman supplied input and inspiration. Jack Silverman read numerous iterations of the introduction and manuscript, fielding a steady onslaught of questions about timelines, context and punctuation in spite of how much we disagree about the Grateful Dead.

I am thankful for Vanderbilt University Press — especially editor Beth Kressel Itkin, for patiently guiding this project to completion; Betsy Phillips, for conspiring on strategies for spreading the word; Zack Gresham, for a painstaking copyedit; and Dariel Mayer, for attentive design direction. I'm also grateful to my family, who endured countless piles of unfolded laundry and unwashed dishes in the name of this work.

A note: In the original published review of *Boys Don't Cry* (Chapter 5), Brandon Teena is described as a "cross-dresser." This has been changed, in this volume, to "transgender man," in order to reflect current standards. Additionally, the term "sex-change" has been replaced with "gender reassignment surgery." Both of these changes were made in following with GLAAD's Media Reference Guide, which Jim would have happily observed.

Certainly, I would not be a person who was capable of assembling this book without the generosity and unswerving love of the man himself. Whatever I thought I knew when I started working at the *Nashville Scene*, Jim Ridley taught me to be an editor.

I remember a night when we trudged out of the office together. It was after midnight, and we'd been working on the Best of Nashville issue, the biggest and most important of the year, for 16 hours. Our wives and kids had long since gone to sleep; a halfhearted rain sputtered down on us and on the only two cars left in the parking lot. As we paused at the midpoint between our respective vehicles, I offered wearily, "See you in a few hours." Jim laughed a muted, exhausted version of his usual laugh. He had a way of fixing his eyes on you, with his lips pursed tightly, to let you know there was more he wanted to say than he was about to say. A silence passed between us, then he smiled and said sweetly, "See you in a few hours."

I miss you, my friend.

Index

8MM, 210
300, 65

absurdity, 19, 175, 177, 182, 187, 190, 213
Academy Awards, 113, 228. *See also* Oscar
acting, 52, 143, 162, 223, 227
Actress, 97–100
African-American, 68, 180, 235
Afterglow, 159–60
After Life, 230–31
Akeelah and the Bee, 138, 144–46
Alcaine, José Luis, 93
Allen, Dede, 49
allusion, 15, 17, 24–25, 203
Altman, Robert, 32–33, 160, 186, 235, 236–39
alt-weekly, 3–4, 103, 197
ambiguity, 50, 88, 214
American History X, 215–18
American Indian, 31, 39
Anderson, Wes, 137, 150–52
anime, 65
archetypes, 15, 27, 51, 150
Army of Shadows, 218–20
art, 154, 187, 209, 215, 226, 233
arts, 3–5, 118–19
Asian, 97, 178–180, 191
  -American, 6
assassin, 44–46, 60, 109, 238
Atchison, Doug, 144–46
attention, 7, 93, 111, 183, 199, 226, 237
audience, 51, 78, 118–19, 177, 190, 209–11, 214–15,
  225
auteur, 30, 61, 62, 211, 232
authenticity, 74, 112

Bad Boys II, 196, 198–200
Badham, John, 85–87
Ballad of Little Jo, The, 37–38
Ballard, Lucien, 35
Band of Outsiders, 16–19, 26
Batman Begins, 42–43
Bay, Michael, 9, 198–200
Beatty, Warren, 33, 44, 49–50, 187, 237

Beauchamp, Keith A., 220–22
Belcourt Theatre, 4–5, 12, 114–22, 123, 134, 159,
  197. *See also* Watkins Belcourt
Besson, Luc, 85–87, 191–93, 204–6
Biddle, Adrian, 53
Bigelow, Kathryn, 63
Big Lebowski, The, 64–65
Blanchett, Cate, 172–73
Blauvelt, Christopher, 39
blaxploitation, 68
blood, 29, 34, 50, 165, 180–82, 205, 207–8
B movie, 85–86, 94
bodies, 31, 34, 43, 89, 164, 167, 209, 221
Bonnie and Clyde, 44, 48–50, 52, 245
boys, 54, 80–83, 90, 148–49, 232
Boys Don't Cry, 80–83
Boyz N the Hood, 148–50
Bridges, Jeff, 65, 203, 233
Buñuel, Luis, 168, 182, 184
Bush, George W., 39, 65

Cahiers du Cinema, 85
camera, 91, 162, 186, 191, 210, 222, 240
  angle, 110, 243
  digital, 25, 76
  movement, 23, 69, 86, 96, 152, 160, 193, 237
  placement, 166, 178, 224
  -work, 23, 76, 188, 209, 217, 241
Campion, Jane, 163–66
Cannes, 84, 100, 119, 225, 227, 241
Carlito's Way, 68, 85
Carmike, 116, 120
Carol, 172–74
cartoons, 17, 63, 138, 141, 175, 176, 179
casting, 6, 51, 89, 98, 166, 169, 191, 219
Castro Theatre, 241
celebrity, 42, 75, 105, 110, 154, 183–84
censorship, 36, 116, 147–48, 168, 228
CGI, 43, 75, 205, 233. *See also* computers; special
  effects
Chan, Jackie, 98, 177–80
Chen, Joan, 222–23
Cheung, Maggie, 98–100

Chicago, 220–21
Chicago, 77–78
Chicago Reader, 9, 98
childhood, 12, 19, 67, 137, 148, 153, 164
Chinese, 37, 46–47, 98–99, 145, 222, 226–28
cinema, 9, 16, 25, 116, 140–41, 193–94, 199
Cinemascope. *See* 'Scope
cinematographer, 39, 44, 93, 162, 165, 208, 223, 232. *See also specific individuals*
cinematography, 33, 38, 149
Citizen Kane, 2, 94, 117
civilization, 30, 35, 79, 88, 224
Civil Rights, 66, 108
Clash of the Titans, 62
clip, 24–25, 94
codes, 35, 44, 181, 186
Coen Brothers, 64–65
Cohen, Leonard, 33, 147
Cohen, Rob, 46–48
color
    as related to race, 6, 66
    use in film, 22, 76, 90, 92, 143, 162, 170, 209
commerce, 31, 33, 79
commercial, 97, 106, 109, 116, 198–99, 202, 237–38
compassion, 70, 166, 228
computers, 62, 65, 91. *See also* CGI; special effects
conservatism, 112, 217
contempt, 83, 144, 183, 190
Contempt, 18, 117
context, 3, 100–101, 103, 161
contradictions, 49, 84, 89, 148, 173
controversy, 104, 114, 225
convention, 15, 45, 76, 78, 86, 146, 194, 242. *See also* genre
Corbucci, Sergio, 30–32
costume, 42, 64, 98, 152, 153–54, 165, 169–70, 190
country music, 105, 106, 107–8, 109, 111–14, 155, 238
Coutard, Raoul, 15, 17, 23
Criterion, 176
critics, 2, 7–9, 13, 97, 104–5, 186, 193, 207
Cronenberg, David, 2, 87–89
crosscut, 96, 209
culture, 24, 47, 60, 64, 83, 144, 182
    pop, 17, 80, 138, 180, 185, 187, 188
cut, 95, 99, 104, 199
cutting, 8, 34, 36, 49, 75, 84, 99, 145
cynicism, 28, 31, 50, 77, 238

Darin, Bobby, 217
dark, 42, 54, 89, 163, 170, 186, 208, 216
darkness, 25–26, 54, 95, 101, 234
Darwin's Nightmare, 79–80
Dash, Julie, 235–36
Daughters of the Dust, 235–36

Dayton, Jonathan, 200–202
death, 7, 36, 149, 208–9, 229, 230, 234, 236
debut, 8, 94, 150, 235
Decae, Henri, 44, 46
democracy, 110, 209
democratic, 26, 122, 182
demographic, 138, 188
Demy, Jacques, 11, 13–16, 137, 230, 241–46
Deneuve, Catherine, 21, 241, 243, 245
De Palma, Brian, 2, 56, 83–85, 91–94
desire, 15, 23, 148, 157, 160, 164, 166, 169
devil, 56, 148, 202, 204
Devil's Rejects, The, 61
dialogue, 14, 143, 146, 204, 237, 241
diversity, 6
documentary, 79, 98, 144, 184, 209, 214, 219, 220
Dogme 95, 74, 154
Doinel, Antoine, 19
Donen, Stanley, 77–78
doppelganger, 25, 29, 73
double, 73, 83–84
Dragon: The Bruce Lee Story, 46–48
dreams, 83, 101–2, 108, 117, 140, 159, 230, 232
dress-up, 45, 101, 141, 161
Dryburgh, Stuart, 165
DVD, 1, 65, 93, 146, 176, 195, 237
Dylan, Bob, 24, 124–25

Eastwood, Clint, 30, 51
economy, 38, 57, 203
editing, 18, 25, 36, 59, 94–96, 110, 195, 226
emotion, 15, 53–56, 58, 125, 164–65, 170, 222, 231
erotic, 15, 53, 86, 92, 147, 164, 168
evil, 29, 42, 54–55, 88, 187, 208, 211, 220
exploitation, 48, 50
Eyes Wide Shut, 168–71

fake, 22, 74–75, 78, 102, 112, 154, 195
fantasy, 62, 78, 92, 144, 148, 161–62, 170, 230–31
Faris, Valerie, 200–202
fascism, 55, 83, 209, 215, 217
father, 43, 68, 217, 225, 232, 243
fear, 42–43, 47, 74, 139, 169–70, 210, 217
feminism, 50, 80, 161
Femme Fatale, 83–85, 93
Femme Nikita, La, 51, 85–87, 193, 206
Fifth Element, The, 191–94
Fight Club, 80–83
Filac, Vilko, 224
Film Comment, 9, 97–98, 231
Fincher, David, 80–83
flashback, 43, 59, 70, 216, 219
flawed, 168, 201, 227, 228
flaws, 43, 142, 148, 149
formula, 14, 54, 177–78, 198
Foster, Jodie, 60, 142–44

fragmentation, 59, 84, 98, 111, 235
frame, 16, 35, 39, 55, 58, 92, 150, 240
freedom, 56, 70, 147, 190, 201
French New Wave, 13, 50, 241. *See also* Nouvelle Vague
fringe, 60, 154, 238
Fuller, Samuel, 25, 45
Full Frontal, 74–76

gadget, 43, 56, 83, 92, 171, 218
gangster, 17–18, 44–45, 48–49, 85, 146, 149, 195, 203
Gautier, Eric, 23
gender, 6, 37, 51, 81–82, 190–91
genre, 15, 29, 33, 57, 75, 185, 194, 242. *See also* convention
Gloria, 166–67
God, 35, 60, 61, 75, 187, 205, 208, 236
Godard, Jean-Luc, 16–19, 24–26, 50, 85, 87, 117, 190, 241
Goldblum, Jeff, 109, 113
grandmother, 28, 246
Grand Ole Opry, 105, 107–9, 112, 115
Greenwald, Maggie, 37–38
grief, 21, 43, 234
Grizzly Man, 79–80
Guffey, Burnett, 49
guns, 39, 49, 52, 85, 86, 186, 217, 219

Harron, Mary, 160–62
Harryhausen, Ray, 62–63
hate, 56, 77, 80, 82, 89, 153, 216–18
Hawks, Howard, 27, 57–58, 202, 232
Haynes, Todd, 172–74
hell, 25, 36, 59, 60, 79, 202, 206
hero, 31, 41–56, 60, 87–88, 178–79, 204, 219
heroine, 52–53, 64, 98, 167, 173, 222
Herzog, Werner, 79–80, 154
history, 44, 90, 104, 115, 124, 189, 216, 219–22
History of Violence, A, 87–89
Hollywood, 47–48, 56, 60, 77, 87, 100–101, 183, 232
homage/*hommage*, 17, 50, 64, 85, 87, 194, 245
Hong Kong, 47, 98
hope, 16, 56, 114, 144, 152, 228, 246
horror, 50, 61, 89, 97, 101, 166, 181, 207–8
Hot Fuzz, 194–96
human, 22, 42, 52, 70, 165, 211, 231, 242

icon, 29, 48, 161
iconic, 147, 232
iconography, 45, 52, 196
identity, 81, 88, 101–2, 112, 115, 153
Ikiru, 70–71
I Like It Like That, 67–68
illusion, 18, 63, 74, 77–78, 102, 122, 169, 242–43

imitation, 16, 35, 48, 49, 86, 97, 193
innocence, 51, 101–2, 108, 137, 153, 161, 232
interactive, 32, 177
International Black Film Festival of Nashville, 6
ironic, 15, 50, 60, 77, 82, 92, 165, 225
irony, 98, 113, 149, 190–91, 200, 203

Jackass: The Movie, 183–84
Jennings, Garth, 140–42
journalism, 2–3, 27, 103
Jules and Jim, 2, 19–21, 119, 137, 152, 230

Kael, Pauline, 2, 9, 18, 104, 246
Kaminski, Janusz, 208
Karina, Anna, 17–18
Kaye, Tony, 215–18
Keitel, Harvey, 52, 86–87, 163, 166, 171, 185, 187
Keller, Harry, 95
Kelly, Gene, 14, 77–78, 178, 241
Khouri, Callie, 52
Kiarostami, Abbas, 117, 229, 231, 239–40
kids, 5, 47, 121, 127, 138–42, 145, 148–49, 151
Kids, 154
Kore-eda Hirokazu, 229, 230–31
Korine, Harmony, 11, 153–55, 184
Kubrick, Stanley, 20, 83, 168–71, 186
Kuleshov, Lev, 18
Kuras, Ellen, 90
Kurosawa, Akira, 2, 70–71
Kusturica, Emir, 223–25
Kwan, Stanley, 97–100

Lachman, Ed, 173
Lanzmann, Claude, 207, 220
Lasseter, John, 138–39
Last Picture Show, The, 202–3, 229, 232–33
Lee, Bruce, 41, 46–48, 178, 193
Lee, Jason Scott, 46–48
Lee, Spike, 89–91, 186
Legrand, Michel, 14, 19, 243, 244, 245
Lelio, Sebastián, 166–67
Leone, Sergio, 28–32, 38–39
Little Man Tate, 142–44
Little Miss Sunshine, 200–202
location, 17, 77, 90, 170, 179
Lola, 14–16, 243
Lucas, George, 53–56
Luna, Diego, 154
Lü Yue, 223, 228
Lynch, David, 2, 100–102, 202, 237

macho, 35–37, 61, 81–82, 195, 199
magic, 11, 14, 63, 109, 155, 176, 203
Mann, Anthony, 39
Mara, Rooney, 172–73
Marshall, Rob, 77–78

Martin, Darnell, 6, 67–68
masculinity, 35, 80
Mathis, Samantha, 147
McCabe & Mrs. Miller, 32–33, 37, 107, 187, 235, 237, 238
McGuffin, 58
media, 3–4, 6, 81, 93, 110–11, 183, 184
    mass, 2, 90, 182
Meek's Cutoff, 38–39
Meet Me in St. Louis, 12, 23, 58–59, 242
Melville, Jean-Pierre, 44–46, 196, 218–20
memory, 6, 11, 19, 69, 139, 225, 230–31
men, 37, 52, 80–82, 161, 163, 178, 199, 221
Messenger, The, 204–6
metaphor, 69, 82, 112, 114, 154, 201, 228, 231
Miller, Frank, 65
Minnelli, Vincente, 23, 58, 242
misfits, 3, 17, 62, 90, 140, 186
misogyny, 82–83, 162
Mister Lonely, 153–55
modernism, 21, 92, 176
montage, 26, 49, 85, 91, 139, 145, 245
Moonrise Kingdom, 137, 150–52
Morricone, Ennio, 29, 31
mother, 12, 17, 20, 199, 221, 233–34
Mother and Son, 233–34
motif, 15, 29, 30, 57, 111, 170, 175, 235
movie theater. *See* screens; theater; *specific theaters*
Moyle, Allan, 146–48
Mulholland Drive, 100–102
murder, 59, 68, 80–81, 90, 108, 194, 220–22
Murray, Noel, 7, 123, 229
music, 24, 29, 119, 123, 145, 146–47, 163, 227
    musical, 14–15, 58, 77–78, 107, 180, 241–46
    theme, 29, 31, 96, 188, 243
    score, 29, 32, 165
    See also country music; sound; soundtrack
Music City, 105, 107, 238
myth, 28–29, 51–52, 56, 63, 66–67, 87, 214, 225

Nashville, 2, 10, 104, 108, 115, 147, 161, 233
Nashville, 104–14, 237–38
Nashville Banner, 106, 107
Nashville Public Radio, 123
Nashville Scene, 1–11, 119, 123, 213
Nashvillian, 52, 105, 111–12, 118, 126, 214
Nazi, 28, 206–10, 214–15, 217, 218–19, 220, 224–25
Neeson, Liam, 42, 206
New York, 3, 89–91, 118, 121, 162, 171, 179, 192
New Yorker, 3, 9, 69, 104, 150, 193
New York Times, 241
nightmare, 45, 79, 101, 159, 183, 237
nihilism, 31, 68, 86, 218
Nolan, Christopher, 42–43

Norton, Edward, 82–83, 151, 215–18
nostalgia, 139, 161, 218, 232
Notorious Bettie Page, The, 160–62
Notre Musique, 24–26
Nouvelle Vague, 46, 59, 73, 152, 241. *See also* French New Wave

obsession, 20, 56, 80, 85, 87, 161, 200, 245
Once Upon a Time in the West, 28–30, 31, 137
order, 43, 70, 81, 84, 88, 152, 181, 195
Order of Myths, The, 66–67
Orlando, 189–91
Oscar, 160, 195, 207, 210, 228. *See also* Academy Awards
outsiders, 3, 18, 111, 186, 238

Palme d'Or, 119, 225, 241
paranoid, 83, 219
Parillaud, Anne, 51, 86
Paris, 17, 22, 26, 44, 57, 124, 176
Parmet, Phil, 61
parody, 36, 112, 165, 193, 195
passion, 16, 19, 21, 55, 91, 164, 169, 242–43
Passion, 91–94
Passion de Jeanne d'Arc, La, 204
Peckinpah, Sam, 34–36
Peirce, Kimberly, 80–83
Penn, Arthur, 48–50
performance, 37, 48, 53, 55, 143, 167, 191, 223
perspective, 44, 83–84, 219
Phantom of the Liberty, The, 168, 184
Piano, The, 163–66
Playtime, 176–77, 245
plot, 57, 110, 152, 175, 178, 194, 224, 227
Point Blank, 44, 59–60
Point Break, 63
Point of No Return, 85–87
pop, 8, 48, 53, 112
porn, 23, 48, 161, 168, 171, 210–11
Potter, Sally, 189–91
Private Fears in Public Places, 22–24
progress, 51, 119, 240
progressive, 3, 126
protagonist, 54, 148, 151, 166, 172, 226
provocation, 26, 56, 146, 154, 185, 217, 234
psychology, 47, 161
pulp, 19, 44, 59, 85, 88, 95, 161, 186
Pulp Fiction, 185–87
Pump Up the Volume, 146–48

Quinn, Declan, 38

Rabier, Jean, 243
racism, 67, 90, 213, 221, 238
rape, 37, 50, 51, 81–82, 168, 193, 235
realism, 12, 22, 74, 77–78, 159, 194, 242

redemption, 35, 60, 85, 187
Reed, Rex, 105, 112, 114
Regal, 116, 118–19
Reichardt, Kelly, 38–39
Resnais, Alain, 14, 22–24, 59, 209
Revenge of the Sith, 53–56
reviewers, 3, 8–11, 50, 89, 103–5, 114, 183, 209
Reynolds, Burt, 8, 30–32
rhythm, 25, 29, 36, 171, 245
Riefenstahl, Leni, 214–15
Rio Bravo, 27, 57–58
Rock 'n' Roll High School, 64, 147
Rodionov, Alexei, 190
romanticism, 43, 137, 160, 163
Ruan Ling-yu, 98–100
Rudolph, Alan, 113, 159–60
Rumble in the Bronx, 177–80

Samouraï, Le, 44–46, 218
satire, 81–83, 111, 182, 225, 237
Sauper, Hubert, 79–80
scale, 28, 39, 43, 56, 143, 176, 231, 242
Scent of Green Papaya, The, 69–70
Schindler's List, 197, 206–10
Schumacher, Joel, 168, 206, 210–11
science fiction, 31, 56, 62, 74, 175, 237, 245
'Scope, 15, 24, 167
Scorsese, Martin, 2, 20, 46, 60, 110, 115, 149, 203
Scott, Ridley, 50–53
screens, 84–85, 92, 94, 177, 228
    movie theater, 36, 116, 118–19, 120–21, 206
Sekula, Andrzej, 185
sequel, 42, 54, 61, 138
sequence, 8, 18, 93, 153, 170, 200, 226, 245
Serial Mom, 180–82
set, 1, 22–23, 110, 141, 210, 211
set piece, 84, 96, 178, 203
setting, 15, 54, 67, 77, 107, 165, 194, 231
sex, 21, 89, 92, 148, 158, 164–65, 169–71, 210–11
sexuality, 15, 101, 166, 169, 232
Shalit, Gene, 3, 61
Shepherd, Cybill, 203–4, 233
shot, 17, 25, 80, 84, 140, 143, 171, 192
    close-up, 28, 29, 99
    exterior, 198, 240
    final, 53, 80, 228, 240
    long, 29, 95, 153, 155
    opening, 44, 46, 96, 148, 155, 214
    point of view, 101, 139
    slow-motion, 15, 36, 50
Shyamalan, M. Night, 74–76
Signs, 74–76
Silence of the Lambs, The, 114, 143
Singin' in the Rain, 77–78
Singleton, John, 148–50
Sinking Creek Film Festival, 107, 197

Slater, Christian, 146–47
slow motion, 34, 85, 151, 153, 194–95, 199, 217, 236
small screen, 94, 116. *See also* television; TV
Smith, Larry, 170
Snyder, Zack, 65
Soderbergh, Steven, 74–76
Sokurov, Aleksandr, 233–34
Son of Rambow, 140–42
sound, 33, 59, 75, 78, 93, 95–96, 110–11, 209
soundtrack, 33, 53, 112, 147, 185, 199, 237–38, 243
South, the, 30, 66–67, 111, 220, 235
spaghetti Western, 30–32, 38
special effects, 55, 62, 75, 231. *See also* CGI;
    computers
Spheeris, Penelope, 187–89
Spielberg, Steven, 56, 110, 206–10
Springsteen, Bruce, 7, 123–27, 172
Stallone, Sylvester, 140, 178
Star Wars, 7, 41, 53–56
stereotypes, 180, 208, 219
structure, 74, 95, 109, 165, 185, 216
studios, 6, 33, 76, 95–96, 113, 158, 193–94, 217
Sturges, Preston, 114, 117, 201
stylization, 77, 82, 243, 245
stylized, 22, 49, 63, 82, 88, 152, 159, 225
Sugar Hill, 68–69
Summer of Sam, 89–91
surveillance, 45, 84, 91, 183
suspense, 44, 83, 95, 202, 239
Suspiria, 117
Swept From the Sea, 66
Swinton, Tilda, 152, 190–91
Systad Jacobsen, Jannicke, 158–59

taboo, 61, 157, 161, 167, 170, 182
Tarantino, Quentin, 17, 28, 30, 46, 61, 185–87
Taste of Cherry, 11, 117, 119, 229, 239–40
Tati, Jacques, 159, 176–77, 245
Taxi Driver, 60
Taylor, Steve, 119–20
technology, 56, 92
teens, 11, 21, 146–49, 158–59, 161, 187–89, 220–21
television, 36, 114, 116, 236. *See also* small screen;
    TV
Tennessean, 2, 3, 105, 108, 122
Tewkesbury, Joan, 103, 107–8, 110–11, 113
Texasville, 202–4
theater, 94, 223
    movie, 28, 49, 105–6, 114–22, 170, 180, 203,
    230
Thelma & Louise, 50–53
theme, 25, 35, 44, 93, 118, 143, 218, 231
Thurman, Uma, 185, 187
To Live, 226–28
Tong, Stanley, 177–80
Tony Takitani, 69

torture, 31, 61, 193, 211, 218–19, 222, 224
Touch of Evil, 94–97, 117
Toy Story 2, 138–39
transgender, 7, 81, 247
Tremain, Jeff, 183–84
trilogy, 55–56, 240
Triumph of the Will, 53, 209, 214–15
Truffaut, François, 2, 19–22, 85, 117, 119
Trump, Donald, 80
Turner, Kathleen, 182
Turn Me On, Dammit!, 158–59
TV, 23, 36, 74–75, 80, 91–93, 101, 117, 183. *See also* small screen; television
Two English Girls, 19–22

Umbrellas of Cherbourg, The, 11, 14, 16, 19, 22, 230, 241–46
Underground, 223–25
Untold Story of Emmett Louis Till, The, 220–22

Vanderbilt University, 2, 107, 119, 121, 197, 214
Varda, Agnès, 14, 243
VHS, 23, 140, 197, 241
video, 21, 74–76, 116, 120, 183, 191, 211, 230
viewings, 13, 26, 111, 151, 177, 233, 244
vigilante, 42, 51, 89, 90
Village Voice, 3, 4, 233

villain, 42, 43, 50, 90, 147, 193, 195
violence, 34, 49, 82, 88, 148–49, 170, 186, 208–9
voyeurism, 83–84, 91, 168, 170, 183, 210

war, 25, 36, 45, 88, 193, 206, 218, 224–25
Warriors, The, 63
Waters, John, 180–82, 184
Watkins Belcourt, 62, 114–22. *See also* Belcourt Theatre
Wayne's World, 187–89
Welles, Orson, 75, 94–97, 115, 176, 237
Western, 58, 60, 87–88, 107, 126, 232, 237
white, 6, 37, 66–67, 80, 89, 109, 215–18, 220
Wiest, Dianne, 142, 144
Wild Bunch, The, 29, 33, 34–36, 49, 115
Willis, Bruce, 151, 185, 192, 193, 194
women, 6, 37, 50–52, 80–82, 163, 190–91, 235, 244
Wong Kar-wai, 8, 99
Wright, Edgar, 194–96

Xiu Xiu: The Sent-Down Girl, 222–23

Yeoman, Robert, 152
YouTube, 2, 92

Zhang Yimou, 10, 226–28